# LET'S MAKE RAMEN!

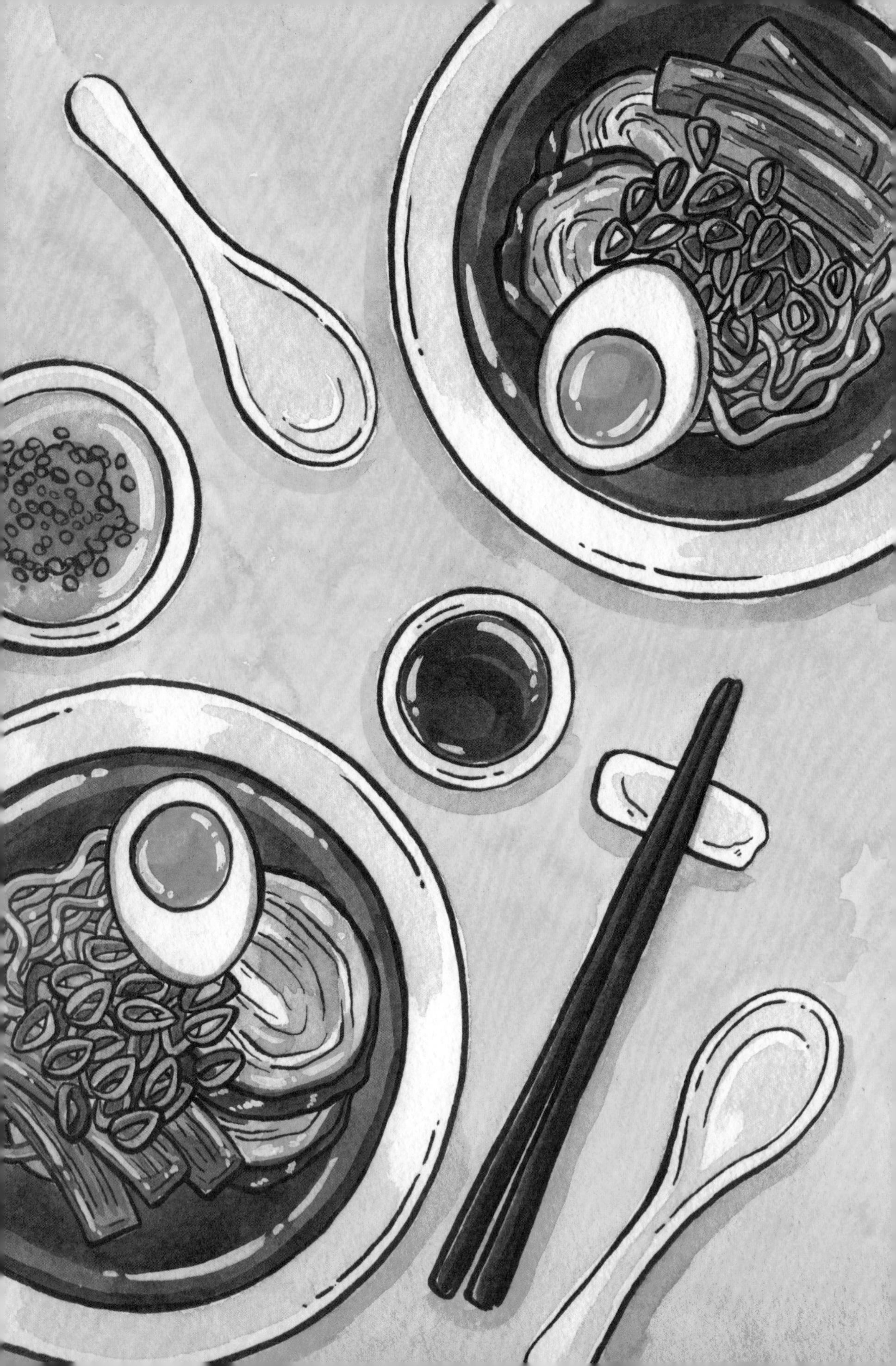

# LET'S MAKE RAMEN!

## A COMIC BOOK COOKBOOK

### HUGH AMANO
### AND SARAH BECAN

TEN SPEED PRESS
CALIFORNIA | NEW YORK

# TABLE OF

# CONTENTS

## ACCOMPANIMENTS

## OFFSHOOTS & RIFFS

# INTRODUCTION

HI! I'M HUGH!

AND I'M SARAH!

AND WELCOME TO OUR WORLD OF RAMEN!

HUGH IS A CHEF AND WRITER,

AND SARAH IS AN ILLUSTRATOR AND COMICS ARTIST.

FUELED BY A COMMON LOVE OF THE ALCHEMY OF CHEWY NOODLES, NUANCED BROTHS, AND DELICIOUS TOPPINGS,

WE'VE JOINED FORCES TO GUIDE YOU ALONG A TASTY PATH TO MAKING A DELICIOUSLY SLURPABLE BOWL RIGHT IN YOUR HOME KITCHEN.

RAMEN TWIN POWERS... ACTIVATE!

WE'LL GIVE RAMEN'S HISTORY AND CULTURE A PEEK

BEFORE DIVING INTO STOCKING YOUR RAMEN PANTRY AND KITCHEN AT HOME.

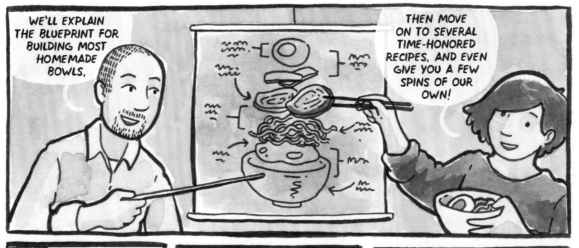

WE'LL EXPLAIN THE BLUEPRINT FOR BUILDING MOST HOMEMADE BOWLS,

THEN MOVE ON TO SEVERAL TIME-HONORED RECIPES, AND EVEN GIVE YOU A FEW SPINS OF OUR OWN!

YOU'LL LEARN HOW TO MAKE SIMPLE STOCKS AND TURN THEM INTO FLAVORFUL BROTHS,

WHAT TO LOOK FOR WHEN BUYING PREMADE NOODLES AND HOW TO ROLL YOUR OWN,

AND HOW TO MAXIMIZE FLAVOR, AROMA, AND TEXTURE WITH A NUMBER OF APPROACHABLE RECIPES FOR TOPPINGS AND GARNISHES.

WE'VE EVEN GOT A FEW TITANS OF THE RAMEN WORLD DROPPING BY TO ENLIGHTEN YOU ON YOUR JOURNEY.

SO LET'S GO!

FULL SLURP AHEAD!

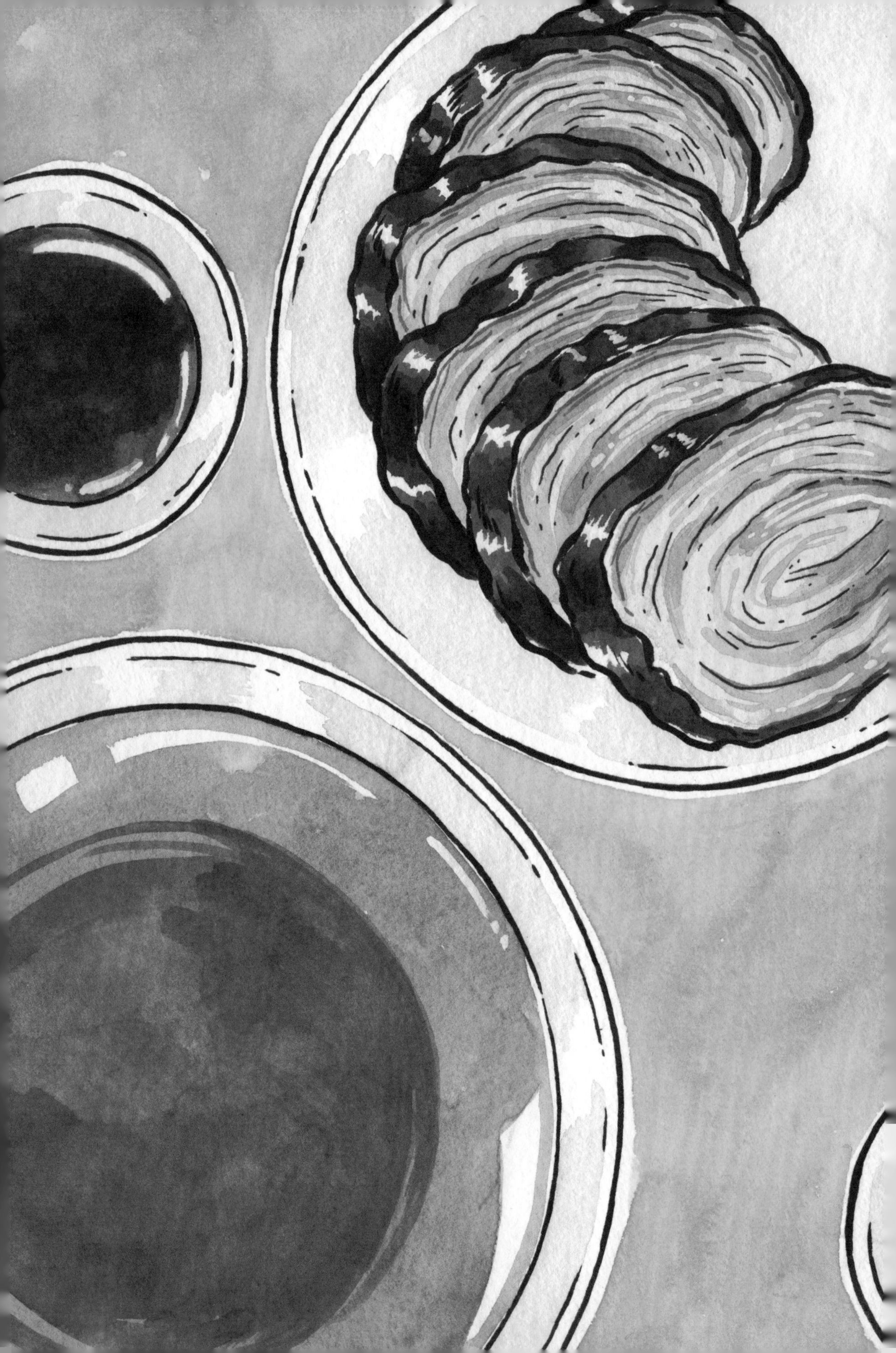

# RAMEN 101

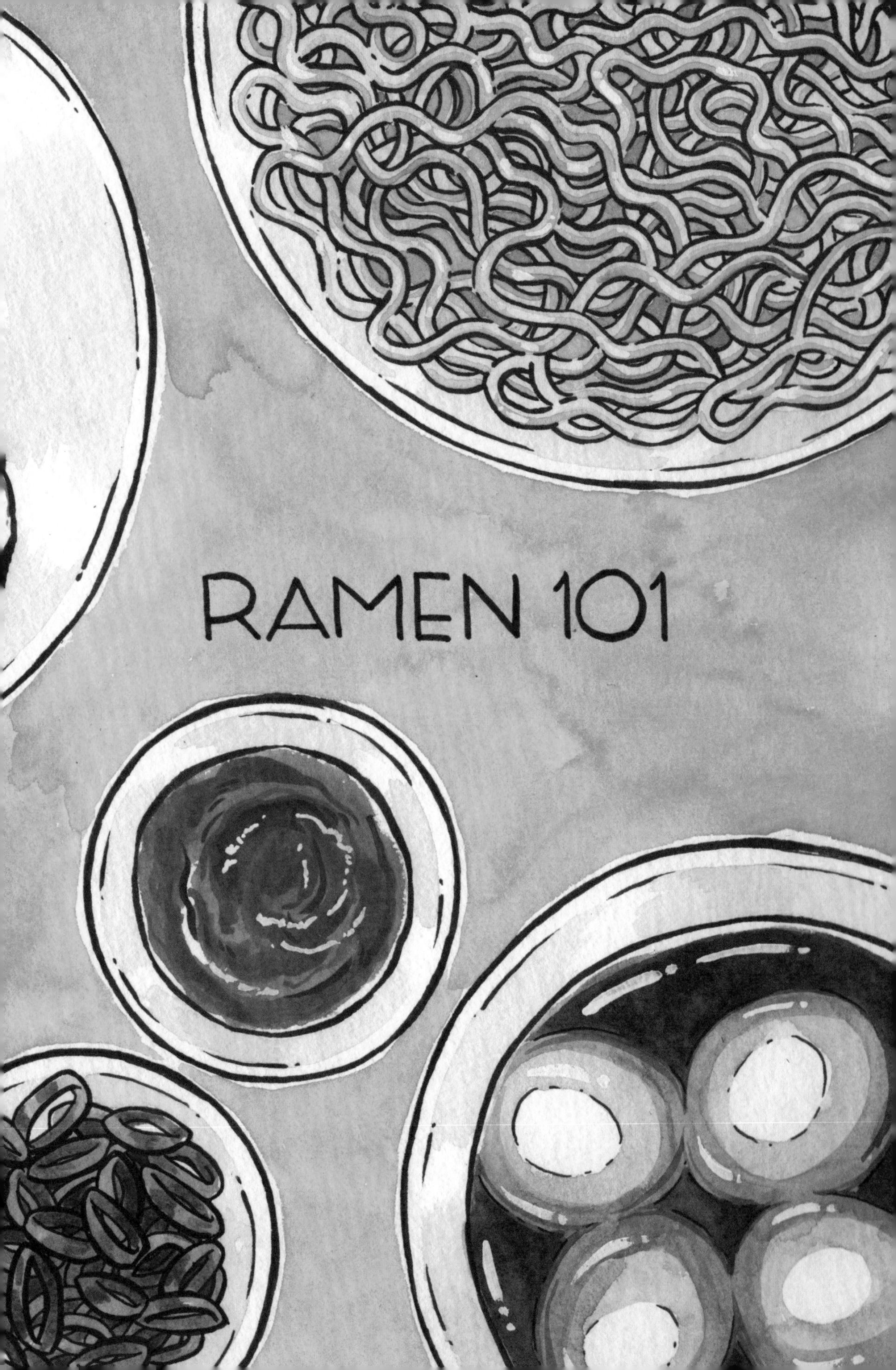

# A BRIEF HISTORY OF RAMEN

IN 1868, JAPAN ADVANCED FROM THE FEUDAL SHOGUNATE OF THE EDO PERIOD TO THE IMPERIAL RULE OF THE MEIJI PERIOD.

PREVIOUSLY CLOSED OFF ECONOMICALLY AND SOCIALLY, JAPAN OPENED ITSELF TO THE REST OF THE WORLD.

THE TECHNIQUE FOR HAND-PULLED *LAMIAN* NOODLES CAME FROM CHINA

AND EVENTUALLY MORPHED INTO HAND-CUT *RAMEN* NOODLES.

SOMEWHERE AROUND THE TURN OF THE TWENTIETH CENTURY, VENDORS IN PORT CITIES STARTED SELLING BOWLS OF NOODLES,

BLOWING THEIR DISTINCTIVE *CHARUMERAS* TO ANNOUNCE THEIR PRESENCE TO LOCAL WORKERS.

ACCUSTOMED TO WIDE UDON NOODLES AND THIN SOBA NOODLES IN SUBTLE DASHI BROTHS,

THE WORKING CLASS QUICKLY TOOK TO THE CHEWY ALKALINE NOODLES IN THE BIG FLAVORS OF FISH- AND MEAT-BASED BROTHS.

FOOD RATIONING DURING WORLD WAR II MADE WHEAT SCARCE (FOOD IN GENERAL BECAME SCARCE, FOR THAT MATTER),

BUT WHEAT RETURNED IN FORCE VIA AMERICAN FOOD AID, AND THE STAGE WAS SET FOR WHEAT NOODLES LIKE RAMEN TO SURGE IN POPULARITY.

AS THE COUNTRY RECOVERED, RAMEN SHOPS POPPED UP, OFFERING DELICIOUS, EASILY ACCESSIBLE, AND AFFORDABLE BOWLS.

ULTIMATELY MAKING THEM INEXPENSIVE, DURABLE, AND WILDLY POPULAR ACROSS THE GLOBE.

MEANWHILE, IN 1958, A TAIWANESE IMMIGRANT TO JAPAN NAMED MOMOFUKU ANDO DEVELOPED A METHOD TO FLASH-FRY — AND THEREFORE PRESERVE — RAMEN NOODLES.

THIS EARNED RAMEN A REPUTATION
OF COLLEGE DORM-STYLE,
TEN-FOR-A-DOLLAR CHEAPNESS;

IN THE 80'S, HOWEVER,
COOKS BEGAN TO APPLY
CERTAIN JAPANESE PRINCIPLES
TO THE BOWLS OF RAMEN
THEY WERE CREATING.

*SHOKUNIN:* SINGULAR FOCUS
ON ONE'S CRAFT

*KAIZEN:* SUSTAINED FOCUS
ON IMPROVEMENT

*KODAWARI:* PASSIONATE FOCUS
ON PERFECTING ONE'S ART

THE FACT THAT
THERE WAS NOT A
MASSIVE AMOUNT OF
JAPANESE HISTORY
BEHIND RAMEN
HELPED IT BREAK
FREE FROM THE
USUAL CONSTRAINTS
OF TRADITION,

ALLOWING FOR
FLEXIBILITY IN HOW
IT IS INTERPRETED
AND CREATED.

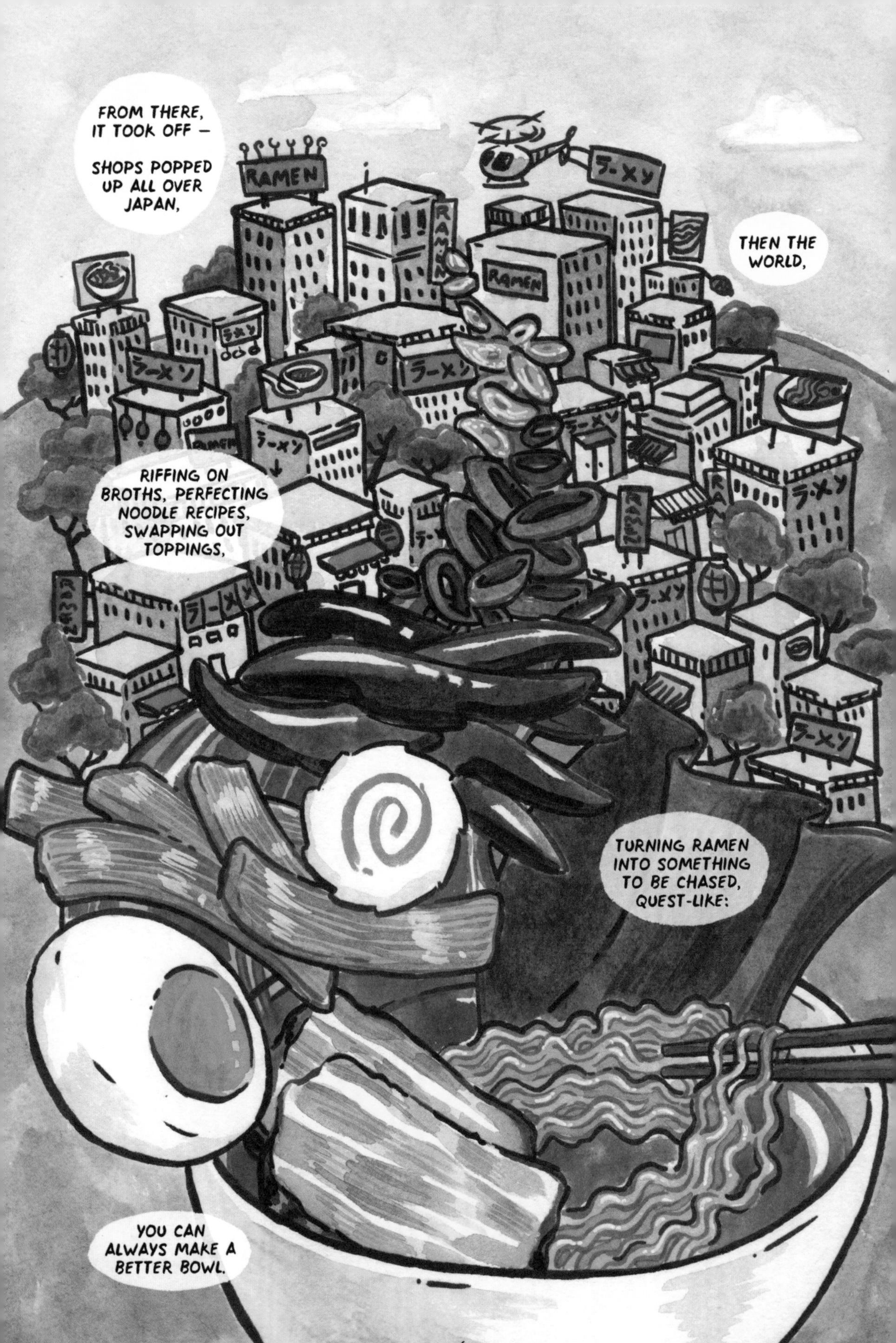
FROM THERE, IT TOOK OFF —
SHOPS POPPED UP ALL OVER JAPAN,
RAMEN
RAMEN
THEN THE WORLD,
RIFFING ON BROTHS, PERFECTING NOODLE RECIPES, SWAPPING OUT TOPPINGS,
TURNING RAMEN INTO SOMETHING TO BE CHASED, QUEST-LIKE:
YOU CAN ALWAYS MAKE A BETTER BOWL.

# HOW TO ENJOY RAMEN

A GOOD BOWL OF RAMEN IS A SYMPHONY OF FLAVOR AND AROMA, TEXTURE AND TEMPERATURE.

FROM CHEWY NOODLES TO CRUNCHY *MENMA*, SHARP *NEGI* TO RICH AND UNCTUOUS *CHASHU*, STEAMING HOT BROTH TO COOL EGGS, RAMEN IS RARELY SUBTLE;

MOST COMPONENTS PLAY THEIR RESPECTIVE PARTS LOUDLY, ABLY FILLING THEIR ROLES AMONGST A CREW OF BOISTEROUS COMRADES.

SO WHEN A BOWL ARRIVES IN FRONT OF YOU, GO AHEAD AND GET IN TUNE WITH IT BEFORE PLUNGING IN!

7

FIRST, TAKE IN THE BEAUTY OF THE COMPOSITION AS A WHOLE.

A GOOD-LOOKING BOWL OF RAMEN COMES TOGETHER FAIRLY SIMPLY:

INGREDIENTS ADORNING LOVELY NOODLES, FOCUSED BY A ROUND BOWL, MAKES FOR A STRIKING VISUAL PALETTE.

REVEL IN THE CLARITY OR THICKNESS OF THE BROTH, THE WAVY OR STRAIGHT NOODLES, THE GRAIN OF THE MENMA AND THE CHASHU.

THEN, AS YOU'RE MARVELING AT THE BEAUTIFUL BOWL, GET YOUR WHOLE HEAD IN THERE.

LET THE STEAM RISE TO YOUR FACE TO FEEL THE BROTH'S ENERGY AND SMELL ITS COMPLEXITY.

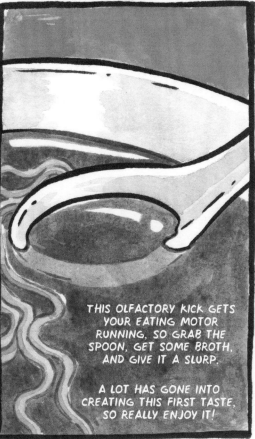

THIS OLFACTORY KICK GETS YOUR EATING MOTOR RUNNING, SO GRAB THE SPOON, GET SOME BROTH, AND GIVE IT A SLURP.

A LOT HAS GONE INTO CREATING THIS FIRST TASTE, SO REALLY ENJOY IT!

**SLURPING IS AN ART!** AS IT HELPS COOL THE SCREAMING HOT BROTH AND NOODLES ENTERING YOUR MOUTH, IT AERATES THE BOWL'S AROMATIC COMPONENTS, ENHANCING YOUR EXPERIENCE OF ALL THE WONDERFUL INGREDIENTS.

WE KNOW, WE KNOW — IN WESTERN CULTURE IT MAY SEEM RUDE TO SLURP YOUR SOUP AND NOODLES — BUT THROW THOSE INHIBITIONS OUT THE WINDOW, AND LET GO!

SLURPING IS AN INTEGRAL PART OF THE RAMEN EXPERIENCE AND SHOWS THE COOK — EVEN IF THE COOK IS YOU — THAT YOU'RE EATING WITH GUSTO!

OFTEN YOUR BOWL WILL BE SO LOADED UP THAT YOU MIGHT FORGET THE NOODLES ARE DOWN THERE!

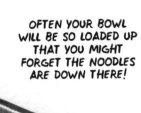

USE YOUR CHOPSTICKS TO PULL SOME OUT OF THE BOWL AND SAVOR THEIR LOVELY LINES.

SOME ARE CURVED AND WAVY, SOME ARE STRAIGHT. NOTICE ANY INTERESTING GRAINS OR TEXTURES.

LET A LITTLE STEAM RISE OFF THEM, LEAN IN, AND SLURP AWAY.

RAMEN NOODLES HAVE GREAT BODY, DISTINCT IN THEIR CHEWINESS FROM NON-ALKALINE NOODLES, WHICH FALL APART IN HOT SOUP. ENJOY THE SATISFYING CHEW OF A GOOD NOODLE.

RUBBING YOUR CHOPSTICKS TOGETHER IS CONSIDERED BAD ETIQUETTE; IT IMPLIES TO YOUR HOST THAT THEY ARE SERVING YOU WITH CHEAP CHOPSTICKS (OR EVEN INDICATES THAT YOU USUALLY DINE AT LOW-QUALITY ESTABLISHMENTS!).

NOW, GET AT THOSE TOPPINGS. THESE WILL VARY WILDLY, BUT THERE WILL USUALLY BE A BIG, DELICIOUS SLAB OF CHASHU TO PICK UP WITH YOUR CHOPSTICKS AND ENJOY BITE BY BITE.

IN JAPANESE CULTURE AND RELIGIONS, A BOWL OF RICE WITH A PAIR OF CHOPSTICKS STICKING OUT OF IT IS OFTEN OFFERED TO THE DEAD.

THERE SHOULD BE AN EGG PRESENT AS WELL; PICK IT UP IN YOUR SPOON AND GENTLY CLUTCH IT WITH YOUR CHOPSTICKS TO BRING IT TO YOUR MOUTH FOR THE FIRST BITE.

DEPENDING ON THE FIRMNESS OF THE EGG, EITHER IT WILL HOLD TOGETHER OR YOU'LL STRIKE A MOTHER LODE OF GOLDEN SOFT YOLK (ESPECIALLY WITH *ONSEN* EGGS).

DON'T FRET! YOU CAN CONTAIN THIS DELICIOUSNESS IN YOUR SPOON, OR LET IT RUN ONTO THE NOODLES OR OTHER TOPPINGS, OR EVEN INTO THE BROTH.

SO TO LEAVE YOUR CHOPSTICKS LYING IN YOUR BOWL OF RAMEN (OR ANY OTHER FOOD, FOR THAT MATTER) CAN TEETER ON BEING OFFENSIVE — AND EVEN SPOOKY!

IF THE EGG IS MORE FIRMLY COOKED, LET IT HANG OUT IN THE HOT BROTH BETWEEN BITES!

SIMPLY LAY YOUR CHOPSTICKS ACROSS A CORNER OF YOUR BOWL WHEN NOT IN USE.

NOW, IN SENSORY OVERDRIVE, YOU'LL FEEL A NATURAL PULL TO KEEP YOUR HEAD TUCKED DOWN OVER THE BOWL, REALIZING WHY RAMEN IS A RATHER INDIVIDUAL EXPERIENCE.

THE SUFFIX -YA INDICATES A SHOP SELLING THE WORD THAT CAME BEFORE IT.

*RAMEN-YA* SIMPLY MEANS RAMEN SHOP!

ラーメン屋

WHILE IT'S FUN TO MAKE AND SHARE RAMEN WITH OTHERS AT HOME, IN A TYPICAL RAMEN-YA IN JAPAN, SEATS DON'T FACE OTHER CUSTOMERS, AND IF THEY AREN'T AT A BAR FACING THE KITCHEN, THEY ARE AT A BAR FACING A WALL.

YOU AREN'T THERE TO CATCH UP WITH AN OLD FRIEND, OR TO LINGER A LONG WHILE OVER DRINKS.

IT'S A QUICK MEAL; YOU WANT TO EAT EVERYTHING WHILE IT'S HOT, REMEMBERING THAT WHEN BROTH IS THAT SCORCHING HOT, THE NOODLES ARE STILL COOKING.

OF COURSE THINGS MIGHT MOVE AT A SLOWER PACE IN THE AT-HOME EXPERIENCE, BUT YOU CAN ALWAYS CATCH UP WHEN THE BOWL IS EMPTY!

HOW WAS WORK TODAY?

CAN'T TALK — RAMEN.

## WHAT TO DRINK TO WASH IT ALL DOWN?

IN GENERAL, LOOK TO BEVERAGES THAT WILL BE REFRESHING AND NOT COMPETE WITH THE FLAVORS OF THE SOUP.

COLD WATER IS A GREAT CLEANSER BETWEEN SLURPS, AND YOUR MOUTH WILL APPRECIATE THE RELIEF.

LIGHTER, JAPANESE-STYLE BEER DOES WELL IN THIS ROLE AS WELL.

BIG IPAS AND FINE WINES MIGHT BE BETTER ENJOYED BEFORE — OR SAVED FOR AFTER — THE MEAL!

AND REMEMBER, IT'S OKAY TO PICK UP THAT BOWL TO SLURP DOWN EVERY LAST DROP AND USE YOUR CHOPSTICKS TO SLIDE EVERY LAST NOODLE INTO YOUR MOUTH!

EAT WITH RELISH! ENJOY! AND WHEN YOU'VE REACHED THE DEEP BOTTOM OF YOUR BOWL, SIT BACK, WIPE YOUR MOUTH (AND FACE!),

AND REVEL IN THE WARMTH YOU JUST PUT IN YOUR BELLY.

# NAVIGATING a JAPANESE RAMEN-YA
## with BRIAN MACDUCKSTON of RAMEN ADVENTURES

BRIAN MACDUCKSTON IS *THE* GO-TO GUY TO MAKE SENSE OF JAPAN'S VAST RAMEN OFFERINGS.

HE'S LIVED IN TOKYO SINCE 2006, SLURPING NOODLES IN 1,000+ SHOPS AND GIVING TOURS OF HIS FAVORITES — CHECK HIM OUT ON THE INDISPENSABLE RAMEN ADVENTURES (RAMENADVENTURES.COM).

HERE'S HIS RUNDOWN ON HOW TO NAVIGATE A JAPANESE RAMEN-YA.

A LONG LINE IS AN INDICATION OF A GOOD SHOP!

BUY A TICKET AT THE VENDING MACHINE. WHEN IN DOUBT, GO FOR THE UPPER LEFT BUTTON — THIS IS USUALLY THE SHOP'S MOST CELEBRATED BOWL.

ラーメン = RAMEN!

EACH SEAT INSIDE IS PRECIOUS — DON'T HOLD SPOTS IN LINE!

RAMEN-YAS ARE CASH ONLY!

ASK "OSUSUME?" (OH-SU-SU-MEH) TO GET THE SHOP'S RECOMMENDATION.

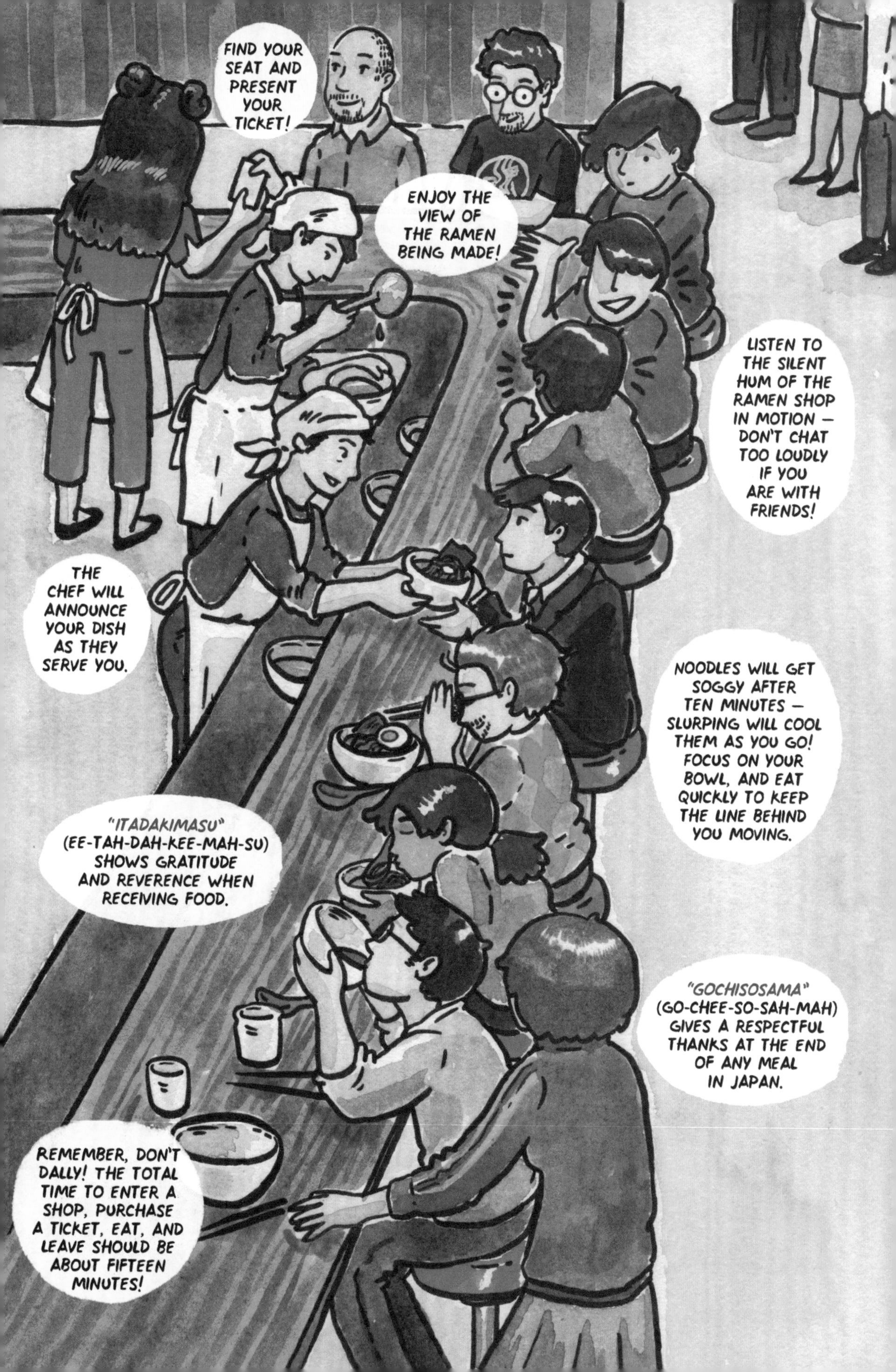
FIND YOUR SEAT AND PRESENT YOUR TICKET!
ENJOY THE VIEW OF THE RAMEN BEING MADE!
LISTEN TO THE SILENT HUM OF THE RAMEN SHOP IN MOTION — DON'T CHAT TOO LOUDLY IF YOU ARE WITH FRIENDS!
THE CHEF WILL ANNOUNCE YOUR DISH AS THEY SERVE YOU.
NOODLES WILL GET SOGGY AFTER TEN MINUTES — SLURPING WILL COOL THEM AS YOU GO! FOCUS ON YOUR BOWL, AND EAT QUICKLY TO KEEP THE LINE BEHIND YOU MOVING.
"ITADAKIMASU" (EE-TAH-DAH-KEE-MAH-SU) SHOWS GRATITUDE AND REVERENCE WHEN RECEIVING FOOD.
"GOCHISOSAMA" (GO-CHEE-SO-SAH-MAH) GIVES A RESPECTFUL THANKS AT THE END OF ANY MEAL IN JAPAN.
REMEMBER, DON'T DALLY! THE TOTAL TIME TO ENTER A SHOP, PURCHASE A TICKET, EAT, AND LEAVE SHOULD BE ABOUT FIFTEEN MINUTES!

# PANTRY

A WELL-STOCKED PANTRY IS LESS COMPLEX THAN YOU MIGHT THINK — IN ADDITION TO KEEPING YOUR FRIDGE AND FREEZER STOCKED WITH STOCKS, TARES, MEAT, TOPPINGS, AND NOODLES, HAVING THESE COMMONLY USED INGREDIENTS AROUND WILL MAKE FOR A SMOOTH RAMEN-MAKING EXPERIENCE!

EVERYTHING HERE CAN BE FOUND IN JAPANESE MARKETS, LARGER ASIAN MARKETS, OR ONLINE.

## SHOYU (SOY SAUCE)

SOY SAUCE VARIETIES RANGE FROM BARGAIN BUCKET TO SUPER ARTISANAL.

JAPANESE SHOYU AND TAMARI ARE THINNER THAN CHINESE SOY SAUCES, SO BE AWARE OF STRENGTH OF FLAVOR WHEN USING AND ADJUST ACCORDINGLY.

FOR COOKING AND BRAISES, STANDARD SUPERMARKET SOY SAUCE FROM JAPAN, CHINA, AND EVEN THE U.S. WILL SUFFICE, BUT BE SURE IT IS BREWED WITH FERMENTED SOY BEANS, NOT HYDROLYZED PROTEINS.

FOR TARES, IT'S WORTH IT TO SPEND A LITTLE MORE ON ARTISANAL PRODUCTS TO SHOWCASE SUBTLE FLAVOR DIFFERENCES.

## MISO

MISO IS MADE FROM SOYBEANS FERMENTED WITH A FUNGUS KNOWN AS *KOJI* AND THEN AGED.

WE USE TWO TYPES OF MISO IN OUR BASIC MISO TARE (P. 48), BUT — AS WITH SHOYU — THE MISO WORLD IS BEAUTIFULLY VAST AND COMPLEX, OFFERING YOUR TARE ENDLESS DYNAMIC POSSIBILITIES!

## GOCHUJANG

WE USE THIS FERMENTED KOREAN CHILE PASTE IN ADDITION TO OR IN PLACE OF MISO WHEN WE WANT THE SALTY RICHNESS WITH A BIT MORE SPICE.

## SANSHO AND SICHUAN PEPPERCORNS
THESE TWO CLOSELY RELATED DRIED BERRIES OFFER A PLEASANTLY NUMBING, CITRUSY ELEMENT, OFTEN USED TO BALANCE CHILE HEAT IN SPICY DISHES — A STRANGELY BEGUILING SENSATION! WE LIKE TO GRIND AND SIFT THE BERRIES BEFORE USING.

## SHICHIMI TOGARASHI (7-FLAVOR CHILI PEPPER)
A BLEND OF SPICES INCLUDING CHILES, SANSHO, NORI, SESAME SEEDS, ORANGE PEEL, AND OTHER SPICES, DEPENDING ON THE MAKER. PERFECT TO SPRINKLE ON TOP OF RAMEN!

## SEA SALT
WE PREFER NATURAL SEA SALT OVER MANUFACTURED KOSHER SALT IN OUR KITCHEN — AND ESPECIALLY IN OUR SHIO TARE (P. 46) — FOR ITS SUBTLE FLAVOR DIFFERENCES ACROSS TYPES. IT'S NOT MANDATORY, BUT THERE'S A HUGE OCEAN OF SALT OUT THERE — EXPLORE IT!

## DRY RAMEN NOODLES
IF YOU'RE FRESH OUT OF HANDMADE RAMEN NOODLES (P. 79), IT DOESN'T HURT TO HAVE DRIED NOODLES IN YOUR PANTRY AS WELL.

USE 2–3 OUNCES DRY NOODLES FOR EACH BOWL OF RAMEN, AND REMEMBER THAT THEY'LL TAKE LONGER TO COOK — FOLLOW THE PACKAGE DIRECTIONS!

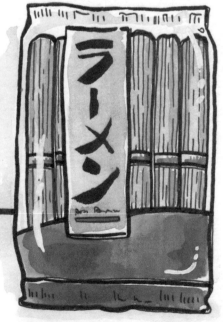

## KATSUOBUSHI

THESE FISH FLAKES ARE MADE FROM DRIED AND SMOKED SKIPJACK TUNA. OFTEN FOUND DANCING ATOP HOT FOODS IN JAPAN, THEY BRING IMMENSE AMOUNTS OF UMAMI TO OUR BROTHS.

ADMIRE THE BEAUTIFUL ARTISAN KATSUOBUSHI SOLD WHOLE (RESEMBLING BLOCKS OF WOOD AND REQUIRING A SPECIAL PLANE TO SHAVE THIN), BUT BUY THE ALREADY SHAVED VARIETY FOR YOUR RAMEN.

## NIBOSHI

THESE TINY SARDINES ADD DEEP UMAMI TO BROTHS, BUT THE FLAVOR CAN BE TOO ASSERTIVE AND FISHY FOR SOME PALATES. FOR THOSE WHO LIKE THEM, THEY ARE GREAT ATOP STEAMED RICE AND OTHER JAPANESE DISHES AS WELL.

## KOMBU

KOMBU IS A THICK KELP, RICH IN GLUTAMIC ACID (AN AMINO ACID RESPONSIBLE FOR ADDING THE PROTEIN-RICH UMAMI TASTE TO FOODS), THAT WE USE TO FORTIFY STOCKS.

## NORI

SHEETS OF DRIED SEAWEED KNOWN FOR THEIR USE IN SUSHI, BUT GREAT FOR THE OCEANIC UMAMI DOSE THEY ADD TO RAMEN. LOOK FOR ROASTED NORI, BUT SKIP THE SEASONED VARIETY, AS THAT IS MORE FOR SNACKING OUT OF THE BAG. FOR MAX CRISPNESS, MAKE NORI ONE OF THE FIRST STOPS WHEN SLURPING YOUR BOWL.

## MIRIN

MIRIN IS A RICE WINE, SWEETER THAN SAKE AND WITH A LOWER ALCOHOL CONTENT, USED TO SEASON OUR TARES (P. 46-48) AND BRAISES.

UBIQUITOUS IN JAPANESE COOKING, YOU'VE MOST LIKELY TASTED IT BEFORE IN SUSHI RICE.

## SAKE

SAKE IS A RICE WINE WE USE WHEN WE WANT A LITTLE MORE FINESSE THAN WHAT MIRIN OFFERS.

AS WITH WINE, THE SAKE YOU USE FOR COOKING SHOULD BE GOOD ENOUGH FOR DRINKING.

## FISH SAUCE

MORE COMMON IN SOUTHEAST ASIA AND UNTRADITIONAL TO THE JAPANESE PANTRY, FISH SAUCE IS A MAJOR PLAYER IN OUR RIFF, ADOBO CHICKEN RAMEN (P. 163), AND WE LIKE TO HAVE IT ON HAND FOR AN EASY UMAMI BOOST IN BROTHS, BRAISES, AND ANYWHERE ELSE IT'S NEEDED.

## NEGI

STANDARD GREEN ONIONS ARE A GREAT SUBSTITUTE FOR THIS SLIGHTLY LARGER COUSIN.

WHEN WE CALL FOR NEGI IN THIS BOOK, WE ARE REFERRING TO THE GREENS ONLY, CUT THINLY AND DIAGONALLY. OTHERWISE, WE'LL REFER TO GREEN ONIONS AND INSTRUCT HOW THEY SHOULD BE CUT ON A RECIPE-BY-RECIPE BASIS.

# EQUIPMENT

YOU DON'T NEED A LOT OF FANCY, SPECIALIZED EQUIPMENT TO COOK WELL, AND CHANCES ARE YOU HAVE EVERYTHING YOU NEED TO MAKE A BOWL OF RAMEN IN YOUR HOME KITCHEN ALREADY.

BUT HERE ARE A FEW TOOLS TO HELP STREAMLINE THE PROCESS, AND MINIMIZING THE MOVING PARTS CAN HELP YOU FOCUS ON WHAT MATTERS — THE RAMEN!

THESE ITEMS ARE AVAILABLE IN JAPANESE MARKETS, LARGER ASIAN STORES, AND ONLINE AS WELL.

## STOCK POT
A 12 TO 16 QUART STOCK POT WILL GIVE YOUR SOUPS PLENTY OF ROOM TO SIMMER AND IS GREAT FOR COOKING NOODLES — THE HIGHER THE RATIO OF HOT WATER TO NOODLES, THE FASTER YOUR WATER WILL RETURN TO A BOIL, AND THE LESS STARCHY THE WATER WILL GET.

## EXTRA POTS
AT GO-TIME, RAMEN CAN BE A MULTI-POT OPERATION, SO IT'S USEFUL TO HAVE A COUPLE OF SAUCE POTS AVAILABLE RANGING IN SIZE FROM 1 TO 2 QUARTS TO 4 TO 6 QUARTS. ALSO, HEAVY, LIDDED DUTCH OVENS WORK GREAT FOR OUR CHASHU (P. 89) AND OTHER BRAISES.

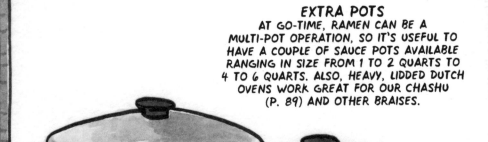

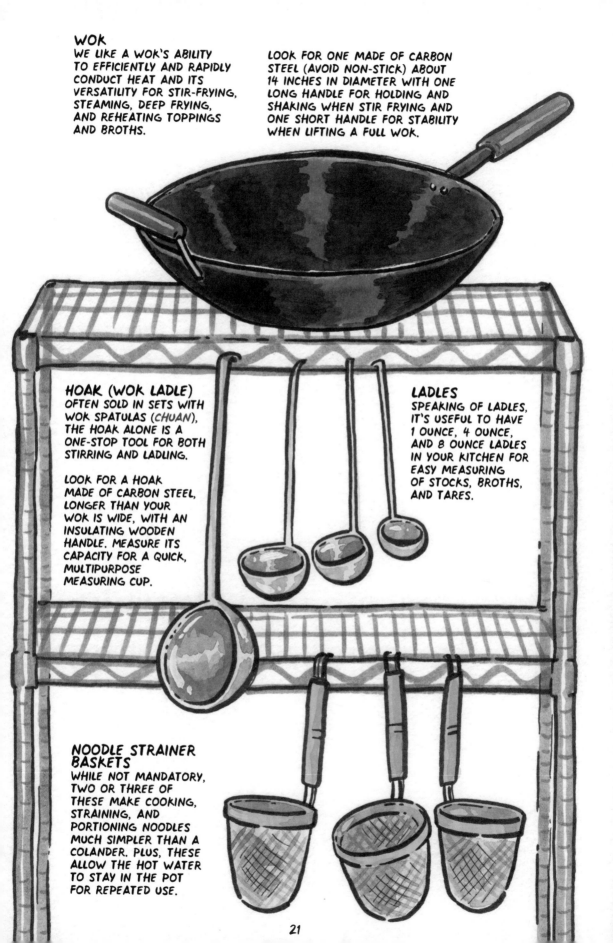

## WOK

WE LIKE A WOK'S ABILITY TO EFFICIENTLY AND RAPIDLY CONDUCT HEAT AND ITS VERSATILITY FOR STIR-FRYING, STEAMING, DEEP FRYING, AND REHEATING TOPPINGS AND BROTHS.

LOOK FOR ONE MADE OF CARBON STEEL (AVOID NON-STICK) ABOUT 14 INCHES IN DIAMETER WITH ONE LONG HANDLE FOR HOLDING AND SHAKING WHEN STIR FRYING AND ONE SHORT HANDLE FOR STABILITY WHEN LIFTING A FULL WOK.

## HOAK (WOK LADLE)

OFTEN SOLD IN SETS WITH WOK SPATULAS (CHUAN), THE HOAK ALONE IS A ONE-STOP TOOL FOR BOTH STIRRING AND LADLING.

LOOK FOR A HOAK MADE OF CARBON STEEL, LONGER THAN YOUR WOK IS WIDE, WITH AN INSULATING WOODEN HANDLE. MEASURE ITS CAPACITY FOR A QUICK, MULTIPURPOSE MEASURING CUP.

## LADLES

SPEAKING OF LADLES, IT'S USEFUL TO HAVE 1 OUNCE, 4 OUNCE, AND 8 OUNCE LADLES IN YOUR KITCHEN FOR EASY MEASURING OF STOCKS, BROTHS, AND TARES.

## NOODLE STRAINER BASKETS

WHILE NOT MANDATORY, TWO OR THREE OF THESE MAKE COOKING, STRAINING, AND PORTIONING NOODLES MUCH SIMPLER THAN A COLANDER. PLUS, THESE ALLOW THE HOT WATER TO STAY IN THE POT FOR REPEATED USE.

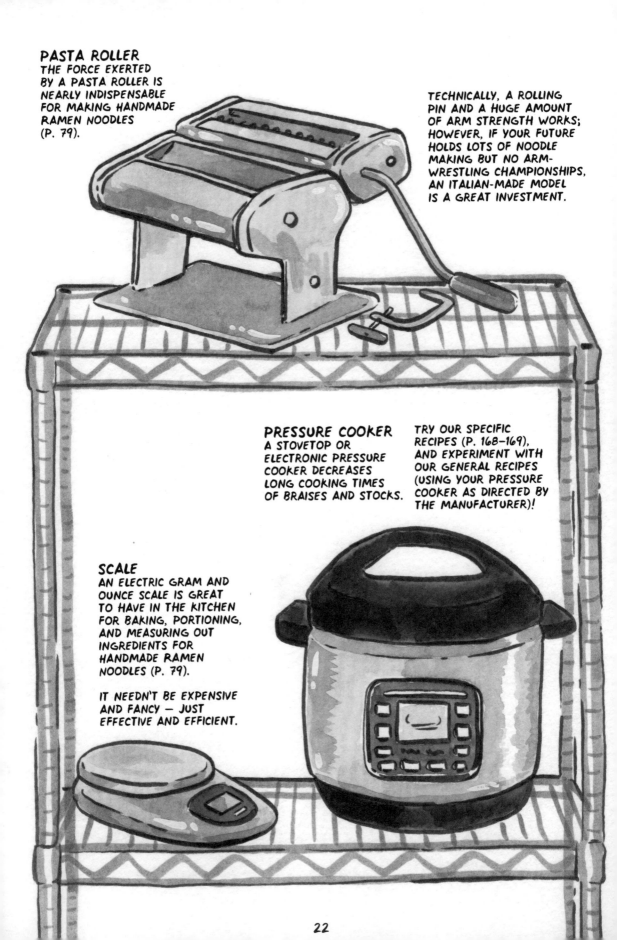

**PASTA ROLLER**
THE FORCE EXERTED BY A PASTA ROLLER IS NEARLY INDISPENSABLE FOR MAKING HANDMADE RAMEN NOODLES (P. 79).

TECHNICALLY, A ROLLING PIN AND A HUGE AMOUNT OF ARM STRENGTH WORKS; HOWEVER, IF YOUR FUTURE HOLDS LOTS OF NOODLE MAKING BUT NO ARM-WRESTLING CHAMPIONSHIPS, AN ITALIAN-MADE MODEL IS A GREAT INVESTMENT.

**PRESSURE COOKER**
A STOVETOP OR ELECTRONIC PRESSURE COOKER DECREASES LONG COOKING TIMES OF BRAISES AND STOCKS.

TRY OUR SPECIFIC RECIPES (P. 168–169), AND EXPERIMENT WITH OUR GENERAL RECIPES (USING YOUR PRESSURE COOKER AS DIRECTED BY THE MANUFACTURER)!

**SCALE**
AN ELECTRIC GRAM AND OUNCE SCALE IS GREAT TO HAVE IN THE KITCHEN FOR BAKING, PORTIONING, AND MEASURING OUT INGREDIENTS FOR HANDMADE RAMEN NOODLES (P. 79).

IT NEEDN'T BE EXPENSIVE AND FANCY — JUST EFFECTIVE AND EFFICIENT.

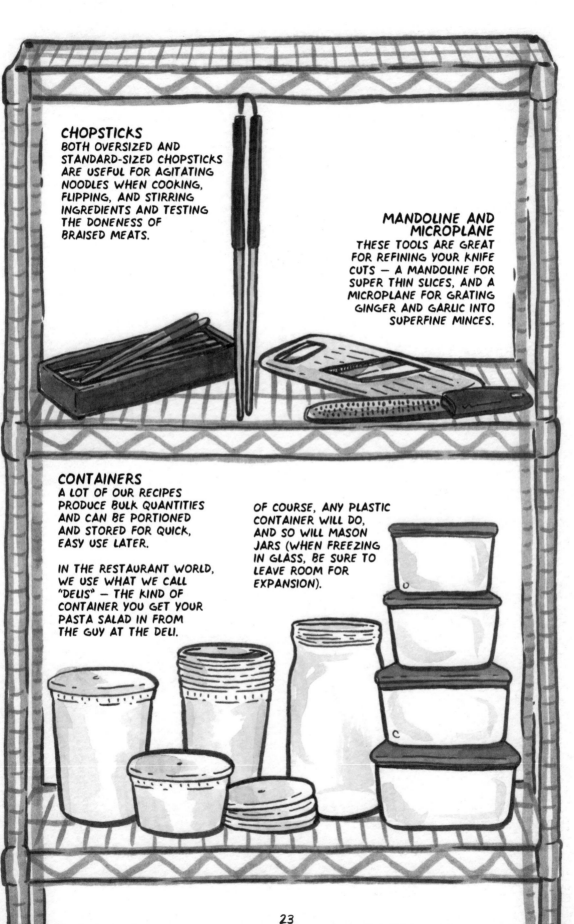

## CHOPSTICKS
BOTH OVERSIZED AND STANDARD-SIZED CHOPSTICKS ARE USEFUL FOR AGITATING NOODLES WHEN COOKING, FLIPPING, AND STIRRING INGREDIENTS AND TESTING THE DONENESS OF BRAISED MEATS.

## MANDOLINE AND MICROPLANE
THESE TOOLS ARE GREAT FOR REFINING YOUR KNIFE CUTS — A MANDOLINE FOR SUPER THIN SLICES, AND A MICROPLANE FOR GRATING GINGER AND GARLIC INTO SUPERFINE MINCES.

## CONTAINERS
A LOT OF OUR RECIPES PRODUCE BULK QUANTITIES AND CAN BE PORTIONED AND STORED FOR QUICK, EASY USE LATER.

IN THE RESTAURANT WORLD, WE USE WHAT WE CALL "DELIS" — THE KIND OF CONTAINER YOU GET YOUR PASTA SALAD IN FROM THE GUY AT THE DELI.

OF COURSE, ANY PLASTIC CONTAINER WILL DO, AND SO WILL MASON JARS (WHEN FREEZING IN GLASS, BE SURE TO LEAVE ROOM FOR EXPANSION).

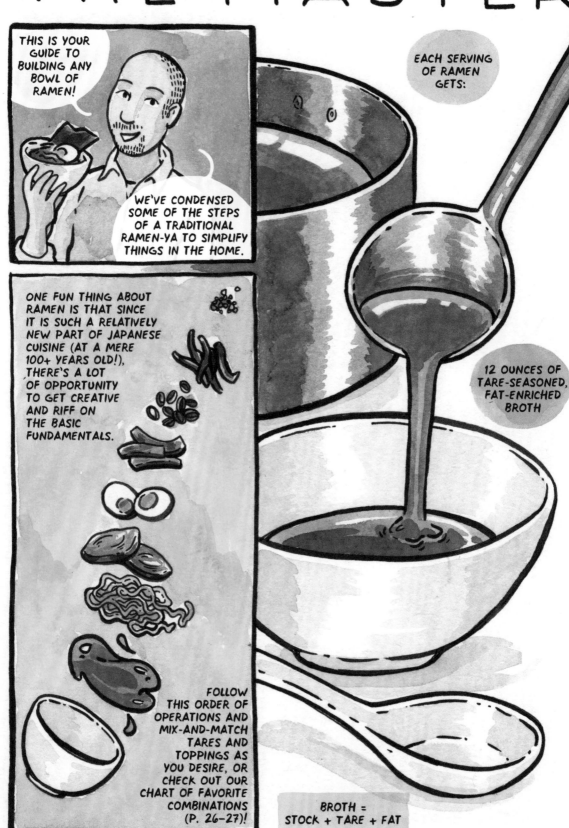

THIS IS YOUR GUIDE TO BUILDING ANY BOWL OF RAMEN!

WE'VE CONDENSED SOME OF THE STEPS OF A TRADITIONAL RAMEN-YA TO SIMPLIFY THINGS IN THE HOME.

ONE FUN THING ABOUT RAMEN IS THAT SINCE IT IS SUCH A RELATIVELY NEW PART OF JAPANESE CUISINE (AT A MERE 100+ YEARS OLD!), THERE'S A LOT OF OPPORTUNITY TO GET CREATIVE AND RIFF ON THE BASIC FUNDAMENTALS.

FOLLOW THIS ORDER OF OPERATIONS AND MIX-AND-MATCH TARES AND TOPPINGS AS YOU DESIRE, OR CHECK OUT OUR CHART OF FAVORITE COMBINATIONS (P. 26-27)!

EACH SERVING OF RAMEN GETS:

12 OUNCES OF TARE-SEASONED, FAT-ENRICHED BROTH

BROTH = STOCK + TARE + FAT

24

# RAMEN BOWL

5 OUNCES HANDMADE RAMEN NOODLES (P. 79),

AND AS MANY TOPPINGS AS YOU LIKE!

# SOME OF OUR

ALL THE FREEDOM IN MIXING AND MATCHING ELEMENTS FOR A BOWL OF RAMEN MAY MAKE IT DIFFICULT TO KNOW WHERE TO START.

THIS CHART LISTS THE COMPONENTS FOR SOME OF OUR FAVORITES AS WELL AS BASIC COMBINATIONS THAT YOU MIGHT SEE ON OFFER IN A RAMEN-YA,

AND BE SURE TO CHECK OUT THE OFFSHOOTS & RIFFS SECTION (P. 127) FOR EVEN MORE START-TO-FINISH GUIDANCE!

| BOWL | | BROTH | |
|---|---|---|---|
| SHIO RAMEN |  |  | SHIO BROTH (P. 46) |
| SHOYU RAMEN |  |  | SHOYU BROTH (P. 47) |
| MISO RAMEN |  |  | MISO BROTH (P. 48) |
| TONKOTSU RAMEN |  |  | TONKOTSU BROTH (P. 52) SEASONED WITH SHIO TARE (P. 46) |
| MEAT HEAD'S DELUXE |  |  | TONKOTSU BROTH (P. 52) SEASONED WITH SHIO TARE (P. 46) |
| VEG HEAD'S DELUXE |  |  | YASAI BROTH (P. 60) SEASONED WITH SHOYU TARE (P. 47) |

# FAVORITE BOWLS

USE 5 OUNCES OF HANDMADE RAMEN NOODLES (P. 79),

5 OUNCES OF STORE-BOUGHT FRESH RAMEN NOODLES,

OR 2 TO 3 OUNCES OF DRIED RAMEN NOODLES IN EACH BOWL.

FINISH EACH BOWL WITH NORI, MENMA (P. 110), AND NEGI!

| MEAT | ACCOMPANIMENTS | | |
|---|---|---|---|
|  CHASHU (P. 89) |  AJITSUKE TAMAGO (P. 104) |  WOK-FRIED BROCCOLI (P. 115) | |
|  CHASHU (P. 89) | ONSEN EGG (P. 108) |  WOK-FRIED MUSHROOMS (P. 114) | |
|  CHASHU (P. 89) |  AJITSUKE TAMAGO (P. 104) |  CRISPY CHICKEN SKINS (P. 117) |  RAYU (P. 124) |
| CHASHU (P. 89) | WOK-FRIED SPINACH (P. 116) | PICKLED SHIITAKE MUSHROOMS (P. 111) | MAYU (P. 125) |
|  CHASHU (P. 89)  YAKITORI (P. 96)  SHREDDED PORK (P. 92)  NIKU DANGO (P. 98) |  AJITSUKE TAMAGO (P. 104)  ONSEN EGG (P. 108) |   CRISPY CHICKEN SKINS (P. 117) |  PICKLED SHIITAKE MUSHROOMS (P. 111)  MAYU (P. 125) |
| :• NONE •: |  AJITSUKE TAMAGO (P. 104)  WOK-FRIED BOK CHOY, RADISH, AND CAULIFLOWER (P. 115) |  PICKLED SHIITAKE MUSHROOMS (P. 111)  RAYU (P. 124) | |

# GET READY

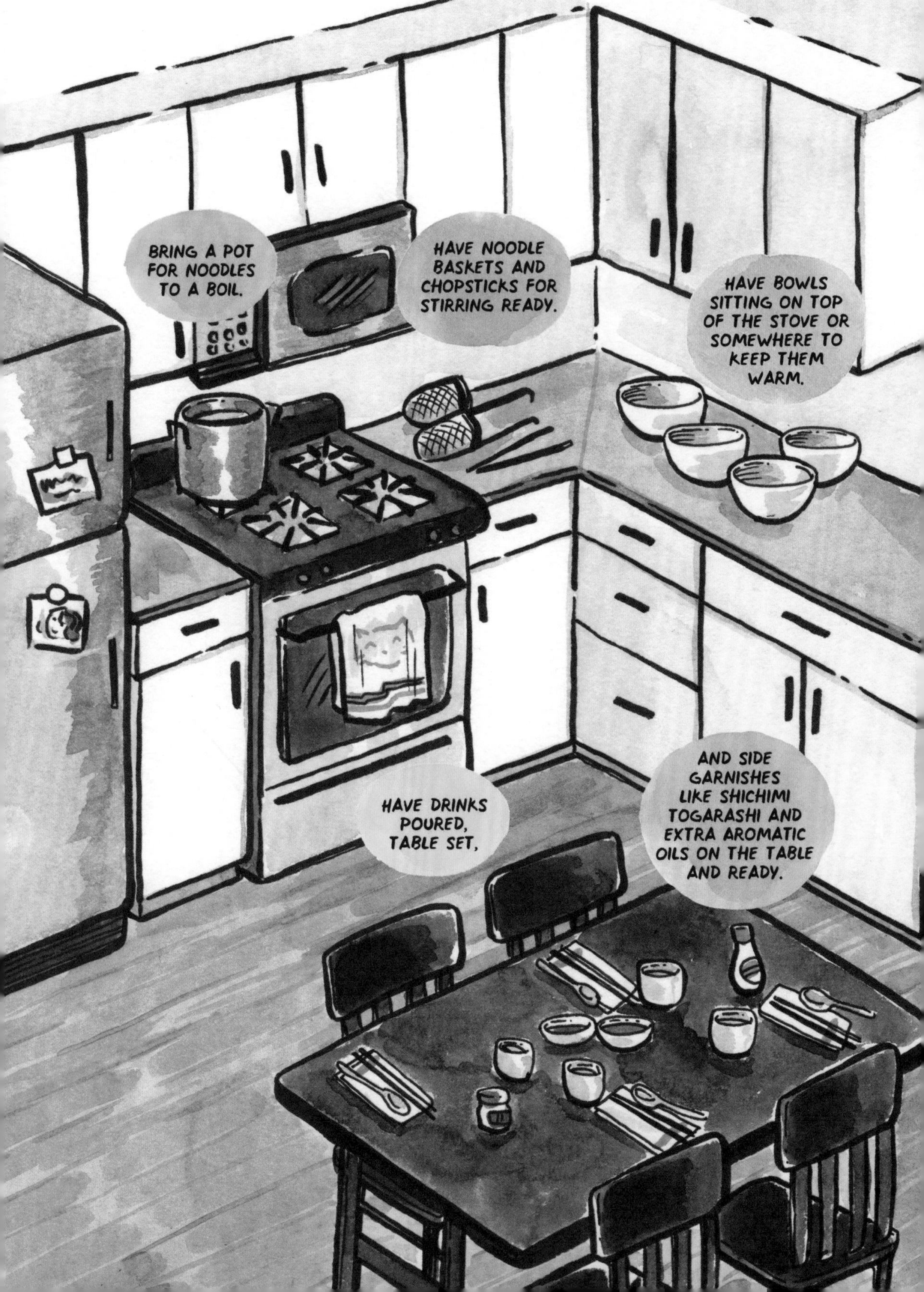
BRING A POT FOR NOODLES TO A BOIL.
HAVE NOODLE BASKETS AND CHOPSTICKS FOR STIRRING READY.
HAVE BOWLS SITTING ON TOP OF THE STOVE OR SOMEWHERE TO KEEP THEM WARM.
HAVE DRINKS POURED, TABLE SET,
AND SIDE GARNISHES LIKE SHICHIMI TOGARASHI AND EXTRA AROMATIC OILS ON THE TABLE AND READY.

# TO RUMBLE

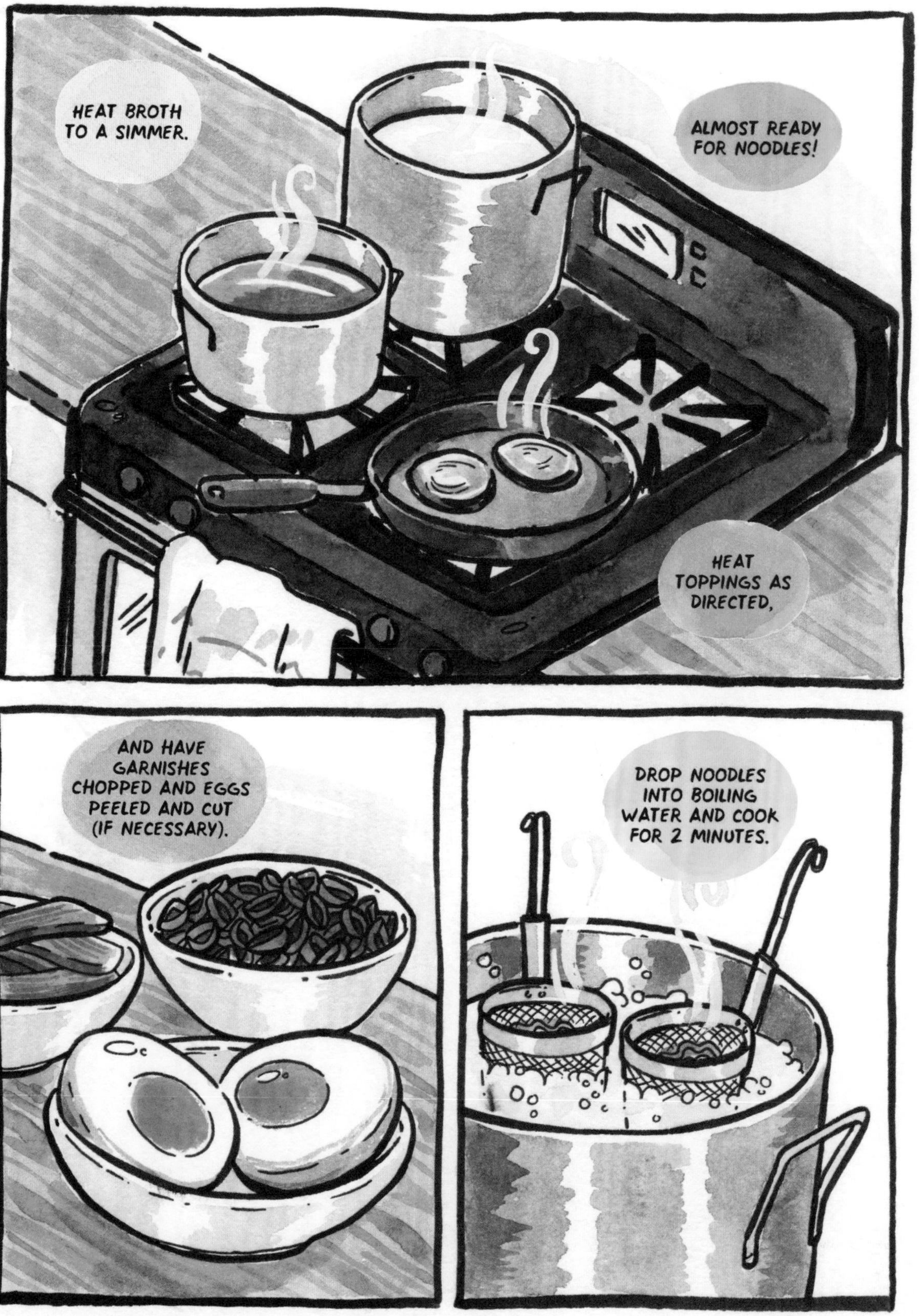

HEAT BROTH TO A SIMMER.
ALMOST READY FOR NOODLES!
HEAT TOPPINGS AS DIRECTED,
AND HAVE GARNISHES CHOPPED AND EGGS PEELED AND CUT (IF NECESSARY).
DROP NOODLES INTO BOILING WATER AND COOK FOR 2 MINUTES.

WITH ONE MINUTE TO GO ON THE NOODLES, LADLE 12 OUNCES OF PIPING HOT BROTH INTO EACH BOWL.

STRAIN NOODLES WELL AND TRANSFER TO BOWLS, ARRANGING NOODLES IN AN ATTRACTIVE MANNER.

PLACE HOT GARNISHES LIKE CHASHU, PULLED CHICKEN, AND WOK-FRIED VEGETABLE AGAINST THE SIDE OF THE BOWL.

NESTLE EGG AGAINST MEAT.

PLACE SMALLER GARNISHES LIKE MENMA, GARI, NEGI, PICKLED SHIITAKE MUSHROOMS, CHARRED SHALLOT AND SCALLION, AND SESAME SEEDS ON TOP OF NOODLES.

DRIZZLE AROMATIC OILS AROUND THE BOWL.

NESTLE CRISPY INGREDIENTS LIKE NORI AND CRISPY CHICKEN SKINS BEHIND NOODLES AND MEATS LAST.

SERVE IMMEDIATELY!

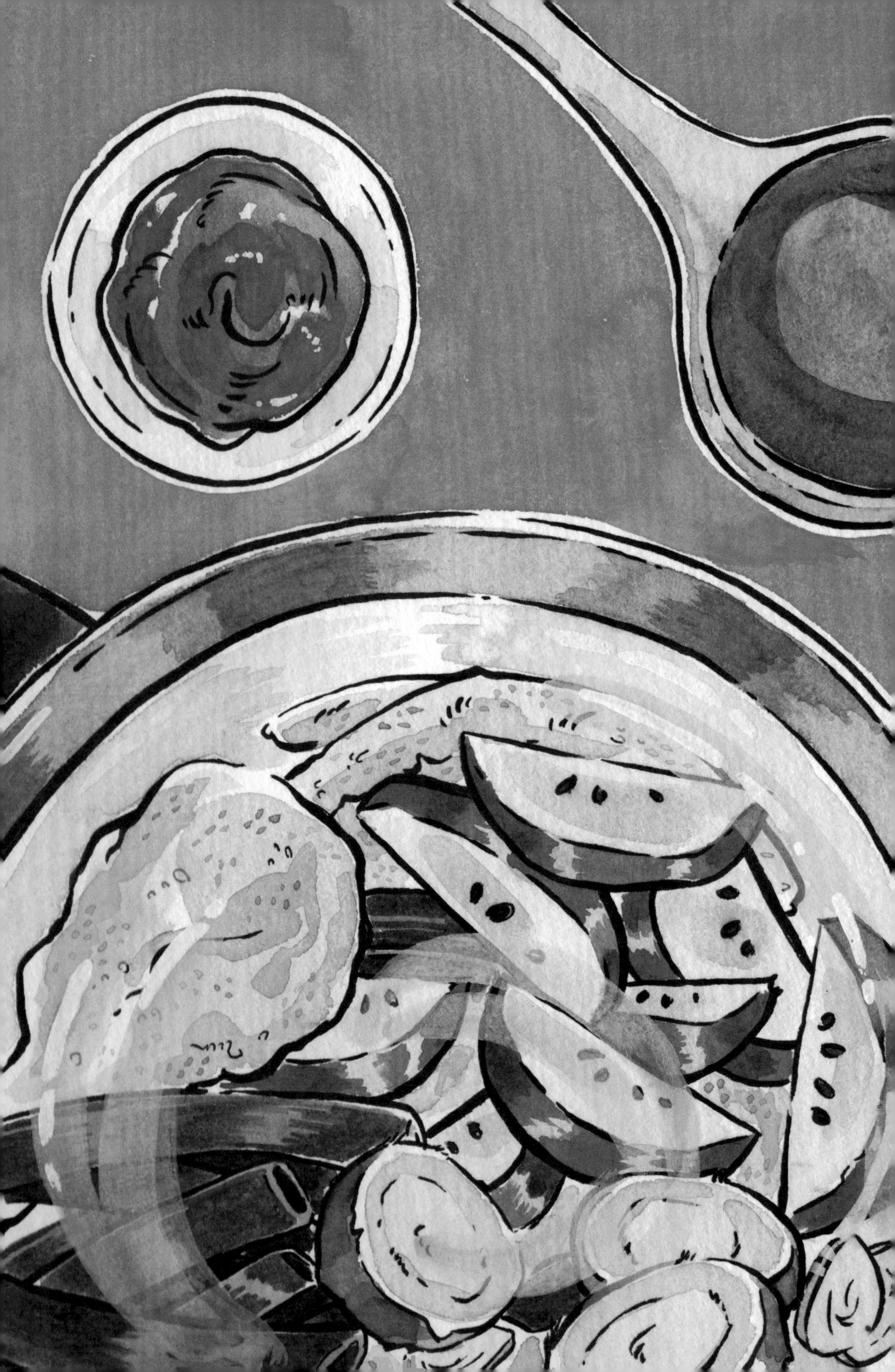

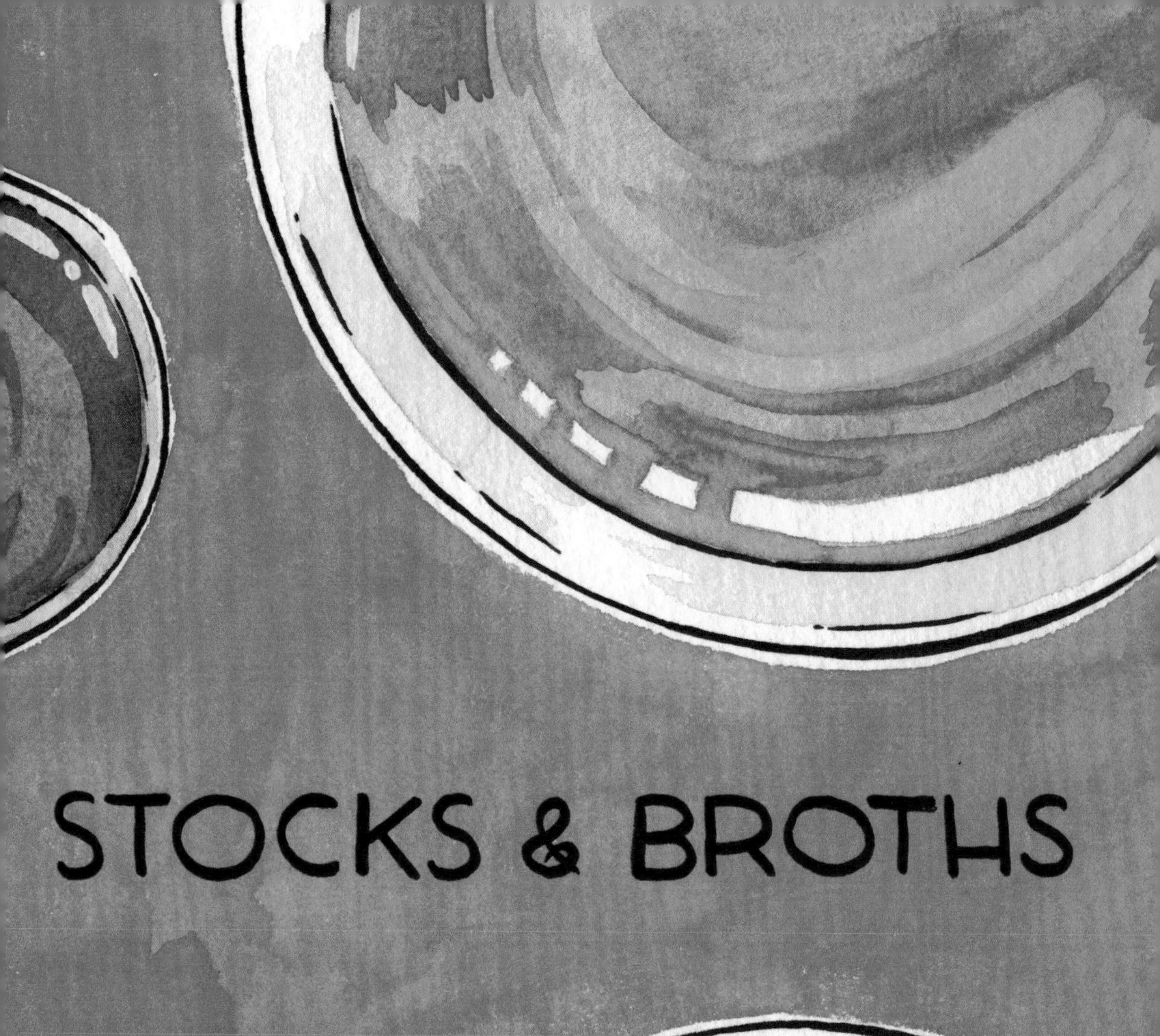

# STOCKS & BROTHS

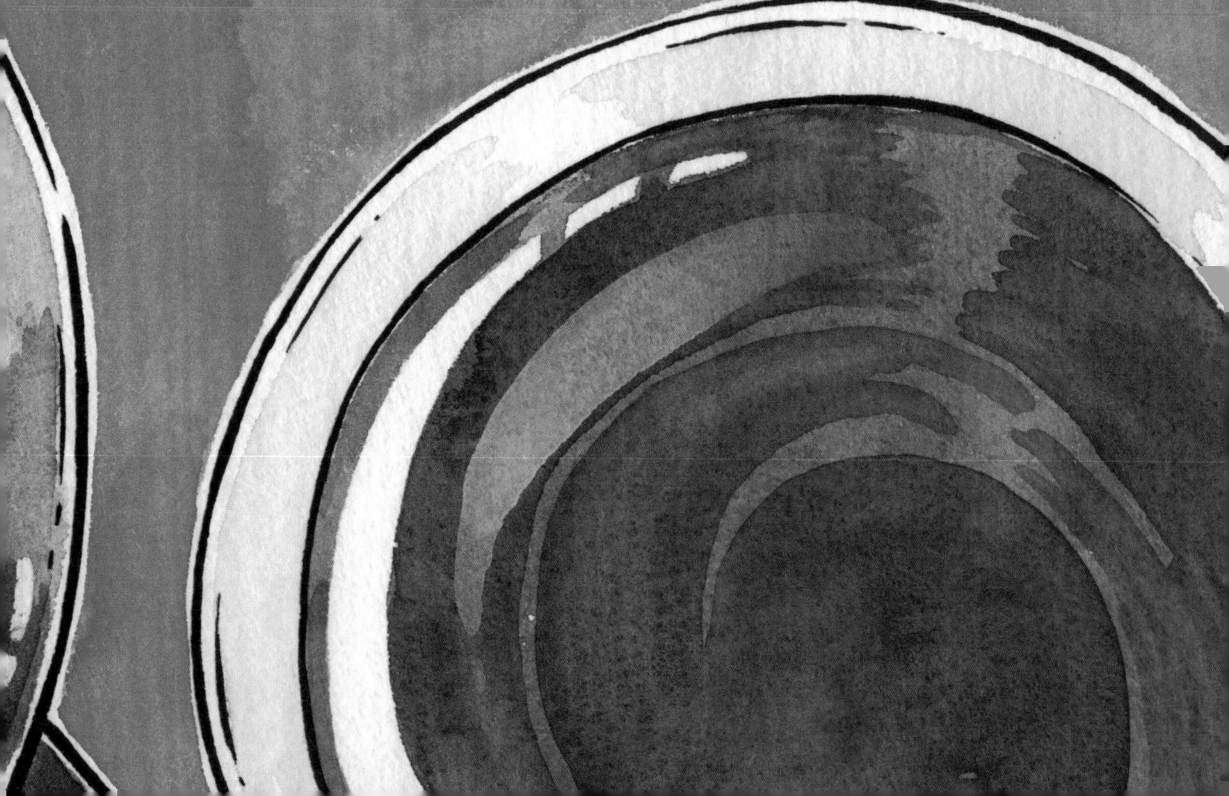

# a word about
# STOCKS, TARES, and BROTHS

WE'LL START WITH THE MOST IMPORTANT FOUNDATION OF A GOOD BOWL OF RAMEN: THE BROTH.

IT STARTS WITH SCENT.

RISING FROM THE SURFACE OF THE SOUP,

THE BROTH'S AROMATIC ELEMENTS DRAW YOU INTO THE DEPTHS OF THE BOWL.

TAKE A FIRST SLURP, AND THE OLFACTORY OPULENCE TURNS INTO A HIGHLY SEASONED RUSH OF SALTY, FATTY DELIGHT.

THE NOODLES AND TOPPINGS ARE INDEED IMPORTANT ELEMENTS AS WELL —

AND WE'LL GET TO THAT —

BUT FOR NOW, LET'S FOCUS ON MAKING OUR BROTHS GREAT.

LET'S DEFINE SOME TERMS BEFORE WE BEGIN. WHAT'S THE DIFFERENCE BETWEEN A STOCK AND A BROTH?

AND TARE — WHAT ON EARTH IS TARE? HERE ARE OUR DEFINITIONS FOR THOSE TERMS:

THE FIRST STEP IS:

## STOCK

A GOOD STOCK IS THE FOUNDATION OF FLAVOR FOR RAMEN. FOR OUR PURPOSES, WE'LL CONSIDER DASHI (P. 45) A STOCK.

IT CONSISTS OF ANIMAL BONES AND/OR AROMATICS THAT ARE SIMMERED IN WATER FOR A LONG TIME,

UNTIL ALL THEIR FLAVOR (AND GELATIN IN THE FORM OF COLLAGEN) HAS BEEN EXTRACTED INTO THE WATER.

THE STOCK ITSELF WILL NOT BE FULLY FLAVORED ENOUGH FOR OUR RAMEN; WE NEED TO SEASON IT WITH:

## TARE

TARE IS THE SEASONING MIXTURE USED TO GIVE RAMEN ITS CHARACTERISTIC DEPTH OF FLAVOR.

IT CAN INCLUDE SALT, MISO, SOY SAUCE, MIRIN, OR EVEN VINEGAR. OPTIONS ARE ENDLESS.

THE MAIN SEASONING IN TARE IS OFTEN WHAT GIVES THE FINAL BROTH (AND THEREFORE BOWL) ITS NAME, SUCH AS SHOYU RAMEN OR MISO RAMEN.

A TARE IS MIXED WITH A STOCK, OR COMBINATION OF STOCKS, TO PRODUCE:

## BROTH

THE FINAL PRODUCT! THE FULLY SEASONED SOUP YOU SLURP WITH YOUR NOODLES AND TOPPINGS IN A BOWL OF RAMEN.

SO!

STOCK   +   TARE   =   BROTH

FIRST, LET'S LEARN ABOUT HOW WE MAKE THESE FOUR WELL-KNOWN BROTHS:

## SHIO
(SALT)

MADE WITH CHICKEN STOCK, DASHI, AND A SALT-BASED TARE.

## SHOYU
(SOY SAUCE)

MADE WITH CHICKEN STOCK, PORK STOCK, DASHI, AND A SOY SAUCE—BASED TARE.

WHILE SHIO, SHOYU, AND MISO ARE MADE WITH STOCKS THAT ARE GENTLY SIMMERED FOR A FEW HOURS,

TONKOTSU IS MADE WITH A STOCK OF PORK BONES THAT ARE BOILED AGGRESSIVELY FOR SEVERAL HOURS, EXTRACTING ALL THE COLLAGEN, FAT, AND PROTEIN AND SUSPENDING IT IN THE LIQUID.

## MISO
(FERMENTED BEAN PASTE)

MADE WITH CHICKEN STOCK, PORK STOCK, DASHI, AND A FERMENTED BEAN PASTE—BASED TARE.

## TONKOTSU
(PORK BONE)

THIS RICH STOCK CAN BE FLAVORED WITH WHATEVER TARE ONE DESIRES.

**ASSARI**
DESCRIBES LIGHTER-BODIED RAMEN

**KOTTERI**
DESCRIBES HEAVIER RAMEN STYLES

NOTE THAT THE PORK AND CHICKEN STOCK RECIPES IN THIS BOOK YIELD FAT AS WELL AS STOCK. KEEP THIS FAT!

THE AMOUNT OF FAT PRODUCED WILL VARY DEPENDING ON HOW MUCH IS ON THE BONES YOU USE TO BEGIN WITH.

A SMALL AMOUNT OF FAT IS A VITAL ADDITION TO ANY BOWL OF RAMEN —

IT NOT ONLY ADDS DEPTH OF FLAVOR AND AROMA, AND COATS THE NOODLES AS YOU SLURP,

BUT ALSO HANGS OUT LIKE A BLANKET ON THE SURFACE OF THE BOWL, KEEPING EVERYTHING UNDERNEATH IT PIPING HOT.

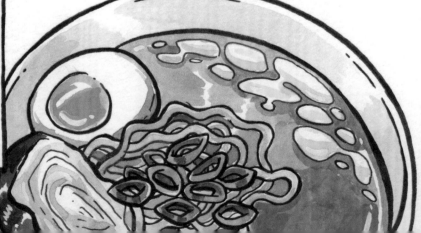

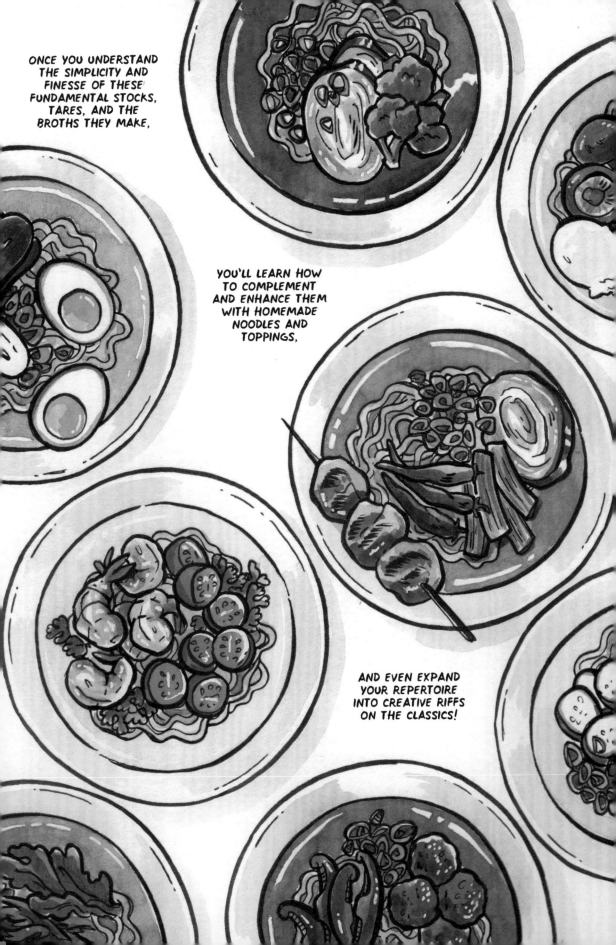

ONCE YOU UNDERSTAND THE SIMPLICITY AND FINESSE OF THESE FUNDAMENTAL STOCKS, TARES, AND THE BROTHS THEY MAKE,

YOU'LL LEARN HOW TO COMPLEMENT AND ENHANCE THEM WITH HOMEMADE NOODLES AND TOPPINGS,

AND EVEN EXPAND YOUR REPERTOIRE INTO CREATIVE RIFFS ON THE CLASSICS!

## SOME TIPS:

WE USE VOLUME MEASUREMENTS FOR THE MOST PART IN THIS BOOK,

BUT FOR SOME INGREDIENTS (LIKE SALT, WHOSE DENSITY VARIES GREATLY DEPENDING ON THE TYPE AND BRAND),

WORKING BY WEIGHT IS MUCH MORE ACCURATE, AND WE'LL GIVE WEIGHT MEASUREMENTS WHEN THIS IS THE CASE.

WHEN CHILLED, THE PORK AND CHICKEN STOCKS WILL BE SOLIDIFIED BECAUSE OF ALL THE LOVELY GELATIN THAT HAS BEEN EXTRACTED FROM THE BONES.

DON'T BE SCARED! THIS IS A GOOD THING THAT WILL ADD BODY TO YOUR BROTHS.

IN ORDER TO QUICKLY ACCOMPLISH THIS IN MANY DIFFERENT WAYS IN A RAMEN-YA, THE FAT IS USUALLY ADDED TO THE BOWL, THEN THE TARE, THEN THE HOT STOCK IS POURED ON TOP OF IT ALL.

HERE, WE SIMPLIFY THINGS BY ADDING THE FAT AND TARE TO THE STOCK WHILE IT HEATS — THIS ALSO ALLOWS YOU TO TASTE AND ADJUST YOUR BROTH BEFORE YOU'VE COMMITTED TO THE WHOLE BOWL OF RAMEN.

OUR STOCK AND TARE RECIPES MAKE LARGE QUANTITIES, ALLOWING YOU TO BUILD A CACHE TO KEEP IN YOUR FRIDGE OR FREEZER;

OUR BROTH RECIPES MAKE ONE BOWL, SO YOU CAN MIX AND MATCH FOR YOUR GUESTS; MULTIPLY AS NECESSARY!

WE USE DIFFERENT TYPES OF MISOS, SALTS, AND SOY SAUCES TO DEVELOP FLAVORS AS WE LIKE AND RECOMMEND.

BUT YOUR TASTES AND THE PRODUCTS AVAILABLE TO YOU MAY BE DIFFERENT, SO FEEL FREE TO ADJUST OUR GUIDELINES TO MAKE YOUR BOWL SUIT YOU!

# IVAN ORKIN

## ON THE BEAUTY of FINESSE VS. THE STRENGTH of BIG FLAVORS

AGAINST ALL ODDS AS AN AMERICAN FROM LONG ISLAND, IVAN ORKIN OPENED HIS EPONYMOUS RAMEN-YA, IVAN RAMEN, IN TOKYO TO TREMENDOUS ACCLAIM IN 2007.

SIX YEARS LATER, HE FOUND THE SAME SUCCESS STATESIDE WHEN HE MOVED THE FRANCHISE TO NEW YORK, OPENING TWO SHOPS IN MANHATTAN.

BUILT ON A STRONG FOUNDATION OF RESEARCH, TESTING, LOVE, AND JUST PLAIN EATING A TON OF RAMEN, IVAN'S RAMEN PROWESS IS KING, AND HE HAS INFLUENCED THE SPREAD OF THE RAMEN GOSPEL WORLDWIDE.

TONKOTSU...

SO FULL...

YOU'VE BEEN EATING TONKOTSU AGAIN, HAVEN'T YOU!

I KNOW HOW YOU FEEL — THE HEAVY SOUPS CAN SEND YOU INTO A PORK FAT-INDUCED STUPOR!

WHEN I FIRST REALLY GOT INTO RAMEN, I'D OFTEN EAT THESE COLLAGEN- AND FAT-LADEN SOUPS AND WONDER WHY I FELT SO TIRED AND BLOATED ALL THE TIME.

THEY WERE SO TEMPTING AND EASY TO LOVE, WITH THEIR RICH, SALTY FLAVORS, BUT TOO MUCH OF THIS DECADENCE WAS MAKING ME LETHARGIC!

I STARTED EATING LIGHTER-BODIED SOUPS — AND IT WAS DISCOVERING THEIR BEAUTIFUL FINESSE THAT LED ME TO SERVE SHIO BROTH IN MY SHOPS.

LIGHTER RAMEN SKILLFULLY BALANCES STRONG FLAVORS LIKE PORK AND DRIED FISH WITH SUBTLE FLAVORS LIKE SEA SALT AND KOMBU, ALLOWING TECHNIQUE TO SHINE.

SOMETIMES HEAVY SOUPS CAN CLOAK POOR TECHNIQUE OR INGREDIENTS, HIDING SHORTCUTS INSTEAD OF SHOWCASING SKILL.

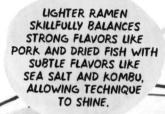

BUT OUR PALATES ARE EASILY DRAWN TO THEIR IMMEDIATELY SATISFYING SALTY AND RICH FLAVORS!

LUCKY PEOPLE AREN'T AS AFFECTED BY A RUSH OF SODIUM AND FAT AS YOU AND ME!

AND WE CAN'T BEGRUDGE PEOPLE'S PERSONAL TASTES, CAN WE?

TAKE ME, FOR EXAMPLE: I *LOVE* MASS-PRODUCED AMERICAN KETCHUP.

I ONCE WENT TO AN AMERICAN-STYLE DINER IN JAPAN CRAVING A TASTE OF HOME.

I ORDERED A BURGER AND FRIES BEFORE I REALIZED THE SHOP SERVED A HOUSEMADE KETCHUP, CHEFFILY DOCTORED UP, INSTEAD OF THE COMMERCIAL PRODUCT I WAS CRAVING.

WORSE, THEY WOULD ONLY SERVE ME A LIMITED, PRECIOUS AMOUNT.

I WAS ANNOYED, BUT THIS LEARNING MOMENT TAUGHT ME THAT SOMETIMES CREATIVE BEAUTY CAN BE OVERSHADOWED BY THE DRAW OF DEEP PERSONAL PREFERENCES.

SO I WON'T TRY TO DICTATE WHAT YOU EAT, BUT DO ME A FAVOR:

AFTER YOU SLEEP THIS ONE OFF, GIVE A LIGHT BOWL OF SHIO RAMEN A TRY!

# CHICKEN STOCK (and fat)

MAKES ABOUT 4 QUARTS STOCK AND 1 CUP FAT

## INGREDIENTS:

5 POUNDS CHICKEN BONES OR CARCASSES, INCLUDING SKIN (IF NOT AVAILABLE, USE 2 WHOLE CHICKENS)

1 POUND CHICKEN FEET (IF AVAILABLE)

1 BUNCH GREEN ONIONS, TRIMMED AND CUT IN HALF CROSS-WISE

2 APPLES (HONEYCRISP, FUJI, OR GALA), QUARTERED

½ POUND FRESH GINGER, UNPEELED, SLICED ¼ INCH THICK

1 BULB GARLIC, CLOVES SMASHED AND PEELED

1 TABLESPOON SALT

PLACE ALL THE INGREDIENTS IN A LARGE POT AND COVER WITH 6 QUARTS OF COLD WATER.

BRING TO A SIMMER OVER MEDIUM-HIGH HEAT, THEN LOWER THE HEAT TO MAINTAIN A SLOW SIMMER.

COOK FOR 4 HOURS, SKIMMING OFF ANY SCUM THAT RISES TO THE SURFACE,

AND AGITATING THE BONES EVERY HOUR OR SO.

AFTER 4 HOURS, THE STOCK WILL HAVE REDUCED TO ABOUT 4 QUARTS; THIS IS NORMAL.

REMOVE FROM THE HEAT AND LET COOL TO ROOM TEMPERATURE.

STRAIN, DISCARD ALL SOLIDS, AND REFRIGERATE, TIGHTLY COVERED, OVERNIGHT.

THE NEXT DAY, REMOVE THE CONGEALED FAT FROM THE TOP OF THE STOCK.

MELT IN A SMALL POT OVER MEDIUM HEAT

AND STORE IN A TIGHT-FITTING JAR IN THE REFRIGERATOR FOR UP TO 1 WEEK,

OR THE FREEZER FOR 6 MONTHS.

1 WEEK

6 MONTHS

REFRIGERATE THE STOCK UNTIL YOU'RE READY TO USE IT, UP TO 1 WEEK, OR FREEZE FOR UP TO 6 MONTHS.

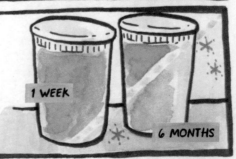

1 WEEK

6 MONTHS

# PORK STOCK (and fat)

MAKES ABOUT 4 QUARTS STOCK AND 1 CUP FAT

## INGREDIENTS:

5 POUNDS PORK BONES, INCLUDING NECK BONES AND TROTTERS (IF NOT AVAILABLE, SUBSTITUTE PORK SHOULDER)

1 POUND CHICKEN FEET (IF AVAILABLE)

1 BUNCH GREEN ONIONS, TRIMMED AND CUT IN HALF CROSS-WISE

2 APPLES (HONEYCRISP, FUJI, OR GALA), QUARTERED

½ POUND FRESH GINGER, UNPEELED, THINLY SLICED

1 BULB GARLIC, CLOVES SMASHED AND PEELED

1 TABLESPOON SALT

PLACE ALL THE INGREDIENTS IN A LARGE POT AND COVER WITH 7 QUARTS OF COLD WATER.

BRING TO A SIMMER OVER MEDIUM-HIGH HEAT, THEN LOWER THE HEAT TO MAINTAIN A SLOW SIMMER.

COOK FOR 6 HOURS, SKIMMING OFF ANY SCUM THAT RISES TO THE SURFACE,

AND AGITATING THE BONES EVERY HOUR OR SO.

AFTER 6 HOURS, THE STOCK WILL HAVE REDUCED TO ABOUT 4 QUARTS; THIS IS NORMAL.

REMOVE FROM THE HEAT AND LET COOL TO ROOM TEMPERATURE.

STRAIN, DISCARD ALL SOLIDS, AND REFRIGERATE, TIGHTLY COVERED, OVERNIGHT.

THE NEXT DAY, REMOVE THE CONGEALED FAT FROM THE TOP OF THE STOCK.

MELT IN A SMALL POT OVER MEDIUM HEAT

REFRIGERATE THE STOCK UNTIL YOU'RE READY TO USE IT, UP TO 1 WEEK, OR FREEZE FOR UP TO 6 MONTHS.

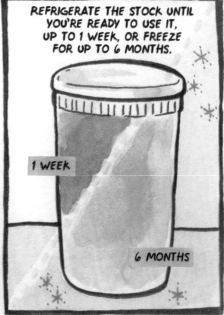

1 WEEK

6 MONTHS

AND STORE IN A TIGHT-FITTING JAR IN THE REFRIGERATOR FOR UP TO 1 WEEK, OR THE FREEZER FOR 6 MONTHS.

1 WEEK

6 MONTHS

# a word about DASHI

DASHI IS A TYPE OF STOCK MADE FROM
*KOMBU* (THICK SEA KELP), DRIED SHIITAKE
MUSHROOMS, AND DRIED FISH SHAVINGS
KNOWN AS *KATSUOBUSHI* (SEE PANTRY,
P. 18 FOR MORE INFORMATION
ON THESE INGREDIENTS).

NOTE! IF YOU ARE
DASHI-CHALLENGED,
KEEP A BOX OF
INSTANT DASHI
IN YOUR PANTRY.

COMMERCIAL INSTANT
DASHIS USUALLY
CONTAIN MSG,
BUT THEY'RE QUICK
AND THEY WORK
WELL TO PROVIDE
AN ESSENTIAL
UMAMI POP TO
RAMEN BROTHS.

DASHI IS AN
INDISPENSABLE
COMPONENT OF
JAPANESE COOKING,
AND ADDS AN UMAMI,
SMOKY DEPTH TO
RAMEN BROTHS.

HONDASHI
BONITO SOUP STOCK

KOMBU

SHIITAKE

KATSUOBUSHI

FOR A STRONGER, MORE
OCEANIC FLAVOR, ADD A
SMALL HANDFUL OF THE
DRIED SARDINES KNOWN
AS *NIBOSHI* (SEE PANTRY,
P. 18) ALONG WITH
THE KATSUOBUSHI.

 # DASHI

MAKES ABOUT 2 QUARTS

**INGREDIENTS:**

5 CUPS (ABOUT 6 OUNCES) DRIED WHOLE SHIITAKE MUSHROOMS

TWO 8 BY 4-INCH SHEETS (ABOUT 1 OUNCE) KOMBU

1 CUP (ABOUT ¼ OUNCE) KATSUOBUSHI (P. 18)

ABOUT 10 NIBOSHI (P. 18), OPTIONAL

PLACE THE MUSHROOMS IN A LARGE POT AND COVER WITH 4 QUARTS OF WATER.

BRING TO A SIMMER OVER HIGH HEAT, THEN LOWER THE HEAT TO MAINTAIN A RAPID SIMMER FOR 30 MINUTES.

REMOVE FROM THE HEAT AND ADD THE KOMBU, KATSUOBUSHI, AND NIBOSHI.

LET STEEP FOR 10 MINUTES, THEN STRAIN.

RINSE THE MUSHROOMS AND RESERVE THEM FOR PICKLED SHIITAKE MUSHROOMS (P. 111) OR DISCARD.

REFRIGERATE THE DASHI UNTIL YOU'RE READY TO USE IT, UP TO 1 WEEK, OR FREEZE FOR UP TO 6 MONTHS.

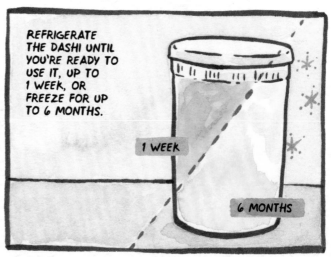

1 WEEK

6 MONTHS

# SHIO BROTH

MAKES 1 SERVING

## INGREDIENTS:

6 OUNCES (¾ CUP) CHICKEN STOCK (P. 42)

6 OUNCES (¾ CUP) DASHI (P. 45)

1 OUNCE (2 TABLESPOONS) SHIO TARE (RECIPE FOLLOWS)

2 TEASPOONS CHICKEN FAT (P. 42)

COMBINE ALL THE INGREDIENTS IN A SAUCEPAN AND BRING TO A SIMMER BEFORE USING FOR THE MASTER RAMEN BOWL (P. 24).

# SHIO TARE

MAKES ENOUGH FOR ABOUT 10 SERVINGS

## INGREDIENTS:

1 OUNCE SEA SALT

4 OUNCES (½ CUP) MIRIN

1 OUNCE (2 TABLESPOONS) RICE WINE VINEGAR

4 OUNCES (½ CUP) WATER

THERE ARE SUBTLE DIFFERENCES ACROSS THE SALT SPECTRUM, AND SHIO RAMEN IS A GREAT PLACE TO EXPLORE THEM BY USING COMBINATIONS OF DIFFERENT SALTS FOR THIS TARE.

SINCE SALTS DIFFER IN DENSITY, SHAPE, AND SIZE, WE HIGHLY RECOMMEND MEASURING BY WEIGHT FOR THIS RECIPE.

STIR ALL THE INGREDIENTS IN A SMALL SAUCEPAN OVER MEDIUM HEAT UNTIL THE SALT DISSOLVES.

USE IMMEDIATELY OR KEEP IN AN AIRTIGHT CONTAINER, REFRIGERATED, FOR UP TO ONE MONTH.

1 MONTH

# SHOYU BROTH

MAKES 1 SERVING

### INGREDIENTS:

4 OUNCES (½ CUP) CHICKEN STOCK (P. 42)

4 OUNCES (½ CUP) PORK STOCK (P. 43)

4 OUNCES (½ CUP) DASHI (P. 45)

2 OUNCES (¼ CUP) SHOYU TARE (RECIPE FOLLOWS)

1 TEASPOON CHICKEN FAT (P. 42)

1 TEASPOON PORK FAT (P. 43)

COMBINE ALL THE INGREDIENTS IN A SAUCEPAN AND BRING TO A SIMMER BEFORE USING FOR THE MASTER RAMEN BOWL (P. 24).

# SHOYU TARE

MAKES ENOUGH FOR ABOUT 10 SERVINGS

### INGREDIENTS:

8 OUNCES (1 CUP) SHOYU

2 OUNCES (ABOUT 3 TABLESPOONS) DARK SOY SAUCE (OR SUBSTITUTE SHOYU)

2 OUNCES (ABOUT 3 TABLESPOONS) MUSHROOM SOY SAUCE (OR SUBSTITUTE SHOYU)

4 OUNCES (½ CUP) MIRIN

2 OUNCES (¼ CUP) RICE WINE VINEGAR

½ OUNCE (1 TABLESPOON) SESAME OIL

2 OUNCES (¼ CUP) WATER

WE MIX DIFFERENT TYPES OF SOY SAUCE HERE FOR MORE COMPLEXITY, ADDING A DARK SOY SAUCE FOR DEPTH OF FLAVOR AND COLOR, AND A MUSHROOM SOY SAUCE FOR EXTRA UMAMI,

BUT FEEL FREE TO ADJUST BASED ON TASTE AND AVAILABILITY.

CHECK THE LABEL TO AVOID FAKE SOY SAUCES MADE OF HYDROLYZED PROTEIN RATHER THAN FERMENTED SOY BEANS.

COMBINE ALL THE INGREDIENTS IN A BOWL AND MIX THOROUGHLY.

USE IMMEDIATELY OR KEEP IN AN AIRTIGHT CONTAINER, REFRIGERATED, FOR UP TO ONE MONTH.

1 MONTH

# MISO BROTH

MAKES 1 SERVING

**INGREDIENTS:**

4 OUNCES (½ CUP)
CHICKEN STOCK
(P. 42)

4 OUNCES (½ CUP)
PORK STOCK (P. 43)

4 OUNCES (½ CUP)
DASHI (P. 45)

2 OUNCES (¼ CUP) MISO
TARE (RECIPE FOLLOWS)

1 TEASPOON CHICKEN
FAT (P. 42)

1 TEASPOON PORK FAT
(P. 43)

COMBINE ALL THE
INGREDIENTS IN
A SAUCEPAN
AND BRING TO A
SIMMER BEFORE
USING FOR THE
MASTER RAMEN
BOWL (P. 24).

 # MISO TARE

MAKES ENOUGH FOR ABOUT 10 SERVINGS

**INGREDIENTS:**

7 OUNCES (⅔ CUP)
AKA MISO

3½ OUNCES (⅓ CUP)
SHIRO MISO

6 OUNCES (¾ CUP) MIRIN

3 OUNCES
(6 TABLESPOONS)
RICE WINE VINEGAR

1½ OUNCES
(3 TABLESPOONS)
SESAME OIL

THIS RECIPE BLENDS RED *AKA
MISO* FOR DEPTH OF FLAVOR
WITH WHITE *SHIRO MISO* FOR
A BIT OF SWEETNESS.

BUT EXPLORE DIFFERENT
MISOS (SEE PANTRY,
P. 16), AND ADJUST
ACCORDING TO YOUR
TASTE.

SHIRO MISO

AKA MISO

STIR ALL THE
INGREDIENTS IN A
SMALL BOWL UNTIL
WELL COMBINED.

USE IMMEDIATELY OR KEEP
IN AN AIRTIGHT CONTAINER,
REFRIGERATED, FOR UP TO
TWO WEEKS.

2 WEEKS

# a word about PAITAN BROTHS

RAMEN CAN BE DESCRIBED AS
*ASSARI* (A LIGHTER-BODIED SOUP)
OR *KOTTERI* (A HEAVIER BROTH).

ASSARI

KOTTERI

SO FAR, THE BROTHS WE'VE
MADE SKEW TO THE ASSARI
SIDE OF THE SPECTRUM,

AND MORE SPECIFICALLY FIT IN
THE CLEAR SOUP CATEGORY
KNOWN AS *CHINTAN*.

NOW, LET'S
TAKE A LOOK
AT A COUPLE
OF KOTTERI
BROTHS —

SPECIFICALLY, TWO
THICK, CREAMY BROTHS
DESCRIBED AS *PAITAN*
(MEANING WHITE SOUP)
THAT ARE QUITE POPULAR
IN THE RAMEN WORLD:
*TONKOTSU* AND
*TORIKOTSU.*

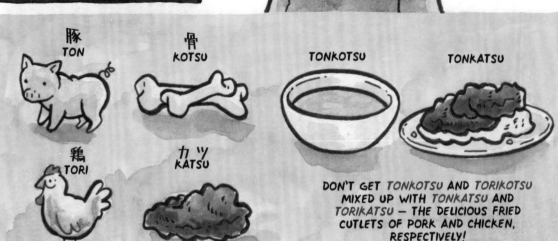

豚
TON

骨
KOTSU

鶏
TORI

カツ
KATSU

TONKOTSU

TONKATSU

DON'T GET *TONKOTSU* AND *TORIKOTSU*
MIXED UP WITH *TONKATSU* AND
*TORIKATSU* — THE DELICIOUS FRIED
CUTLETS OF PORK AND CHICKEN,
RESPECTIVELY!

FOR OUR STANDARD STOCKS AND BROTHS, WE TAKE CARE TO COOK THE BONES AT A SLOW SIMMER TO KEEP THE STOCK NICE AND CLEAR,

BUT STOCKS DESTINED FOR PAITAN BROTHS GET BOILED HARD AND HEAVY.

A HARD BOIL EXTRACTS AS MUCH GELATIN AS POSSIBLE (NOT TO MENTION A BIT OF FAT) FROM THE BONES AND SUSPENDS IT IN THE SOUP,

CREATING A SNOW-WHITE APPEARANCE AND A VERY RICH BASE.

JUST AS WITH OUR OTHER STOCKS, THIS EMULSIFIED STOCK IS THEN SEASONED WITH A TARE BEFORE SERVING;

ANY TARE WOULD BE DELICIOUS, BUT REMEMBER THAT THE CLEAR SHIO TARE (P. 46) WILL KEEP THE COLOR YOU WORKED SO HARD TO CREATE TRUE TO ITS DESCRIPTION AS A PAITAN BROTH.

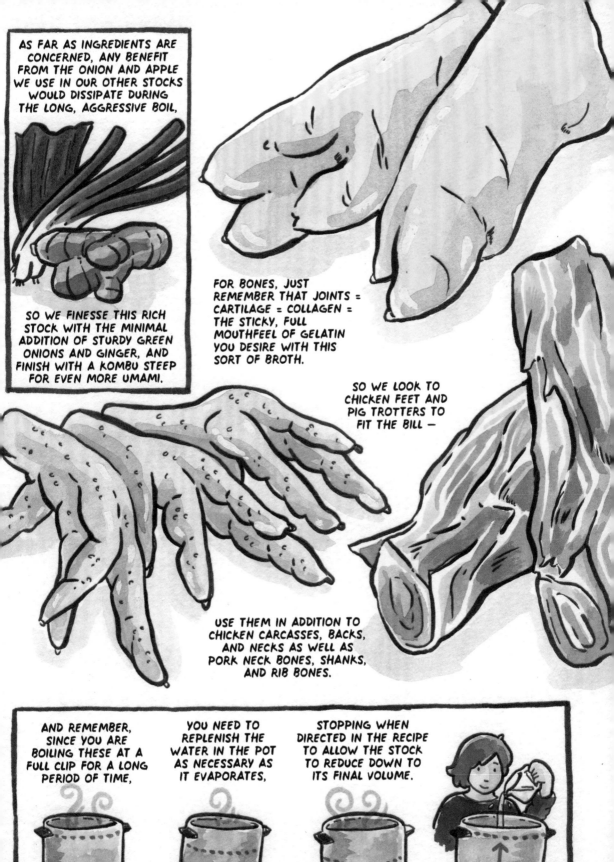

AS FAR AS INGREDIENTS ARE CONCERNED, ANY BENEFIT FROM THE ONION AND APPLE WE USE IN OUR OTHER STOCKS WOULD DISSIPATE DURING THE LONG, AGGRESSIVE BOIL,

SO WE FINESSE THIS RICH STOCK WITH THE MINIMAL ADDITION OF STURDY GREEN ONIONS AND GINGER, AND FINISH WITH A KOMBU STEEP FOR EVEN MORE UMAMI.

FOR BONES, JUST REMEMBER THAT JOINTS = CARTILAGE = COLLAGEN = THE STICKY, FULL MOUTHFEEL OF GELATIN YOU DESIRE WITH THIS SORT OF BROTH.

SO WE LOOK TO CHICKEN FEET AND PIG TROTTERS TO FIT THE BILL —

USE THEM IN ADDITION TO CHICKEN CARCASSES, BACKS, AND NECKS AS WELL AS PORK NECK BONES, SHANKS, AND RIB BONES.

AND REMEMBER, SINCE YOU ARE BOILING THESE AT A FULL CLIP FOR A LONG PERIOD OF TIME,

YOU NEED TO REPLENISH THE WATER IN THE POT AS NECESSARY AS IT EVAPORATES,

STOPPING WHEN DIRECTED IN THE RECIPE TO ALLOW THE STOCK TO REDUCE DOWN TO ITS FINAL VOLUME.

# TONKOTSU BROTH
## (PORK BONE BROTH)
### MAKES 4 QUARTS

**INGREDIENTS:**

2 PORK TROTTERS
(ABOUT 5 POUNDS)

3 POUNDS CHICKEN
BONES, OR
2 CARCASSES

3 POUNDS PORK NECK
BONES OR PORK RIBS

2 BUNCHES GREEN
ONIONS, TRIMMED
AND CUT IN HALF
CROSS-WISE

½ POUND FRESH
GINGER, UNPEELED, CUT
INTO ¼-INCH SLICES

TWO 8 BY 4-INCH
SHEETS (ABOUT
1 OUNCE) KOMBU

TARE OF YOUR CHOICE

TONKOTSU TAKES COMMITMENT (IN SOME RAMEN-YAS THE POTS NEVER STOP BOILING!), AND IT CAN PRODUCE STRONG, PORKY ODORS, SO OPEN YOUR WINDOWS AND STICK AROUND TO CHECK IN ON IT FROM TIME TO TIME!

PLACE ALL THE INGREDIENTS EXCEPT THE KOMBU AND THE TARE IN A LARGE POT AND COVER WITH 2 GALLONS OF COLD WATER, NOTING THE WATER LEVEL IN THE POT.

YOU WILL GET GOOD RESULTS COOKING THIS FOR 6 HOURS AT A RAPID BOIL,

BUT REMEMBER THAT THE LONGER TONKOTSU COOKS — UP TO 16 HOURS — THE MORE COLLAGEN AND FAT WILL BE EXTRACTED AND SUSPENDED IN THE STOCK, AND THE STRONGER THE BROTH WILL BE!

FOR A QUICKER, BUT JUST AS DELICIOUS VERSION, SEE THE PRESSURE COOKER ADAPTATION (P. 168).

BRING TO A RAPID BOIL OVER HIGH HEAT, SKIMMING OFF ANY SCUM THAT RISES TO THE SURFACE,

AND CONTINUE BOILING FOR AT LEAST 6 HOURS AND UP TO 16, REPLENISHING THE WATER TO THE ORIGINAL LEVEL EVERY HOUR OR SO.

ALLOW THE STOCK TO REDUCE WITHOUT REPLENISHMENT DURING THE FINAL HOUR (THE STOCK WILL REDUCE TO ABOUT 4 QUARTS DURING THIS LAST HOUR).

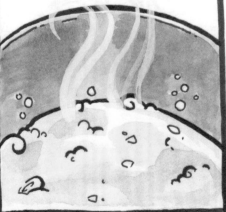

WHEN DONE COOKING, REMOVE FROM THE HEAT, ADD THE KOMBU, AND LET COOL AT ROOM TEMPERATURE FOR ABOUT 1 HOUR.

STRAIN FIRST THROUGH A COARSE-MESH STRAINER,

THEN THROUGH A FINE-MESH STRAINER,

AND REFRIGERATE OVERNIGHT.

THE NEXT DAY, REMOVE THE CONGEALED FAT FROM THE TOP OF THE STOCK AND SAVE IT AS DIRECTED IN PORK STOCK AND FAT (P. 43).

REFRIGERATE THE STOCK UNTIL YOU'RE READY TO USE IT, UP TO 1 WEEK, OR FREEZE FOR UP TO 6 MONTHS.

1 WEEK

6 MONTHS

WHEN READY TO USE, BRING TO A SIMMER BEFORE USING FOR THE MASTER RAMEN BOWL (P. 24)

AND SEASON USING THE FOLLOWING AMOUNTS OF YOUR DESIRED TARE PER 12 OUNCES OF STOCK:

| TARE | AMOUNT PER 12 OUNCES OF STOCK |
|---|---|
| SHIO (P. 46) | 1 OUNCE (2 TABLESPOONS) |
| SHOYU (P. 47) | 2 OUNCES (¼ CUP) |
| MISO (P. 48) | 2 OUNCES (¼ CUP) |

# TORIKOTSU BROTH
## (CHICKEN BONE BROTH)
MAKES 4 QUARTS

**INGREDIENTS:**

5 POUNDS OF A MIXTURE OF CHICKEN BACKS AND FEET, OR 2 CHICKEN CARCASSES

2 BUNCHES GREEN ONIONS, TRIMMED AND CUT IN HALF CROSS-WISE

½ POUND FRESH GINGER, UNPEELED, CUT INTO ¼-INCH SLICES

TWO 8 BY 4-INCH SHEETS (ABOUT 1 OUNCE) KOMBU

TARE OF YOUR CHOICE

PLACE ALL THE INGREDIENTS EXCEPT THE KOMBU AND THE TARE IN A LARGE POT AND COVER WITH 6 QUARTS OF COLD WATER,

NOTING THE WATER LEVEL IN THE POT.

BRING TO A RAPID BOIL OVER HIGH HEAT, SKIMMING OFF ANY SCUM THAT RISES TO THE SURFACE,

AND COOK FOR 4 HOURS, ADDING WATER TO REPLENISH THE LIQUID TO ITS ORIGINAL LEVEL EVERY HOUR FOR THE FIRST 3 HOURS,

ALLOWING THE STOCK TO REDUCE WITHOUT REPLENISHMENT DURING THE FINAL HOUR

(THE STOCK WILL REDUCE TO ABOUT 4 QUARTS DURING THIS LAST HOUR).

WHEN DONE COOKING, REMOVE FROM THE HEAT, ADD THE KOMBU, AND LET COOL FOR ABOUT 1 HOUR.

STRAIN FIRST THROUGH A COARSE-MESH STRAINER,

THEN THROUGH A FINE-MESH STRAINER,

AND REFRIGERATE OVERNIGHT.

THE NEXT DAY, REMOVE THE CONGEALED FAT FROM THE TOP OF THE STOCK AND SAVE IT AS DIRECTED IN CHICKEN STOCK AND FAT (P. 42).

REFRIGERATE THE STOCK UNTIL YOU'RE READY TO USE IT, UP TO 1 WEEK, OR FREEZE FOR UP TO 6 MONTHS.

1 WEEK

6 MONTHS

WHEN READY TO USE, BRING TO A SIMMER BEFORE USING FOR THE MASTER RAMEN BOWL (P. 24)

AND SEASON USING THE FOLLOWING AMOUNTS OF YOUR DESIRED TARE PER 12 OUNCES OF STOCK:

| TARE | AMOUNT PER 12 OUNCES OF STOCK |
|---|---|
| SHIO (P. 46) | 1 OUNCE (2 TABLESPOONS) |
| SHOYU (P. 47) | 2 OUNCES (¼ CUP) |
| MISO (P. 48) | 2 OUNCES (¼ CUP) |

# a word about HOMEMADE INSTANT RAMEN CUBES

THESE CUBES ARE A GREAT TIME AND SPACE SAVER, REMOVING WATER FROM THE STOCKS YOU'VE MADE BY REDUCING THEM OVER HIGH HEAT

AND TURNING THEM INTO EASILY RECONSTITUTED HOMEMADE BROTHS FOR A QUICK BOWL OF RAMEN ANYTIME

(WHAT YOU LOSE IN FINESSE YOU'LL GAIN IN CONVENIENCE).

THIS RECIPE IS WRITTEN FOR SILICONE ICE CUBE TRAYS WITH FIFTEEN 1 BY 1-INCH CUBES, EACH OF WHICH HOLDS ABOUT ONE OUNCE.

IF YOU HAVE DIFFERENTLY SIZED CUBE TRAYS, ADJUST ACCORDINGLY, BUT DON'T OVERTHINK IT UNLESS YOUR TRAYS ARE MASSIVELY DIFFERENT FROM THIS.

YOU MAY WANT A DEDICATED ICE CUBE TRAY FOR THIS, AS THE STRONG FLAVORS CAN LINGER IN A TRAY AFTER WASHING,

AND IT WOULDN'T WORK SO WELL FOR ICE CUBES TO BE USED IN, SAY, LEMONADE.

YOU CAN REALLY TASTE THE PORK!

ALSO, THIS REQUIRES A CLOSE EYE AS THE STOCK GETS CLOSE TO ITS FINAL QUANTITY AFTER REDUCING —

THINGS CAN START TO MOVE QUICKLY, AND YOU DON'T WANT TO OVER-REDUCE AND POSSIBLY BURN THE SOUP YOU'VE SPENT SO MUCH TIME PREPARING.

FEEL FREE TO MIX AND MATCH WHICH TYPE OF TARE YOU USE — JUST BE SURE TO CAREFULLY FOLLOW THE AMOUNTS NEEDED!

# HOMEMADE
# INSTANT RAMEN CUBES
### MAKES ENOUGH CUBES FOR 8 SERVINGS

**INGREDIENTS:**

**1 QUART EACH:**

CHICKEN STOCK (P. 42)

PORK STOCK (P. 43)

AND DASHI (P. 45), OR INSTANT DASHI MADE FROM BOXED POWDER (P. 44)

**OR:**

3 QUARTS UNSEASONED TONKOTSU BROTH (P. 52) OR TORIKOTSU BROTH (P. 54)

**TARE — CHOOSE ONE:**

1 CUP SHIO TARE (P. 46), 2 CUPS MISO TARE (P. 48), 2 CUPS SHOYU TARE (P. 47)

CHICKEN FAT, PORK FAT, OR GARLIC OIL (P. 123) FOR SERVING

PLACE THE STOCKS AND DASHI IN A MEDIUM SAUCEPOT OVER MEDIUM-HIGH HEAT.

BRING TO A BOIL AND CONTINUE TO COOK UNTIL THE LIQUID HAS REDUCED TO ONE QUART (ABOUT ⅓ OF THEIR ORIGINAL VOLUME), ABOUT 30 MINUTES.

REMOVE FROM THE HEAT AND STIR IN THE TARE,

IF IT REDUCES TOO MUCH, SIMPLY ADD WATER SO THE TOTAL VOLUME OF THE STOCK EQUALS ONE QUART (32 OUNCES).

THEN POUR THE CONCENTRATED BROTH INTO ICE CUBE TRAYS,

MAKING SURE THE CONCENTRATION IS STIRRED WELL AND DISTRIBUTED EVENLY,

THEN FREEZE OVERNIGHT.

THIS MAKES 40 CUBES OF 1 OUNCE — OR 2 TABLESPOONS — EACH FOR SHIO BROTH, AND 48 CUBES OF THE SAME SIZE FOR MISO AND SHOYU BROTHS.

DEPENDING ON HOW MANY TRAYS YOU HAVE, YOU MAY HAVE TO DO THIS IN BATCHES — IF SO, TIGHTLY COVER THE UNUSED BROTH AND REFRIGERATE,

THEN STIR WELL (OR REMELT IF GELATIN HAS COAGULATED)

BEFORE POURING THE NEXT BATCH INTO THE ICE CUBE TRAYS.

ONCE FROZEN, TRANSFER THE CUBES TO A ZIPLOCK BAG AND STORE IN THE FREEZER FOR UP TO 6 MONTHS.

6 MONTHS

# HOMEMADE INSTANT RAMEN BROTH

WHEN READY TO USE, PLACE 5 CUBES FOR SHIO OR 6 CUBES FOR MISO AND SHOYU PLUS 8 OUNCES (1 CUP) WATER AND 2 TEASPOONS OF THE DESIRED FAT IN A SAUCEPAN,

THE GELATIN IN THE CUBES WILL MAKE THEM FEEL MORE LIKE RUBBER THAN ICE, BUT DON'T WORRY — THIS IS NORMAL!

BRING TO A SIMMER,

AND USE AS DIRECTED IN THE MASTER RAMEN BOWL (P. 24).

# FAST WEEKNIGHT RAMEN BROTH

MAKES 5 TO 6 SERVINGS

## INGREDIENTS:

32 OUNCES (4 CUPS) CHICKEN STOCK OR BROTH (P. 42)

2 GARLIC CLOVES, PEELED AND GRATED ON A MICROPLANE OR MINCED

2-INCH PIECE FRESH GINGER, PEELED AND GRATED ON A MICROPLANE OR MINCED

1 BUNCH GREEN ONIONS, TRIMMED, CUT INTO 2-INCH PIECES, AND SMASHED WITH THE SIDE OF YOUR KNIFE

24 OUNCES (3 CUPS) DASHI (P. 45), OR INSTANT DASHI MADE FROM BOXED POWDER (P. 44)

2 OUNCES (¼ CUP) SOY SAUCE

1 TABLESPOON RICE WINE VINEGAR

2 TABLESPOONS CHICKEN FAT (P. 42) IF AVAILABLE

COMBINE ALL THE INGREDIENTS IN A SAUCEPAN AND BRING TO A SIMMER OVER HIGH HEAT.

LOWER THE HEAT TO MAINTAIN A SIMMER AND COOK FOR 5 MINUTES, STIRRING OCCASIONALLY.

REMOVE FROM THE HEAT AND DISCARD THE GREEN ONIONS. TASTE AND ADJUST THE SEASONING TO YOUR LIKING.

YOU CAN ADJUST ALL THE FLAVORINGS AND SEASONINGS TO YOUR LIKING — WE USE LOW-SODIUM BROTH SO WE CAN CONTROL THE AMOUNT AND TYPE OF SEASONING THAT GOES IN THE FINAL BOWL.

THIS RECIPE PRODUCES GREAT TASTING BROTH FOR RAMEN IN 5 MINUTES, AND IT'S AS CLEAN AS THE BROTH YOU BUY TO MAKE IT.

LOOK FOR LOW-SODIUM BROTH OR STOCK WITH INGREDIENTS YOU RECOGNIZE.

BRING TO A SIMMER BEFORE USING FOR THE MASTER RAMEN BOWL (P. 24). REFRIGERATE LEFTOVERS UP TO 3 DAYS, OR FREEZE FOR UP TO 6 MONTHS.

THIS MAKES 5 TO 6 SERVINGS; MULTIPLY AS DESIRED AND KEEP SOME IN THE FREEZER.

# YASAI BROTH

## MAKES ABOUT 4 QUARTS

YASAI = 野菜 = VEGETABLES

## INGREDIENTS:

5 CUPS (ABOUT 6 OUNCES) DRIED WHOLE SHIITAKE MUSHROOMS

1 POUND CRIMINI MUSHROOMS, SLICED

1 ONION, COARSELY CHOPPED

2 CARROTS, PEELED AND COARSELY CHOPPED

1 BUNCH GREEN ONIONS, TRIMMED AND CUT IN HALF CROSS-WISE

2 APPLES (FUJI, HONEYCRISP, OR GALA), QUARTERED

½ POUND FRESH GINGER, UNPEELED, CUT IN ¼-INCH SLICES

2 CLOVES GARLIC, SMASHED WITH THE SIDE OF YOUR KNIFE

TWO 8 BY 4-INCH SHEETS (ABOUT 1 OUNCE) KOMBU

TARE OF YOUR CHOOSING

THE SAME MUSHROOMS AND KOMBU THAT GIVE BASIC DASHI (P. 45) ITS UMAMI DEPTH ARE ENHANCED BY AROMATIC VEGETABLES AND THE TARE OF YOUR CHOOSING IN THIS SIMPLE MEAT- AND FISH-FREE BROTH,

PERFECT FOR A NICE CLEAN AND LIGHT BOWL OF RAMEN.

PLACE ALL THE INGREDIENTS EXCEPT THE KOMBU AND TARE IN A LARGE POT AND COVER WITH 6 QUARTS OF COLD WATER.

BRING TO A SIMMER OVER HIGH HEAT, THEN LOWER THE HEAT TO MAINTAIN A RAPID SIMMER FOR 1 HOUR.

REMOVE FROM THE HEAT AND ADD THE KOMBU.

LET THE KOMBU SIT FOR 10 MINUTES, THEN STRAIN THE STOCK.

RINSE THE SHIITAKES AND RESERVE FOR PICKLED SHIITAKE MUSHROOMS (P. 111) IF DESIRED.

REFRIGERATE THE STOCK UNTIL YOU'RE READY TO USE IT, UP TO 1 WEEK, OR FREEZE FOR UP TO 3 MONTHS.

1 WEEK

3 MONTHS

WHEN READY TO USE FOR THE MASTER RAMEN BOWL (P. 24), BRING TO A SIMMER.

AND SEASON USING THE FOLLOWING AMOUNTS OF YOUR DESIRED TARE PER 12 OUNCES OF STOCK:

| TARE | AMOUNT PER 12 OUNCES OF STOCK |
| --- | --- |
| SHIO (P. 46) | 1 OUNCE (2 TABLESPOONS) |
| SHOYU (P. 47) | 2 OUNCES (¼ CUP) |
| MISO (P. 48) | 2 OUNCES (¼ CUP) |

a word about
# GYOKAI BROTH

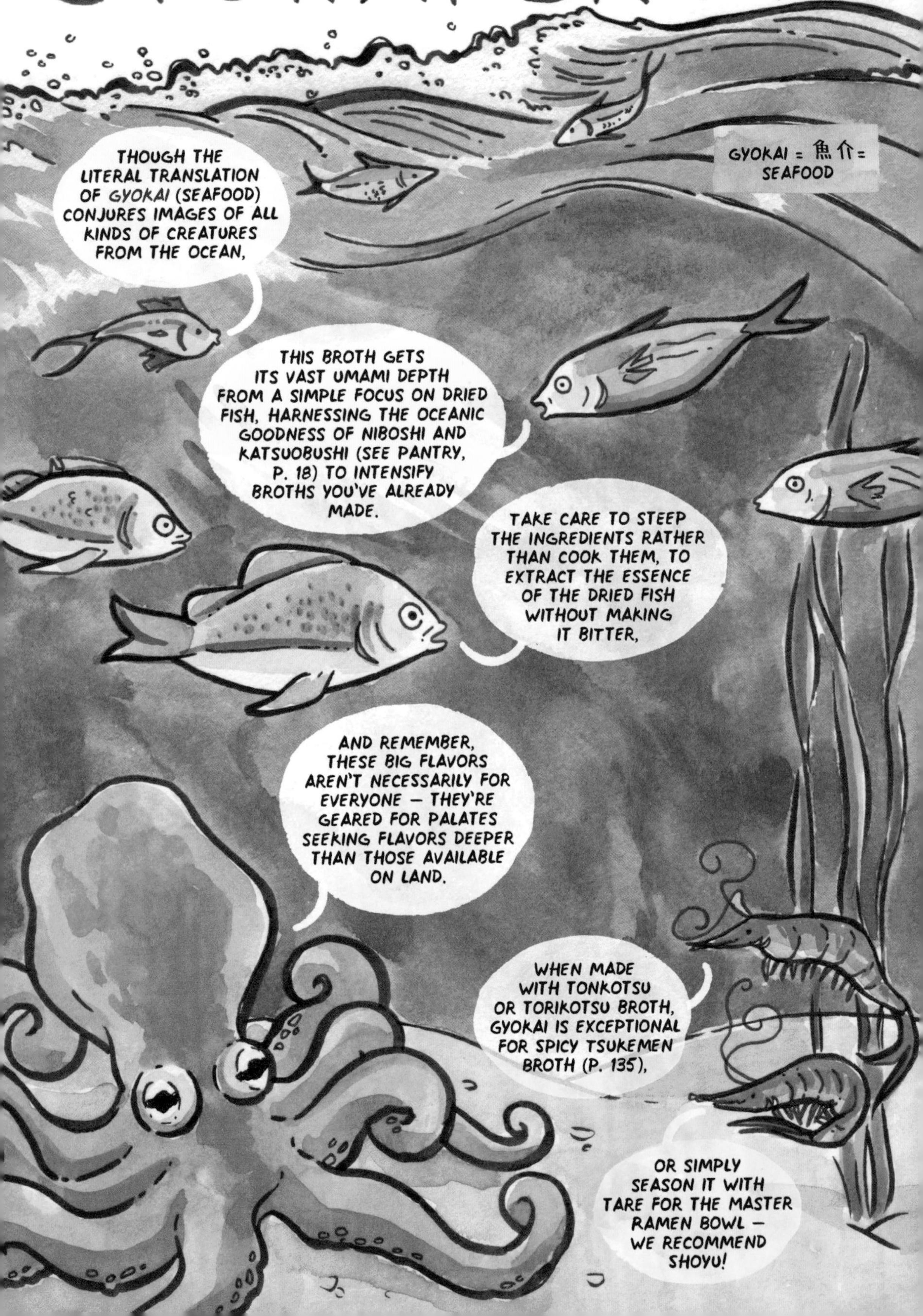
GYOKAI = 魚介 = SEAFOOD
THOUGH THE LITERAL TRANSLATION OF GYOKAI (SEAFOOD) CONJURES IMAGES OF ALL KINDS OF CREATURES FROM THE OCEAN,
THIS BROTH GETS ITS VAST UMAMI DEPTH FROM A SIMPLE FOCUS ON DRIED FISH, HARNESSING THE OCEANIC GOODNESS OF NIBOSHI AND KATSUOBUSHI (SEE PANTRY, P. 18) TO INTENSIFY BROTHS YOU'VE ALREADY MADE.
TAKE CARE TO STEEP THE INGREDIENTS RATHER THAN COOK THEM, TO EXTRACT THE ESSENCE OF THE DRIED FISH WITHOUT MAKING IT BITTER,
AND REMEMBER, THESE BIG FLAVORS AREN'T NECESSARILY FOR EVERYONE — THEY'RE GEARED FOR PALATES SEEKING FLAVORS DEEPER THAN THOSE AVAILABLE ON LAND.
WHEN MADE WITH TONKOTSU OR TORIKOTSU BROTH, GYOKAI IS EXCEPTIONAL FOR SPICY TSUKEMEN BROTH (P. 135),
OR SIMPLY SEASON IT WITH TARE FOR THE MASTER RAMEN BOWL — WE RECOMMEND SHOYU!

# GYOKAI BROTH
## (SEAFOOD BROTH)
MAKES ABOUT 1 QUART

**INGREDIENTS:**

1 QUART TONKOTSU, TORIKOTSU, OR YASAI BROTH, OR CHICKEN OR PORK STOCK (P. 43)

ONE 8 BY 4-INCH SHEET KOMBU

½ CUP NIBOSHI (SEE PANTRY, P. 18)

½ CUP KATSUOBUSHI (SEE PANTRY, P. 18)

TARE OF YOUR CHOOSING

PLACE THE STOCK OR BROTH IN A MEDIUM POT AND BRING TO A SIMMER OVER MEDIUM-HIGH HEAT.

REMOVE FROM THE HEAT AND ADD THE KOMBU, NIBOSHI, AND KATSUOBUSHI.

LET STEEP FOR ONE HOUR,

THEN STRAIN, DISCARDING THE SOLIDS.

REFRIGERATE THE BROTH UNTIL YOU'RE READY TO USE IT, UP TO 3 DAYS, OR FREEZE FOR UP TO 3 MONTHS.

3 DAYS

3 MONTHS

IF MADE WITH TONKOTSU OR TORIKOTSU BROTH, USE AS DIRECTED FOR SPICY TSUKEMEN BROTH (P. 135).

IF USING FOR THE MASTER RAMEN BOWL (P. 24), BRING TO A SIMMER AND SEASON USING THE FOLLOWING AMOUNTS OF YOUR DESIRED TARE PER 12 OUNCES OF STOCK:

| TARE | AMOUNT PER 12 OUNCES OF STOCK |
|---|---|
| SHIO (P. 46) | 1 OUNCE (2 TABLESPOONS) |
| SHOYU (P. 47) | 2 OUNCES (¼ CUP) |
| MISO (P. 48) | 2 OUNCES (¼ CUP) |

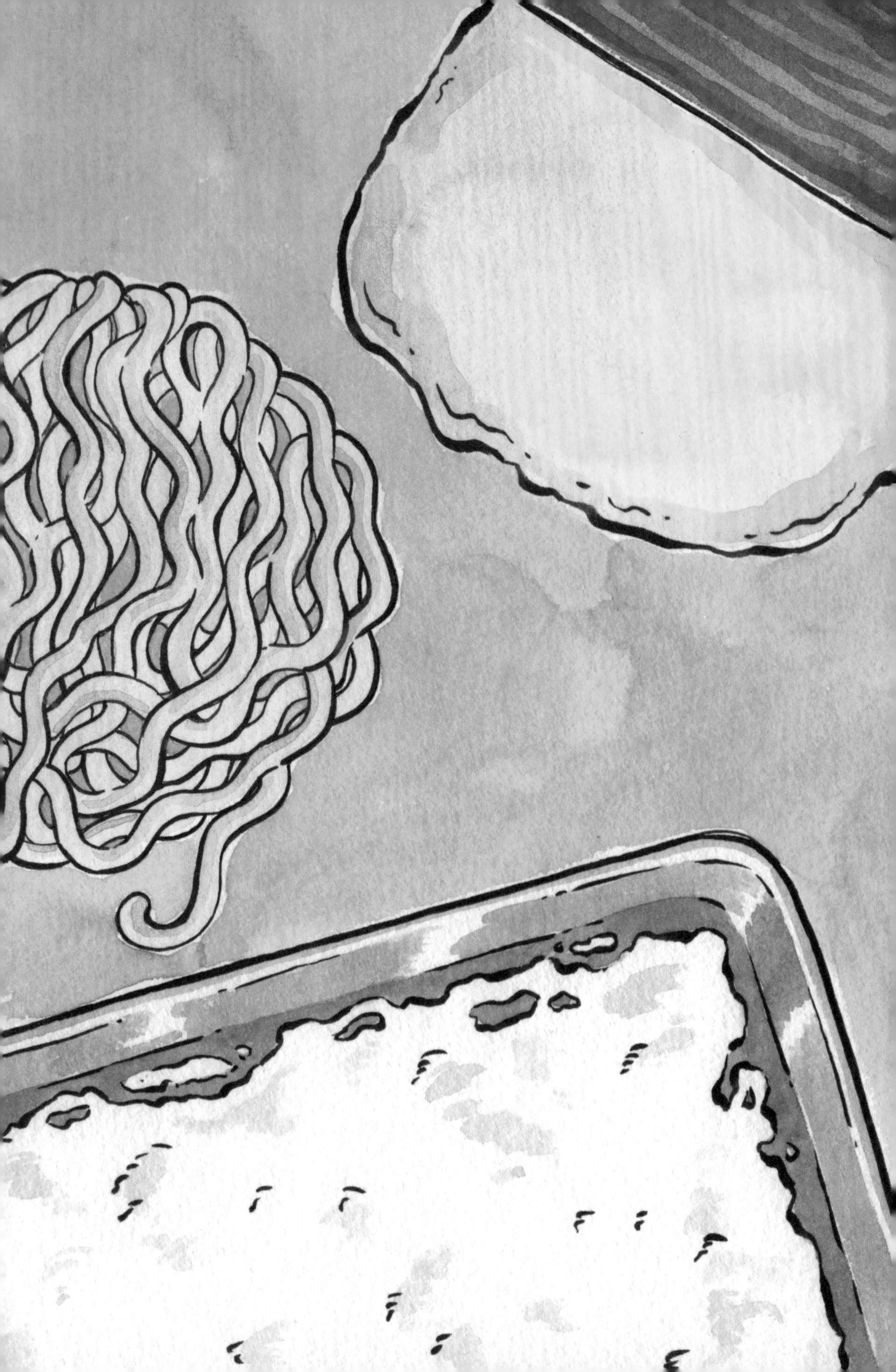

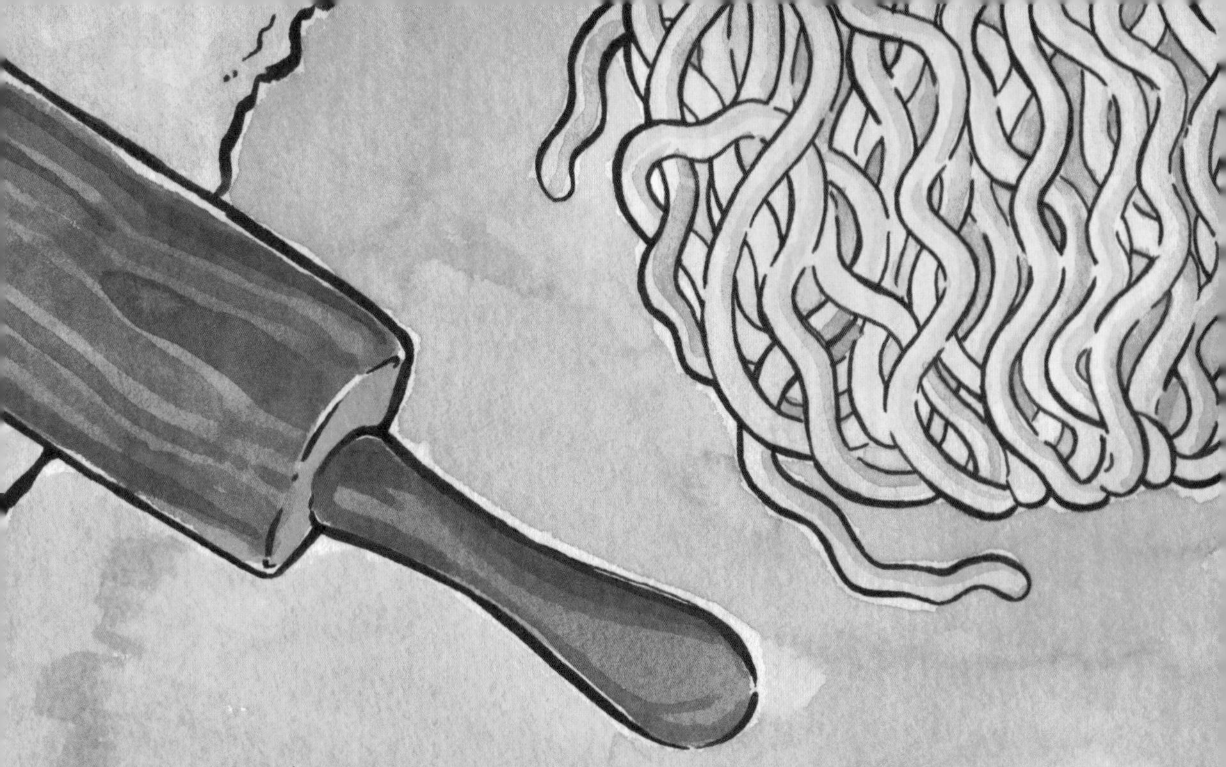

# NOODLES

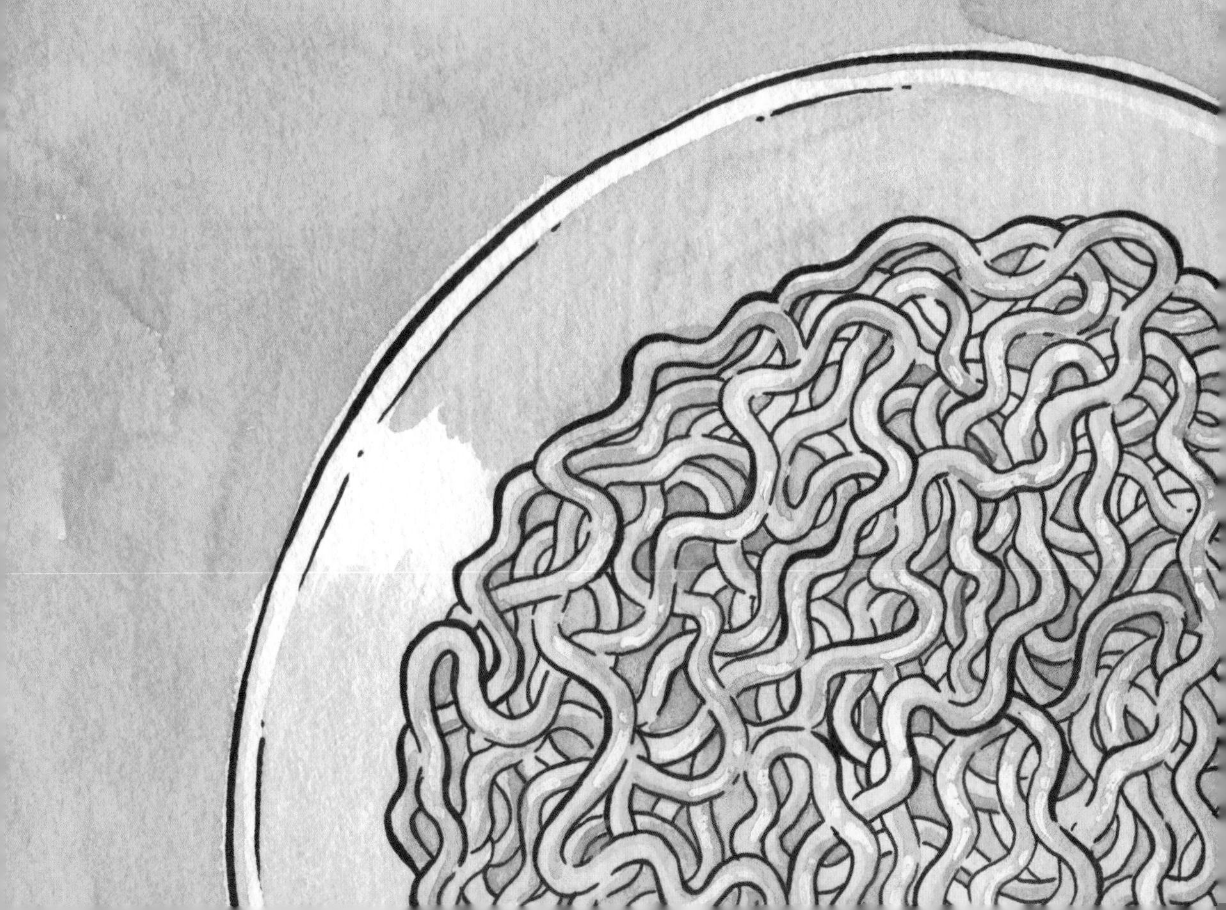

# A NOODLE PRIMER
## WITH KENSHIRO UKI OF SUN NOODLE AND RAMEN LAB

KENSHIRO UKI IS A TOP AUTHORITY ON RAMEN NOODLES — AFTER ALL, HE'S THE VICE PRESIDENT OF SUN NOODLE, PRODUCER OF THE BEST PRE-MADE NOODLES AVAILABLE.

FOUNDED BY KENSHIRO'S FATHER HIDEHITO IN 1981, SUN NOODLE MAKES CUSTOM NOODLES FOR RAMEN-YAS ALL OVER THE COUNTRY AND SUPPLIES MARKETS WITH SEVERAL VARIETIES FOR HOME COOKS.

KENSHIRO ALSO RUNS RAMEN LAB, A KITCHEN SPACE THAT HOSTS BOTH BUDDING AND WELL-ESTABLISHED RAMEN CHEFS IN THEIR MANHATTAN RAMEN-YA.

## ON RAMEN NOODLE TRAITS AND KANSUI

GOOD RAMEN NOODLES MUST HAVE A CLEAN WHEAT AROMA, CHEWY TEXTURE, AND STRENGTH FROM KANSUI FOR A SMOOTH, UNBROKEN SLURP!

KANSUI IS A MIXTURE OF POTASSIUM AND SODIUM CARBONATES, FOUND EITHER AS A POWDER OR MIXED WITH WATER TO FORM AN ALKALINE SOLUTION. MIXED WITH FLOUR, THE HIGH ALKALINE SOLUTION BOLSTERS AN ALREADY STRONG GLUTEN NETWORK IN THE NOODLES.

THIS CREATES A UNIQUE, CHEWY NOODLE, STRONG ENOUGH TO STAND UP TO A BOWL OF HOT SOUP.

A NOODLE MUST HAVE KANSUI TO BE CALLED A RAMEN NOODLE — WITHOUT IT, IT'S JUST A NOODLE.

## COLOR AND INGREDIENTS

RAMEN NOODLES ARE GENERALLY MADE OF REFINED WHEAT FLOUR, BUT SOMETIMES YOU'LL SPOT FLECKS OF WHOLE GRAINS.

THE ADDITION OF KANSUI GIVES THE NOODLES A SLIGHT YELLOW HUE,

TO REPLICATE THIS TODAY, A LITTLE RIBOFLAVIN IS OFTEN ADDED FOR THAT STRONG YELLOW.

BUT THE TRADITIONAL BRIGHT YELLOW WE ASSOCIATE WITH RAMEN COMES FROM A TIME WHEN NOODLE MAKERS ADDED YELLOW COLORING TO COVER UP THE OFF COLOR OF LESS REFINED FLOUR.

NOTHING WRONG WITH A LITTLE EXTRA VITAMIN B2 IN YOUR DIET!

## WHAT KIND OF NOODLE WITH WHAT KIND OF SOUP?

PAIR A THIN NOODLE WITH A LIGHTER SOUP LIKE SHIO OR SHOYU,

AND A THICKER NOODLE WITH A THICKER BROTH LIKE MISO.

THE NOODLE AND BROTH SHOULD NOT OVERPOWER ONE ANOTHER — BALANCE IS KEY.

WHEN NOODLES GET THE SPOTLIGHT, AS IN TSUKEMEN, THICK, CHEWY NOODLES ARE PREFERRED.

AT THE END OF THE DAY, THOUGH, GO WITH WHAT YOU PREFER — YOU REALLY CAN'T CHOOSE A WRONG KIND OF NOODLE!

## KAEDAMA ONEGAISHIMASU!

ONE EXCEPTION IS TONKOTSU RAMEN.

HISTORICALLY COOKED IN THE HAKATA WARD IN SOUTHERN JAPAN BY *YATAI* (STREET CART) VENDORS, TONKOTSU NOODLES WERE THIN AND QUICK-COOKING SO THEY COULD BE PREPARED SPEEDILY FOR CUSTOMERS IN A RUSH.

BUT THEY COULD EASILY OVERCOOK IN HOT SOUP, SO PORTIONS WERE SMALL.

THOSE WANTING MORE COULD CALL OUT "KAEDAMA ONEGAISHIMASU" ("MORE NOODLES, PLEASE!"), A TRADITION THAT CONTINUES IN SOME SHOPS TODAY.

## IT'S YOUR BOWL!

NOODLES AND SOUP SHARE EQUAL IMPORTANCE IN A GOOD BOWL OF RAMEN, AND HARMONY IS KEY.

DON'T FRET TOO MUCH ABOUT THE SHAPE AND SIZE OF THE NOODLE —

WELL-MADE KANSUI NOODLES PAIRED WITH WELL-MADE SOUP BUILD THE FOUNDATION FOR EVERYTHING ELSE!

# a word about RAMEN NOODLES

LIKE KENSHIRO SAYS, NOODLES HOLD AS MUCH IMPORTANCE AS BROTH IN A GOOD BOWL OF RAMEN, AND NOT JUST ANY NOODLE WILL DO.

JUST REMEMBER: AS HE TAUGHT US, KANSUI IS AN ESSENTIAL INGREDIENT IN RAMEN NOODLES THAT PROVIDES THEIR SPRINGY TEXTURE AND STRENGTH IN HOT BROTH.

MANY NOODLES LABELED "RAMEN NOODLES" CONTAIN NO KANSUI

AND THUS ARE NOT SUITABLE TO BE USED FOR RAMEN.

LOTS OF GREAT FRESH RAMEN NOODLES CAN BE FOUND IN THE REFRIGERATED OR FREEZER SECTION OF ASIAN MARKETS (AND SOME AMERICAN MARKETS), AND DRIED NOODLES ARE AVAILABLE AS WELL.

INGREDIENT LISTS USUALLY DON'T USE THE WORD "KANSUI", SO LOOK FOR "MINERAL SALTS", OR SOME VERSION OF THE WORD "CARBONATE" (AS IN BICARBONATE OR POTASSIUM CARBONATE).

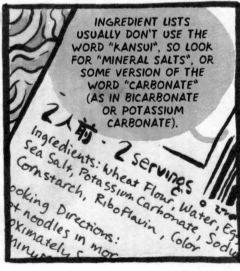

2人前・2 servings

Ingredients: Wheat Flour, Water, Sea Salt, Potassium Carbonate, Egg Cornstarch, Riboflavin, Color, Sodu

ooking Directions:
t noodles in mor
oximately s
inutes

LOOK FOR NOODLES MADE BY SUN NOODLE — OUR ABSOLUTE FAVORITE PRODUCER DUE TO THEIR QUALITY, ACCESSIBILITY, AND REASONABLE COST.

SURE, IF YOU'RE DESPERATE, FIND A CHEAP PACK OF INSTANT RAMEN, THROW AWAY THE SEASONING PACKET, AND USE THE NOODLES IN YOUR RECIPE. BUT HOPEFULLY THINGS AREN'T THAT DIRE!

BUT IF YOU ARE READING THIS, YOU PROBABLY WANT TO MAKE YOUR OWN NOODLES, RIGHT? GREAT!

THIS IS A SIMPLE PROCESS, BUT IT WILL TAKE PRACTICE.

THIS DOUGH LOOKS ROUGH IN THE BEGINNING STAGES, BUT STICK WITH IT — YOU ARE ON THE RIGHT PATH!

IT WILL TAKE MANY TRIES TO "GET" NOODLE-MAKING,

BUT ONCE YOU UNDERSTAND ITS BASICS, YOU WILL SEE WAYS TO EXPLORE AND EXPAND YOUR REPERTOIRE EVEN MORE WITH DIFFERENT FLOURS AND NOODLE WIDTHS.

OUR NOODLE TECHNIQUE HAS BEEN DEVELOPED WITH INFLUENCE FROM MANY GREAT NOODLE MAKERS WHO CAME BEFORE US.

TEN YEARS AGO, WE MADE NOODLES BASED ON DAVID CHANG'S RECIPE IN HIS MOMOFUKU COOKBOOK.

IVAN ORKIN'S (P. 40) BOOK TAUGHT US ABOUT USING FLOURS BEYOND REFINED WHITE FLOUR.

MORE RECENTLY, OUR UNDERSTANDING OF FLOUR HYDRATION HAS BEEN INFLUENCED BY THE OBSESSIVE RESEARCH OF THE RAMEN_LORD, MIKE SATINOVER (P. 170).

WE'VE EVEN MADE SOBA NOODLES WITH AKIYAMA-SAN, A CHEF IN THE FOOTHILLS OF MT. FUJI, WHOSE HAND-MIXING TECHNIQUE TAUGHT US TO DITCH THE STANDING MIXER AND HYDRATE THE FLOURS BY HAND.

THEY ARE ALL OWED OUR GRATITUDE, AND WE HOPE THEIR INSPIRATION PASSES ON TO YOU.

## TECHNICAL STUFF:

WE GIVE VOLUME MEASUREMENTS IN ADDITION TO WEIGHT MEASUREMENTS IN OUR NOODLE RECIPE, BUT HIGHLY RECOMMEND THE WEIGHT MEASUREMENTS.

A GRAM AND OUNCE SCALE IS A GREAT TOOL TO KEEP IN A WELL-STOCKED KITCHEN.

WE USE AN UNBLEACHED, HIGH-GLUTEN BREAD FLOUR PLUS A SMALL AMOUNT OF WHOLE WHEAT FOR TEXTURE AND VISUAL APPEAL. GLUTEN IS THE PROTEIN FOUND IN WHEAT THAT, WHEN HYDRATED AND WORKED, GIVES A NOODLE ITS STRONG YET ELASTIC STRUCTURE

(TOO MUCH MORE COARSE WHOLE GRAIN WOULD INHIBIT GLUTEN FORMATION).

IF THE MOOD STRIKES YOU, GET YOUR HANDS ON SOME RIBOFLAVIN (OFTEN SOLD AS VITAMIN $B_2$). LOOK FOR POWDER, OR USE A ROLLING PIN TO GRIND UP THE BRIGHT YELLOW TABLETS IN A PLASTIC BAG — THEY'LL STAIN OTHERWISE —

AND ADD A PINCH TO THE WATER TO GIVE YOUR NOODLES THAT TRADITIONAL YELLOW HUE.

DON'T FORGET KANSUI! IT MAY BE HARD TO FIND,

SO WE'VE INCLUDED A SIMPLE RECIPE TO MAKE YOUR OWN (P. 85).

RAMEN DEVOTEES WILL TALK AT LENGTH ABOUT HYDRATION PERCENTAGES (THE RATIO OF FLOUR TO LIQUID IN THE NOODLE DOUGH) FOR DIFFERENT TYPES OF NOODLE APPLICATIONS.

IN THE INTEREST OF KEEPING THINGS SIMPLE, WE GO WITH A STRAIGHTFORWARD 40% HYDRATION FOR OUR NOODLES (40 GRAMS OF WATER PER 100 GRAMS OF FLOUR).

THOSE WELL-VERSED IN ITALIAN PASTA MAKING SHOULD KEEP IN MIND THAT RAMEN IS MADE FROM A MUCH, MUCH DRIER DOUGH,

SO DON'T BE ALARMED IF IT SEEMS CRUMBLY AT FIRST.

THIS DOUGH WILL GO FROM SOMETHING THAT LOOKS UNSIGHTLY AND SEEMS ALL WRONG

TO BEAUTIFUL ONCE IT STARTS COMING TOGETHER.

WE RECOMMEND USING CORNSTARCH TO PREVENT THE DOUGH FROM STICKING WHEN ROLLING AND THE NOODLES FROM STICKING WHEN STORING.

CORNSTARCH DOESN'T TEND TO WORK ITSELF INTO THE DOUGH LIKE WHEAT FLOUR, AND IT LEAVES A LESS SLIPPERY COATING ON THE NOODLES WHEN COOKED.

SHAKE OFF ANY EXCESS BEFORE COOKING YOUR NOODLES.

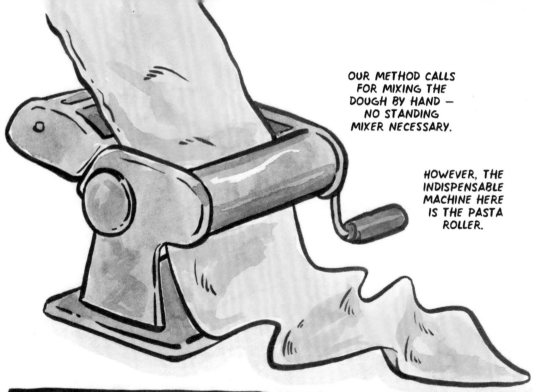

OUR METHOD CALLS FOR MIXING THE DOUGH BY HAND — NO STANDING MIXER NECESSARY.

HOWEVER, THE INDISPENSABLE MACHINE HERE IS THE PASTA ROLLER.

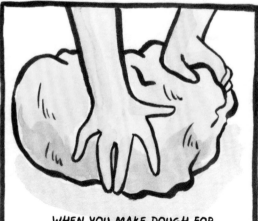

WHEN YOU MAKE DOUGH FOR BREAD OR FRESH PASTA, IT TAKES A LOT OF KNEADING TO DEVELOP THE GLUTEN IN THE FLOUR.

BUT FOR OUR RAMEN NOODLES, MOST OF THIS DEVELOPMENT HAPPENS DURING A TYPE OF KNEADING WE CALL COMPRESSION —

WHERE THE DOUGH GETS PRESSED TOGETHER BY THE IMMENSE PRESSURE CREATED BY A PASTA ROLLER.

THE NEXT FEW PAGES EXPLAIN THE STEPS TO MAXIMIZE GLUTEN DEVELOPMENT FOR DELICIOUSLY CHEWY RAMEN NOODLES.

HYDRATION
+
COMPRESSION
+
RESTING

= GLUTEN DEVELOPMENT

# HYDRATION

WHEN WE MIX BY HAND, AS AKIYAMA-SAN SHOWED US, WE ARE ALLOWING THE FLOUR TO SLOWLY PICK UP THE MOISTURE IN THE BOWL AND SLOWLY HYDRATE.

AS WE PROGRESS, WE SEE THE CLUMPS OF FLOUR GROW A BIT AND BECOME A BIT MORE UNIFORM.

WE ALLOW THIS TO HAPPEN GRADUALLY AND EVENLY.

AND IF YOU'RE INTO THIS SORT OF THING, THIS PROCESS PUTS A WHOLE LOT OF GOOD MOJO AND ENERGY INTO YOUR DOUGH.

WE THEN COVER THE SHAGGY DOUGH CRUMBLES WITH PLASTIC WRAP TO PREVENT DRYING OUT,

THEN LET THE FLOUR CONTINUE TO ABSORB THE WATER AND HYDRATE ON ITS OWN FOR ABOUT HALF AN HOUR.

# COMPRESSION

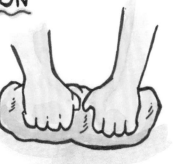

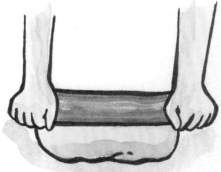

NEXT, WE START TO COMPRESS MANUALLY. WE PRESS THE DOUGH TOGETHER WITH OUR HANDS,

THEN, IN WORKABLE CHUNKS, WE PRESS IT MORE, WITH OUR WEIGHT

OR WITH THE HELP OF A ROLLING PIN.

FOR THE LAST STAGE OF COMPRESSION, WE NEED THE MECHANICAL POWER OF A PASTA ROLLER.

COMPRESSING THESE NOODLES WOULD BE QUITE DIFFICULT WITHOUT ONE.

AN ELECTRIC PASTA ROLLER OR ATTACHMENT FOR A STANDING MIXER WILL MAKE THINGS EXPONENTIALLY EASIER FOR YOU.

SO RETURN THE FAVOR AND FLATTEN THE DOUGH AS MUCH AS POSSIBLE BEFORE SENDING IT THROUGH THE MACHINE —

YOU DON'T WANT TO BURN OUT THE MOTOR (OR YOUR ARM, IF YOU ARE USING A HAND-CRANK MODEL)!

ON THE DOUGH'S FIRST PASS THROUGH THE ROLLER IT WILL TEAR, AND CRUMBLE, AND LOOK ROUGH. BUT DON'T FRET. STAY WITH IT.

EACH TIME THE DOUGH PASSES THROUGH THE ROLLER, THE GLUTEN IN IT WILL STRENGTHEN, AND THE DOUGH WILL BECOME SMOOTHER.

# RESTING

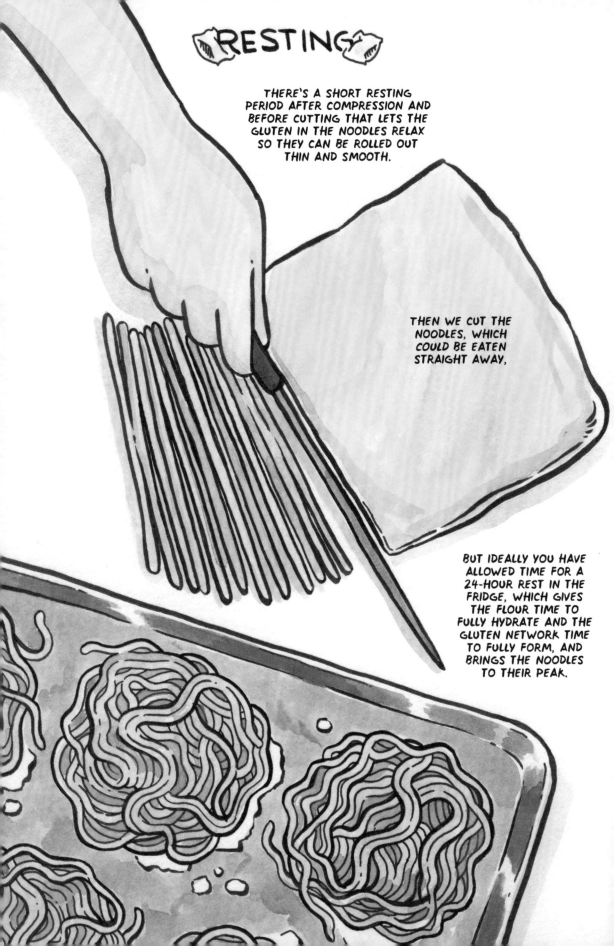

THERE'S A SHORT RESTING PERIOD AFTER COMPRESSION AND BEFORE CUTTING THAT LETS THE GLUTEN IN THE NOODLES RELAX SO THEY CAN BE ROLLED OUT THIN AND SMOOTH.

THEN WE CUT THE NOODLES, WHICH COULD BE EATEN STRAIGHT AWAY,

BUT IDEALLY YOU HAVE ALLOWED TIME FOR A 24-HOUR REST IN THE FRIDGE, WHICH GIVES THE FLOUR TIME TO FULLY HYDRATE AND THE GLUTEN NETWORK TIME TO FULLY FORM, AND BRINGS THE NOODLES TO THEIR PEAK.

## A FEW NOODLE NOTES:

THIS IS AN ALL-PURPOSE NOODLE RECIPE.

ROLL YOUR NOODLES TO DIFFERENT THICKNESSES AND CUT TO DIFFERENT WIDTHS AS YOU LIKE BEST FOR YOUR RECIPES, AND REMEMBER TO ADJUST YOUR COOKING TIME ACCORDINGLY.

COOK NOODLES IN PLENTY OF UNSALTED WATER — USE A 6-QUART OR LARGER POT FULL OF WATER AT A ROLLING BOIL.

INSUFFICIENT WATER WILL CAUSE STARCH FROM THE NOODLES TO CONCENTRATE IN THE POT, LEADING IN TURN TO SLIMY NOODLES AND TOUGH-TO-CLEAN BOIL-OVERS.

AND DON'T SALT THAT WATER! THE NOODLES ALREADY CONTAIN SALT AND WILL BE GOING INTO HIGHLY SEASONED BROTH.

DRAIN YOUR NOODLES WELL — WE COOK OURS IN WIRE MESH NOODLE BASKETS (SEE EQUIPMENT, P. 21) TO KEEP PORTIONS EASILY SEPARATED.

WITH A CONTROLLED MOTION, RAISE THE BASKET HIGH

AND LET IT DROP LOW TO SHAKE OFF AS MUCH EXCESS WATER AS POSSIBLE.

COOK YOUR NOODLES ONLY WHEN ALL OTHER COMPONENTS OF YOUR BOWL ARE READY TO GO,

THEY SHOULD GO INTO THE BOWL AFTER THE BROTH, GENTLY SEPARATED AND ARRANGED WITH CHOPSTICKS BEFORE FINISHING WITH TOPPINGS.

AGAIN, GIVE YOURSELF THE TIME TO GET THE HANG OF THIS SIMPLE NOODLE-MAKING METHOD, AND EXPERIMENT WITH DIFFERENT BLENDS OF FLOURS AS YOU SEE FIT — GET CREATIVE!

EXPLORE DIFFERENT TEXTURES AND THICKNESSES FOR DIFFERENT BROTHS, AND FREEZE EXTRA TO STOCKPILE FOR A RAINY DAY!

AFTER ALL, HOMEMADE NOODLES MAKE YOUR BOWL OF RAMEN REALLY YOURS.

# HANDMADE RAMEN NOODLES

MAKES ABOUT FIVE 5-OUNCE SERVINGS

## INGREDIENTS:

200 GRAMS (ABOUT 1 CUP WITH 2 TABLESPOONS REMOVED) WATER

5 GRAMS (ABOUT 1 TEASPOON) BAKED BAKING SODA (P. 85)

5 GRAMS (ABOUT 1 TEASPOON) SALT

PINCH OF RIBOFLAVIN (OPTIONAL)

25 GRAMS (3 TABLESPOONS PLUS 1 TEASPOON) WHOLE WHEAT FLOUR

475 GRAMS (ABOUT 3½ CUPS) BREAD FLOUR

CORNSTARCH FOR DUSTING

MAKE THE KANSUI LIQUID: PLACE THE WATER IN A SMALL BOWL,

ADD THE BAKED BAKING SODA, SALT, AND RIBOFLAVIN, AND STIR WELL UNTIL DISSOLVED.

PLACE THE FLOURS IN A LARGE MIXING BOWL AND MIX TOGETHER WITH YOUR HANDS.

USING YOUR FINGERTIPS, MIX THE FLOUR IN A CIRCULAR MOTION AS YOU SLOWLY ADD THE KANSUI LIQUID.

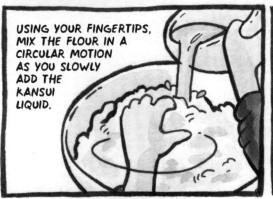

WHEN ALL THE LIQUID HAS BEEN ADDED, USE BOTH HANDS TO CONTINUE MIXING IN A CIRCULAR FASHION FOR ONE MINUTE, DRAGGING YOUR HANDS THROUGH THE DOUGH IN OPPOSING CIRCLES,

OCCASIONALLY RUBBING ALL THE DOUGH COLLECTED ON YOUR HANDS BACK INTO THE BOWL.

THE DOUGH WILL LOOK LIKE A CLUMPY MESS.

THAT'S OKAY!

COVER THE DOUGH WITH PLASTIC WRAP, AND LET IT REST FOR 30 MINUTES.

POUR THE RESTED DOUGH ONTO A WORK SURFACE AND SQUEEZE IT TOGETHER INTO ONE COHESIVE PIECE, MAKING SURE TO INCORPORATE ANY ERRANT CRUMBS.

CUT INTO FOUR ROUGHLY EQUAL PIECES, COVER THEM WITH PLASTIC WRAP, AND SET UP A PASTA ROLLER AND CUTTER.

FLATTEN ONE PIECE OF DOUGH AS MUCH AS POSSIBLE WITH YOUR HAND OR A ROLLING PIN, KEEPING THE OTHERS COVERED.

SET THE PASTA MACHINE TO ITS THICKEST SETTING, AND CRANK THE DOUGH THROUGH THE MACHINE.

IT WILL TEAR AND GENERALLY LOOK TERRIBLE. DON'T WORRY!

BUMP THE MACHINE'S THICKNESS DOWN A NOTCH, AND ROLL THE DOUGH THROUGH AGAIN.

REDUCE THE MACHINE'S THICKNESS ONCE MORE AND FEED THE DOUGH THROUGH AGAIN.

FOLD THE DOUGH LENGTHWISE (IN ABOUT THIRDS) SO THAT IT IS ABOUT THE WIDTH OF THE PASTA ROLLER, GIVING IT STRAIGHT SIDES.

PRESS THE DOUGH DOWN AS MUCH AS POSSIBLE WITH YOUR HAND OR A ROLLING PIN,

THEN ROTATE THE DOUGH 90 DEGREES SO THAT AN OPEN SIDE FEEDS INTO THE PASTA ROLLER,

RESET THE PASTA MACHINE TO ITS THICKEST SETTING. (IMPORTANT!)

AND RUN THE DOUGH THROUGH THE THREE SETTINGS AGAIN.

THE DOUGH WILL BEGIN TO COME TOGETHER MORE AND LOOK SMOOTHER.

NEXT, RESET THE MACHINE AND REPEAT THE FOLDING AND ROLLING PROCESS ONE MORE TIME.

SET THIS QUARTER OF DOUGH ASIDE AND COVER WITH PLASTIC WRAP TO LET IT REST WHILE WORKING ON THE REST OF THE DOUGH.

REPEAT THIS PROCESS WITH THE REMAINING THREE QUARTERS OF DOUGH.

MAKE SURE TO KEEP ANY DOUGH NOT IN USE COVERED WITH PLASTIC WRAP.

RESET THE MACHINE, AND RETURNING TO THE FIRST QUARTER OF DOUGH, ROLL THE DOUGH, ONE SETTING AT A TIME, TO YOUR DESIRED THICKNESS.

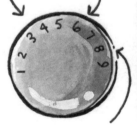

ON A MACHINE WITH 9 THICKNESS SETTINGS,

WE LIKE TO ROLL TO 4 OR 5 FOR THICK NOODLES,

6 FOR MEDIUM NOODLES,

AND ANYTHING HIGHER FOR THIN NOODLES.

CUT DOUGH INTO ROUGHLY 12-INCH SHEETS,

TIP: IN THE FINAL STAGE OF COMPRESSING DOUGH, STOP ROLLING WITH ABOUT 3 INCHES OF DOUGH NOT YET RUN THROUGH THE MACHINE.

FOLD THE OPPOSITE END OVER AND PRESS THE TWO ENDS TOGETHER TO FORM A LOOP,

THEN CONTINUE TO ROLL THE DOUGH UNTIL YOU'VE COMPRESSED THE NEW SEAM TWICE,

NOW YOU CAN USE A PARING KNIFE TO CUT THE DOUGH TO RELEASE IT FROM THE MACHINE,

GIVING IT PERFECTLY STRAIGHT ENDS.

THEN RUN THROUGH THE THINNER CUTTER ON YOUR PASTA ROLLER,

OR CUT BY HAND TO YOUR DESIRED WIDTH.

OPTIONAL!

TO MAKE WAVY NOODLES, COMPRESS CUT NOODLES IN YOUR HANDS,

SHAKE OUT,

AND REPEAT UNTIL THEY'RE AS WAVY AS YOU LIKE.

SET ASIDE AND REPEAT THE PROCESS WITH THE REMAINING SHEETS OF DOUGH.

DIVIDE THE DOUGH INTO 5-OUNCE PORTIONS (MORE OR LESS DEPENDING ON YOUR PREFERENCE).

YOU CAN COOK THESE NOODLES RIGHT AWAY, BUT THEY WILL BE BETTER AFTER RESTING AND FULLY HYDRATING FOR 24 HOURS.

IF RESTING, TOSS WITH A LIGHT AMOUNT OF CORNSTARCH AND PLACE ON A SHEET PAN,

THEN WRAP TIGHTLY WITH PLASTIC WRAP,

OR PLACE INDIVIDUAL PORTIONS IN ZIPLOCK BAGS AND REFRIGERATE.

WHEN READY TO USE, GET ALL THE OTHER COMPONENTS OF YOUR DISH READY TO GO,

THEN COOK THE NOODLES LAST, IN BOILING UNSALTED WATER, FOR 2 MINUTES AND USE AS DIRECTED IN THE MASTER RAMEN BOWL (P. 24).

USE NOODLES WITHIN 5 DAYS OF MAKING, OR FREEZE IN AIRTIGHT PLASTIC BAGS FOR UP TO 1 MONTH.

1 MONTH

IF USING FROZEN NOODLES, DO NOT THAW BEFORE USE — JUST COOK THEM STRAIGHT FROM THE FREEZER, FOR THE SAME AMOUNT OF TIME.

# BAKED BAKING SODA
## (KANSUI)
### MAKES ABOUT ½ CUP

INGREDIENTS:

½ CUP BAKING SODA

THE COMBINATION OF POTASSIUM AND SODIUM CARBONATES USED IN COMMERCIAL RAMEN NOODLE MAKING CAN BE HARD TO FIND FOR THE AVERAGE CONSUMER.

LUCKILY, REVERED FOOD SCIENTIST HAROLD MCGEE UNLOCKED THE MYSTERY OF KANSUI'S INACCESSIBILITY WHEN HE DISCOVERED THAT BAKING BAKING SODA INCREASES ITS ALKALINITY ENOUGH TO CREATE AN EFFECTIVE, ACCESSIBLE KANSUI SUBSTITUTE.

PREHEAT THE OVEN TO 275°F.

SPREAD ½ CUP OF BAKING SODA ON A SHEET PAN,

AND BAKE FOR 1 HOUR.

LET COOL BEFORE USING, AND STORE IN AN AIRTIGHT CONTAINER AT ROOM TEMPERATURE INDEFINITELY.

THE HIGH ALKALINITY OF BAKED SODA MAY IRRITATE SKIN SLIGHTLY;

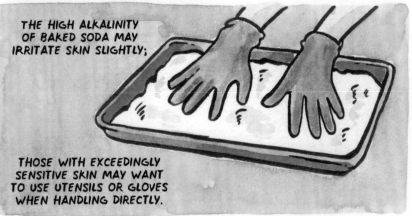

THOSE WITH EXCEEDINGLY SENSITIVE SKIN MAY WANT TO USE UTENSILS OR GLOVES WHEN HANDLING DIRECTLY.

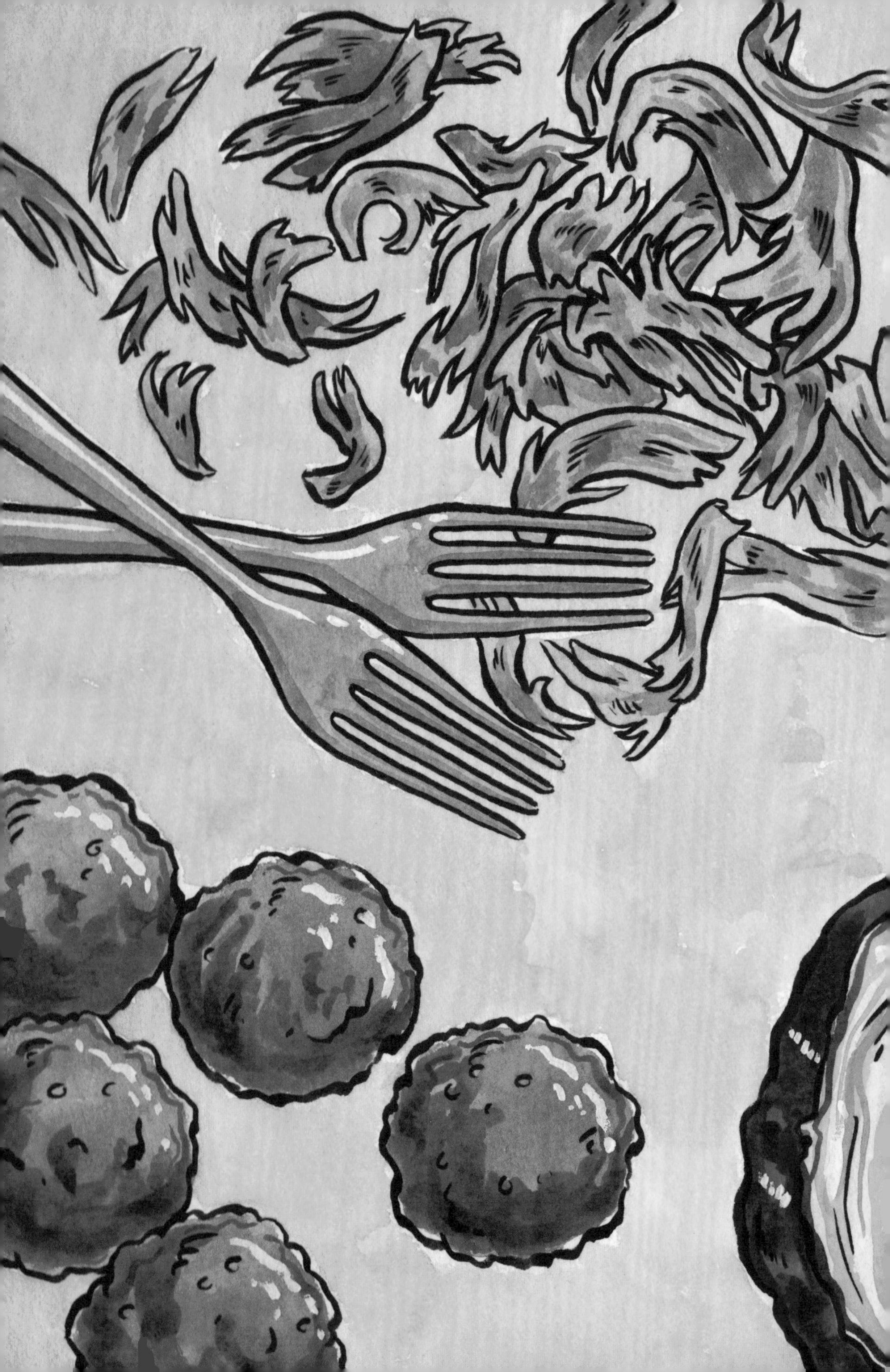

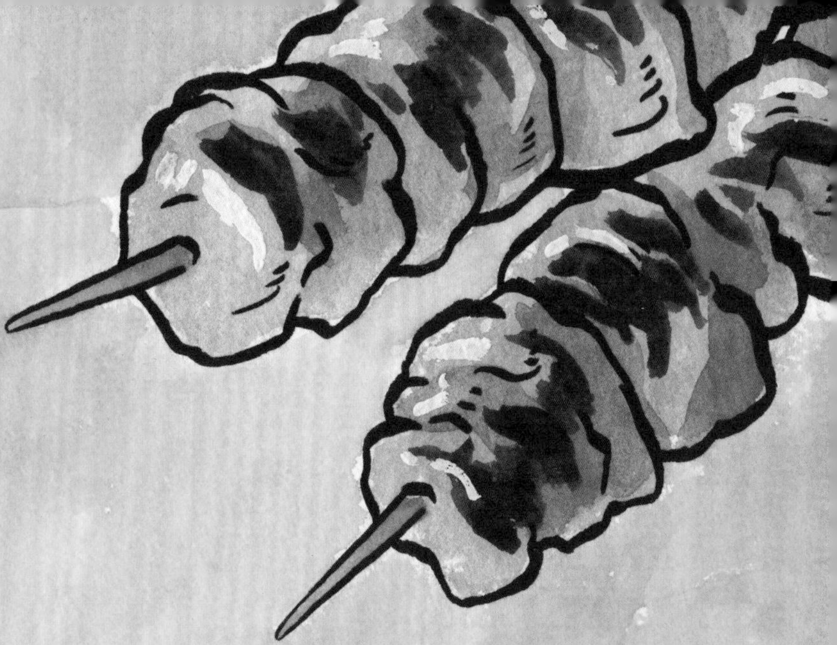

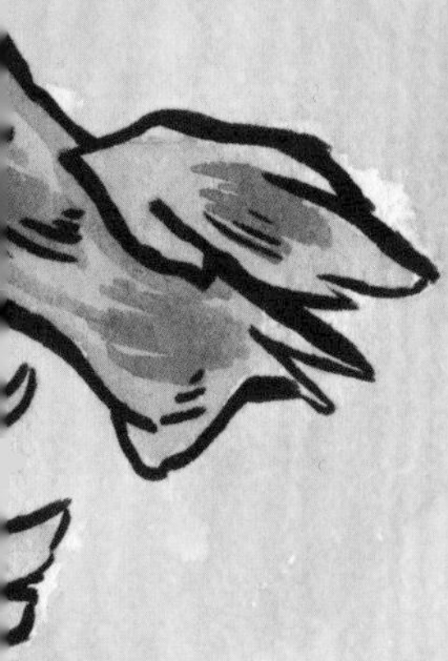

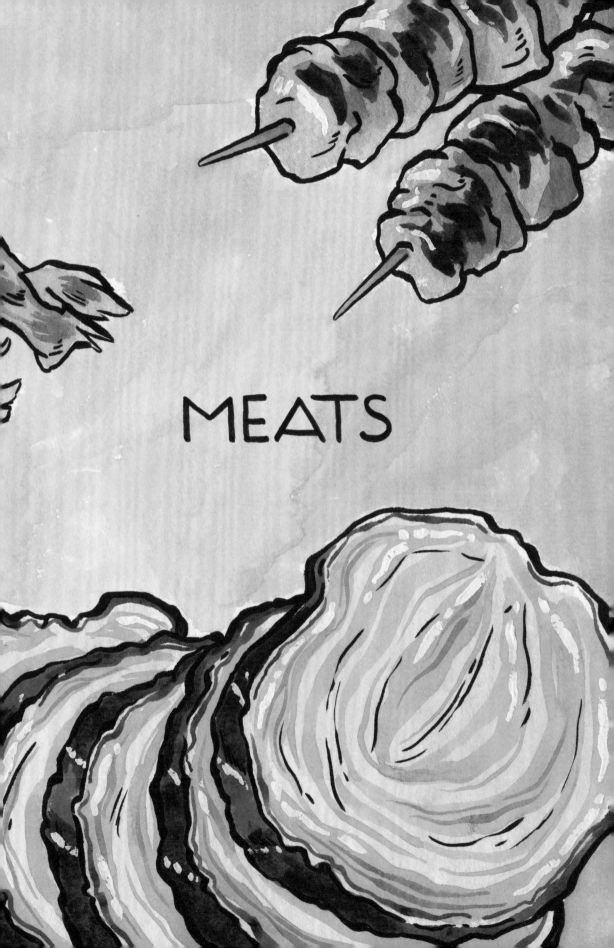

# MEATS

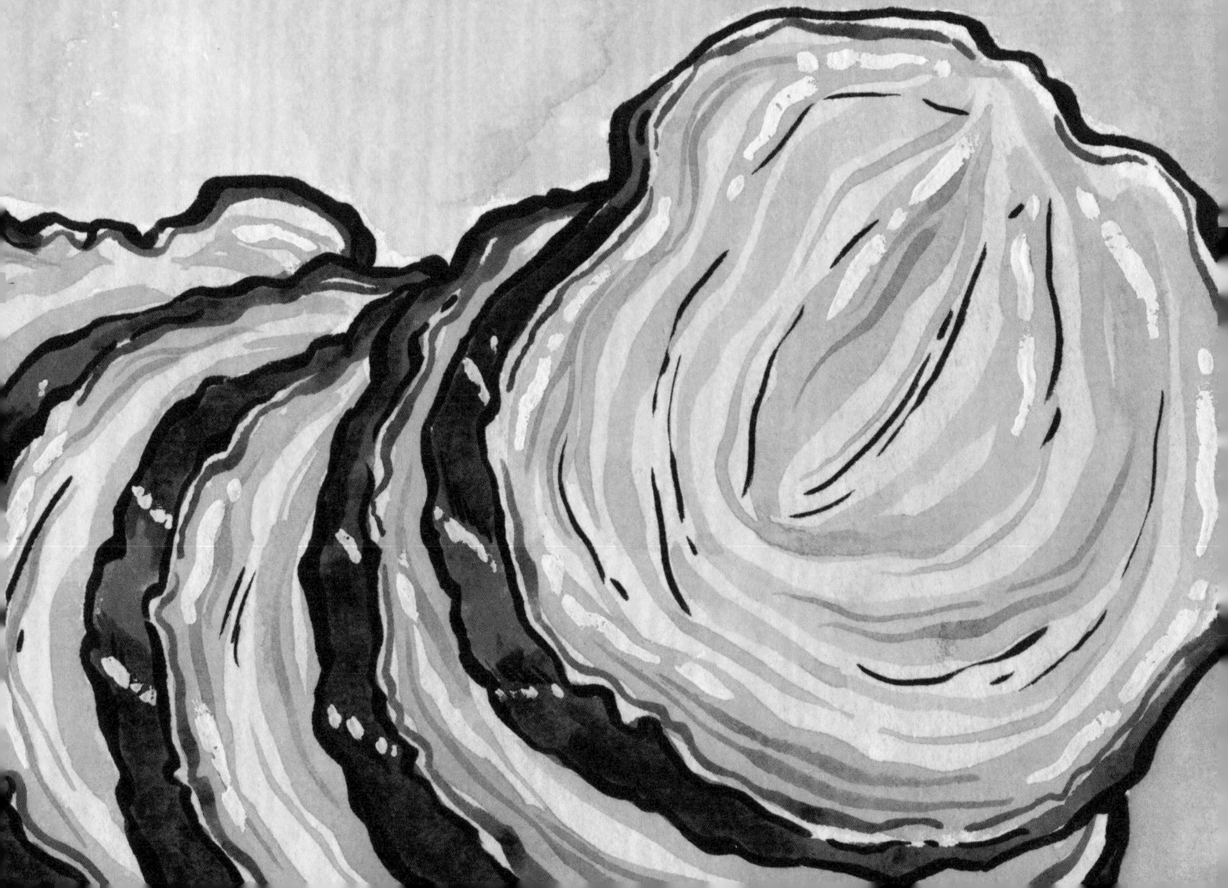

# a word about CHASHU

CHASHU'S NAME ISN'T THE ONLY THING THAT HAS BEEN ADAPTED FROM THE ORIGINAL CHINESE;

THE STYLE OF COOKING AND, ULTIMATELY, THE END PRODUCT HAVE EVOLVED INTO SOMETHING UNIQUE TO JAPAN AS WELL.

CHINESE CHAR SIU — SUCCULENT AND DELICIOUS IN ITS OWN RIGHT — IS MADE BY ROASTING OR GRILLING SKEWERED PORK AFTER MARINATING IN A SWEET RED SAUCE.

CHAR 叉 = FORK
SIU 燒 = ROAST

OVER TIME IN JAPAN. THIS MORPHED INTO A PIECE OF PORK SIMPLY BRAISED TO MELTING TENDERNESS IN SWEETENED SOY SAUCE, THINLY SLICED TO ADORN A BOWL OF RAMEN.

CHAR SIU

CHASHU

CHASHU ADDS DEPTH TO A BOWL OF RAMEN AND CAN BE MADE WITH EITHER RICH PORK BELLY OR (RELATIVELY) LEANER PORK SHOULDER, TRUSSED OR UNTIED, DEPENDING ON YOUR PERSONAL PREFERENCE FOR SHAPE AND COOKING TIME. UNTRUSSED PORK SHOULDER IS EASIER TO FIND.

# CHASHU

MAKES ENOUGH FOR
8 TO 10 BOWLS OF RAMEN

## INGREDIENTS:

2 TABLESPOONS PORK FAT FROM PORK STOCK AND FAT (P. 43) OR CANOLA OIL

3 POUNDS BONELESS PORK SHOULDER, SKIN REMOVED, OR 3 POUNDS PORK BELLY (ABOUT 10 BY 12-INCHES)

6 GARLIC CLOVES, SMASHED AND PEELED

TWO 2-INCH PIECES GINGER, UNPEELED AND SLICED ¼ INCH THICK

1 ARBOL CHILE

1 BUNCH GREEN ONIONS, TRIMMED AND CUT IN HALF CROSS-WISE

1 CUP MIRIN

¼ CUP RICE WINE VINEGAR

¾ CUP SOY SAUCE

¼ CUP BROWN SUGAR, PACKED

1 CUP SAKE

THIS RECIPE GIVES DIRECTIONS FOR PORK SHOULDER,

AND TWO STYLES OF PORK BELLY: TRUSSED IN A NICE TIGHT CYLINDER,

OR LEFT IN A NATURAL RECTANGLE, OFTEN CALLED *KAKUNI*.

TO TRUSS THE PORK BELLY, LAY IT FLAT, FAT SIDE DOWN WITH A SHORT SIDE FACING YOU.

ROLL IT LENGTHWISE INTO A TIGHT CYLINDER

AND TIE WITH BUTCHER'S TWINE AT ABOUT 1-INCH INTERVALS, KEEPING THINGS AS TIGHT AS POSSIBLE.

OVER MEDIUM-HIGH HEAT, HEAT A POT WITH A TIGHT-FITTING LID THAT WILL SNUGLY FIT THE PORK.

WHEN IT'S HOT, ADD THE FAT.

WHEN THE FAT IS MELTED, ADD THE PORK AND SEAR UNTIL GOLDEN BROWN ON AT LEAST 2 SIDES, 3 TO 4 MINUTES PER SIDE.

REMOVE THE PORK FROM THE POT AND SET IT ASIDE.

IF USING PORK BELLY, A LOT OF FAT WILL LIKELY RENDER OUT DURING THIS SEARING STAGE, SO POUR OUT ANY EXCESSIVE FAT, LEAVING A FEW TABLESPOONS IN THE PAN.

ADD THE GARLIC, GINGER, CHILE, AND GREEN ONIONS TO THE POT AND STIR, COOKING UNTIL AROMATIC, ABOUT 1 MINUTE.

CAREFULLY ADD THE REMAINING INGREDIENTS, STIRRING UNTIL THE SUGAR IS DISSOLVED.

RETURN THE PORK TO THE POT, NESTLING IT AMONGST THE OTHER INGREDIENTS.

RETURN TO A SIMMER, THEN LOWER THE HEAT TO MAINTAIN A SLOW, STEADY SIMMER, AND COVER TIGHTLY.

COOK, FLIPPING AND BASTING EVERY 30 MINUTES,

UNTIL THE PORK IS TENDER ENOUGH TO EASILY YIELD TO A POKE FROM A CHOPSTICK

OR HAS REACHED AN INTERNAL TEMPERATURE OF 180°F,

ABOUT 1½ TO 2 HOURS FOR SHOULDER

2 TO 2½ HOURS FOR TRUSSED BELLY,

OR 1 HOUR FOR KAKUNI.

IF A LOT OF THE COOKING LIQUID EVAPORATES FROM UNDER THE LID, JUST ADD A BIT OF WATER TO KEEP THINGS SCORCH-FREE!

THE PORK CAN, OF COURSE, BE EATEN STRAIGHTAWAY,

BUT IT IS MUCH MORE FLAVORFUL AND SLICEABLE IF LEFT TO COOL IN ITS COOKING LIQUID AT ROOM TEMPERATURE, THEN OVERNIGHT IN THE REFRIGERATOR.

STORE THE PORK WHOLE AND SLICE AS NEEDED INTO PIECES ABOUT ¼-INCH THICK

(KAKUNI CAN BE CUT INTO ¼-INCH BY 1½-INCH SQUARES)

AND REHEAT WITH A QUICK SEAR IN A HOT PAN OR A BLAST WITH A KITCHEN TORCH.

EXTRA CHASHU CAN BE REFRIGERATED, SLICED AND TIGHTLY WRAPPED, FOR UP TO 4 DAYS, OR FROZEN FOR UP TO 3 MONTHS.

SAVE THAT DELICIOUS LIQUID!

STRAIN THE COOKING LIQUID AND REFRIGERATE FOR UP TO 2 WEEKS TO USE AGAIN AS THE BRAISING LIQUID FOR MORE CHASHU, AS A BRINE FOR AJITSUKE TAMAGO (P. 104), OR AS TSUKEMEN BROTH (P. 135).

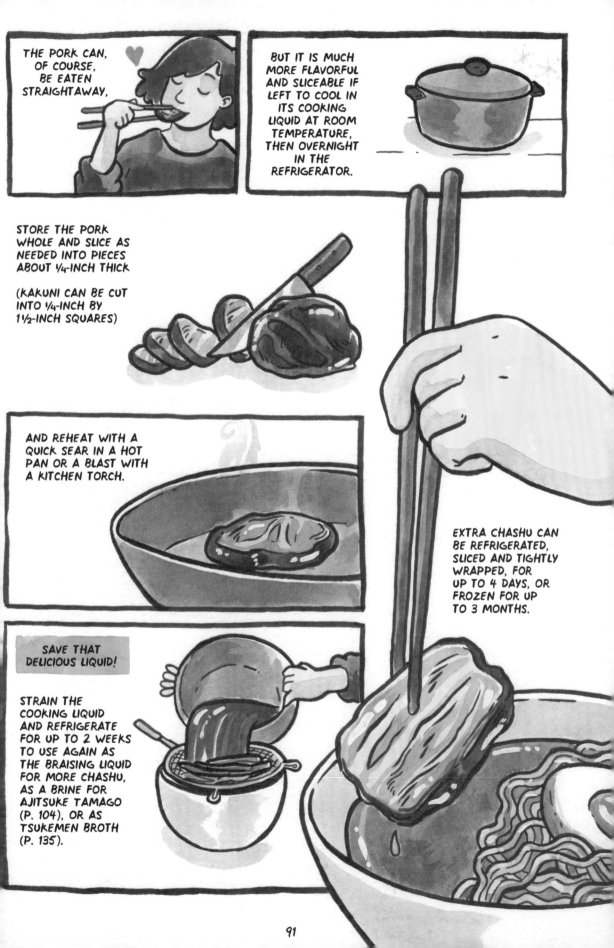

# SHREDDED PORK

MAKES ENOUGH FOR 6 BOWLS OF RAMEN

**INGREDIENTS:**

1 TABLESPOON SALT

1 TABLESPOON SUGAR

2-INCH PIECE FRESH GINGER, PEELED AND GRATED ON A MICROPLANE OR MINCED

2 CLOVES GARLIC, GRATED ON A MICROPLANE, OR MINCED

2 POUNDS BONELESS PORK SHOULDER

¼ CUP SOY SAUCE

½ CUP SAKE

1 CUP WATER

2 TABLESPOONS MISO OF YOUR CHOICE OR GOCHUJANG (SEE PANTRY, P. 16)

1 BUNCH GREEN ONIONS, TRIMMED AND CUT INTO 2-INCH PIECES

MIX THE SALT, SUGAR, GINGER, AND GARLIC IN A BOWL,

THEN RUB ALL OVER THE PORK.

COVER AND REFRIGERATE FOR 4 HOURS OR UP TO OVERNIGHT.

PREHEAT THE OVEN TO 375°F.

MIX THE SOY SAUCE, SAKE, WATER, AND MISO OR GOCHUJANG IN A SMALL BOWL

AND PLACE IN A BAKING DISH OR DUTCH OVEN SMALL ENOUGH TO SNUGLY FIT THE PORK.

ADD THE GREEN ONIONS, THEN THE PORK AND ANY JUICES IT'S RELEASED OVERNIGHT, AND COVER TIGHTLY.

PLACE IN THE OVEN AND BRAISE, TURNING AND BASTING EVERY 30 MINUTES OR SO,

UNTIL THE PORK IS TENDER ENOUGH TO EASILY YIELD TO A POKE FROM A CHOPSTICK OR HAS REACHED AN INTERNAL TEMPERATURE OF 190°F, ABOUT 2 TO 2½ HOURS.

REMOVE FROM THE OVEN AND LET COOL, UNCOVERED, UNTIL THE PORK IS COOL ENOUGH TO HANDLE.

SHRED THE PORK WITH YOUR HANDS OR A FORK

AND STRAIN THE COOKING LIQUID, DISCARDING ALL SOLIDS.

TOSS THE PORK WITH THE COOKING LIQUID

AND USE 3-OUNCE PORTIONS (EACH A SMALL HANDFUL) PER RAMEN BOWL IMMEDIATELY,

OR REFRIGERATE FOR UP TO 3 DAYS,

3 DAYS

REHEATING WITH ABOUT ¼ CUP COOKING LIQUID PER PORTION IN A SMALL PAN OVER MEDIUM-HIGH HEAT.

FOR LONGER STORAGE, WE RECOMMEND SEPARATING THE PORK INTO PORTIONS AND PLACING IN INDIVIDUAL ZIPLOCK BAGS WITH ¼ CUP COOKING LIQUID — SAVING ANY EXTRA LIQUID FOR ANOTHER USE — AND FREEZING FOR UP TO 2 MONTHS.

2 MONTHS

TO REHEAT, JUST PLOP THE FROZEN BLOCK INTO A PAN AND PROCEED AS ABOVE.

# PULLED CHICKEN

MAKES ENOUGH FOR 6 BOWLS OF RAMEN

## INGREDIENTS:

2 TABLESPOONS MISO OF YOUR CHOICE

½ CUP SAKE

2 TABLESPOONS SOY SAUCE

1 CUP DASHI (P. 45), CHICKEN STOCK (P. 42), OR PORK STOCK (P. 43), OR WATER

8 CHICKEN THIGHS, PREFERABLY BONE-IN AND SKIN-ON

SALT

2 TABLESPOONS CHICKEN FAT (P. 42) OR CANOLA OIL

4-INCH PIECE FRESH GINGER, UNPEELED AND THINLY SLICED

3 GARLIC CLOVES, SMASHED WITH THE SIDE OF YOUR KNIFE

3 GREEN ONIONS, TRIMMED AND CUT INTO 2-INCH PIECES

WHISK THE MISO, SAKE, SOY SAUCE, AND DASHI OR STOCK TOGETHER AND SET ASIDE.

SEASON THE CHICKEN THIGHS WITH SALT.

HEAT A LARGE DUTCH OVEN OR LIDDED SKILLET OVER MEDIUM-HIGH HEAT AND ADD THE FAT.

LAY THE CHICKEN THIGHS IN THE PAN, SKIN SIDE DOWN.

COOK UNTIL GOLDEN BROWN AND NOT STICKING, 3 TO 4 MINUTES, THEN FLIP.

COOK AN ADDITIONAL 3 MINUTES,

THEN ADD THE GINGER, GARLIC, AND GREEN ONIONS AND STIR UNTIL FRAGRANT, ABOUT 1 MINUTE.

ADD THE DASHI MIXTURE,

THEN COVER THE PAN TIGHTLY AND LOWER THE HEAT TOMAINTAIN A SLOW SIMMER.

COOK UNTIL THE CHICKEN IS TENDER AND PULLS APART EASILY, 20 TO 25 MINUTES (15 MINUTES FOR BONELESS THIGHS).

REMOVE FROM THE HEAT AND LET COOL, UNCOVERED, UNTIL THE CHICKEN IS COOL ENOUGH TO HANDLE.

REMOVE THE SKINS AND USE FOR CRISPY CHICKEN SKINS (P. 117), OR DISCARD.

PULL THE CHICKEN INTO BITE-SIZED CHUNKS, MAKING SURE TO REMOVE THE CARTILAGE CONNECTING THE MEAT TO THE BONE.

SEPARATE INTO ROUGHLY 3-OUNCE PORTIONS

AND USE FOR RAMEN IMMEDIATELY, REHEATING IN YOUR SIMMERING RAMEN BROTH,

OR REFRIGERATE ANY UNUSED CHICKEN IN ITS COOKING LIQUID FOR UP TO 3 DAYS, OR FREEZE INDIVIDUAL PORTIONS (WITH COOKING LIQUID) FOR UP TO 2 MONTHS.

3 DAYS

2 MONTHS

# YAKITORI
## (MARINATED AND GRILLED CHICKEN)
### MAKES ENOUGH FOR 2 TO 4 BOWLS OF RAMEN

**INGREDIENTS:**

3 GARLIC CLOVES, PEELED AND GRATED ON A MICROPLANE OR MINCED

2-INCH PIECE FRESH GINGER, PEELED AND GRATED ON A MICROPLANE OR MINCED

2 GREEN ONIONS, TRIMMED AND MINCED

½ CUP SOY SAUCE

¼ CUP MIRIN

¼ CUP SAKE

1 TABLESPOON SESAME OIL

1 TABLESPOON SUGAR

1 POUND BONELESS, SKINLESS CHICKEN THIGHS, CUT INTO 1-INCH PIECES

CANOLA OIL AS NEEDED

THESE CHICKEN SKEWERS ARE DELICIOUS ON THEIR OWN, A BELOVED BAR SNACK STAPLE ACROSS JAPAN.

YAKI 焼き = GRILLED
TORI 鳥 = CHICKEN

IF YOU ARE EVER IN TOKYO, WALK THROUGH GINZA'S YAKITORI ALLEY, MEMORABLE FOR ITS APPETIZINGLY INTENSE SMOKY ATMOSPHERE, INSTANTLY TURNING WHATEVER YOU ARE WEARING INTO A FREE TAKE-HOME SOUVENIR!

PUT ALL THE INGREDIENTS EXCEPT THE CHICKEN IN A SMALL BOWL AND MIX WELL.

PLACE THE CHICKEN IN A ZIPLOCK BAG AND ADD THE MARINADE. SQUEEZE OUT AS MUCH AIR FROM THE BAG AS POSSIBLE AND SEAL.

MASSAGE THE CHICKEN AROUND INSIDE THE BAG TO EVENLY COAT, AND REFRIGERATE FOR AT LEAST 1 HOUR.

THE LONGER THE MARINATING TIME, THE MORE ROBUST, RAMEN-READY FLAVOR FOR YOUR BOWL!

LIGHT A GRILL OR TURN ON A BROILER AND SOAK SOME WOODEN SKEWERS IN WATER FOR ABOUT 15 MINUTES WHILE THINGS HEAT UP.

THREAD THE CHICKEN ONTO SKEWERS, MAKING SURE THE MEAT COVERS THE TIP OF THE SKEWER.

RESERVE THE MARINADE. IF BROILING, COVER ANY EXPOSED WOOD ON THE "HANDLE" OF THE SKEWER WITH ALUMINUM FOIL.

RUB THE GRILL GRATES WITH OIL,

OR IF BROILING, PLACE THE SKEWERED CHICKEN ON AN OILED ALUMINUM FOIL-LINED SHEET PAN.

GRILL (MAKING SURE EXPOSED SKEWER ISN'T OVER DIRECT HEAT) OR BROIL FOR ABOUT 3 MINUTES, BASTING WITH MARINADE FROM TIME TO TIME,

THEN FLIP AND CONTINUE COOKING AND BASTING FOR ANOTHER 3 MINUTES,

AND FLIP AGAIN.

CONTINUE FLIPPING AND BASTING UNTIL THE CHICKEN IS COOKED THROUGH AND DELICIOUSLY CHARRED, A TOTAL OF 9 TO 12 MINUTES DEPENDING ON THE STRENGTH OF YOUR GRILL OR BROILER.

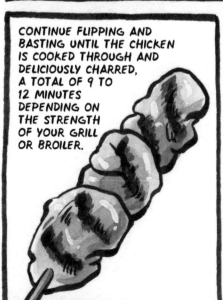

SERVE THE SKEWER ATOP RAMEN, OR SLIDE THE MEAT OFF SKEWERS INTO YOUR BOWL BEFORE SERVING.

REFRIGERATE LEFTOVERS FOR UP TO 3 DAYS, REHEATING WITH A QUICK SEAR IN A HOT PAN OR A BLAST WITH A KITCHEN TORCH — ALSO GREAT COLD IN TSUKEMEN (P. 132)!

# JAPANESE MEATBALLS
## (NIKU DANGO & TSUKUNE)

MAKES ABOUT 2 DOZEN MEATBALLS (4 TO 6 BOWLS OF RAMEN)

**INGREDIENTS:**

1 POUND GROUND PORK OR GROUND CHICKEN

1-INCH PIECE OF GINGER, PEELED AND GRATED ON A MICROPLANE, OR MINCED

2 CLOVES GARLIC, GRATED ON A MICROPLANE, OR MINCED

3 GREEN ONIONS, TRIMMED AND MINCED

1 TABLESPOON TOASTED SESAME SEEDS

1 TEASPOON SHICHIMI TOGARASHI (SEE PANTRY, P. 17)

2 TABLESPOONS SOY SAUCE

1 TEASPOON SESAME OIL

1 TEASPOON RICE WINE VINEGAR

1 TEASPOON MIRIN

1 EGG

1 TEASPOON FISH SAUCE (OPTIONAL)

PLACE ALL THE INGREDIENTS IN A LARGE MIXING BOWL.

STIR VIGOROUSLY IN A CIRCULAR MOTION WITH A GLOVED HAND — THE INGREDIENTS WILL SEEM VERY WET AND LOOSE AT FIRST.

KEEP AT IT — THE MIXTURE WILL BECOME STIFFER AND STICKIER AS IT EMULSIFIES AFTER 1 OR 2 MINUTES.

(YOU CAN ALSO USE A SPOON OR A STAND MIXER WITH THE PADDLE ATTACHMENT ON MEDIUM HIGH.)

FORM BALLS ABOUT 1½ INCHES IN DIAMETER (OR USE A ¾ OUNCE SCOOP) AND COOK IMMEDIATELY.

THESE MEATBALLS CAN BE COOKED THROUGH BY:

FOR MEATBALLS THAT STAY ROUND, BUT DO NOT BROWN

POACHING IN SIMMERING (NOT RAPIDLY BOILING!) WATER FOR 4 TO 5 MINUTES (YOU CAN ALSO USE YOUR RAMEN BROTH FOR A LESS REFINED APPROACH)

FOR LESS ROUND BUT NICELY BROWNED MEATBALLS (THEY FLATTEN OUT A BIT IN THE PAN)

FRYING IN A CAST IRON PAN OVER MEDIUM HEAT WITH A TABLESPOON OF CANOLA OIL, TURNING OCCASIONALLY, FOR 8 TO 10 MINUTES

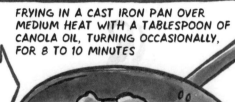

FOR FLAT-BOTTOMED, CONSISTENT, AND NICELY ROUND MEATBALLS

ROASTING ON A PARCHMENT PAPER-LINED SHEET PAN IN A 400°F OVEN FOR 8 TO 10 MINUTES

TO DISTINGUISH BETWEEN THESE MEATBALLS, WE CALL THOSE MADE WITH PORK *NIKU DANGO* (LITERALLY MEAT DUMPLING)

AND THE CHICKEN ONES *TSUKUNE*, THE NAME FOR THE CHICKEN MEATBALLS SERVED BY THE SKEWER SPECIALISTS IN YAKITORI-YAS.

WE OMIT THE TARE SAUCE USUALLY FOUND WITH THESE BEAUTIES, AS THEY WILL BE SWIMMING IN YOUR DELICIOUS SOUP!

WHEN COOKED, USE TO GARNISH RAMEN,

OR COOL AND REFRIGERATE FOR UP TO 3 DAYS, OR FREEZE FOR UP TO 1 MONTH.

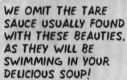

3 DAYS

1 MONTH

GREAT COLD, OR REHEAT WITH A QUICK DIP IN YOUR SIMMERING BROTH!

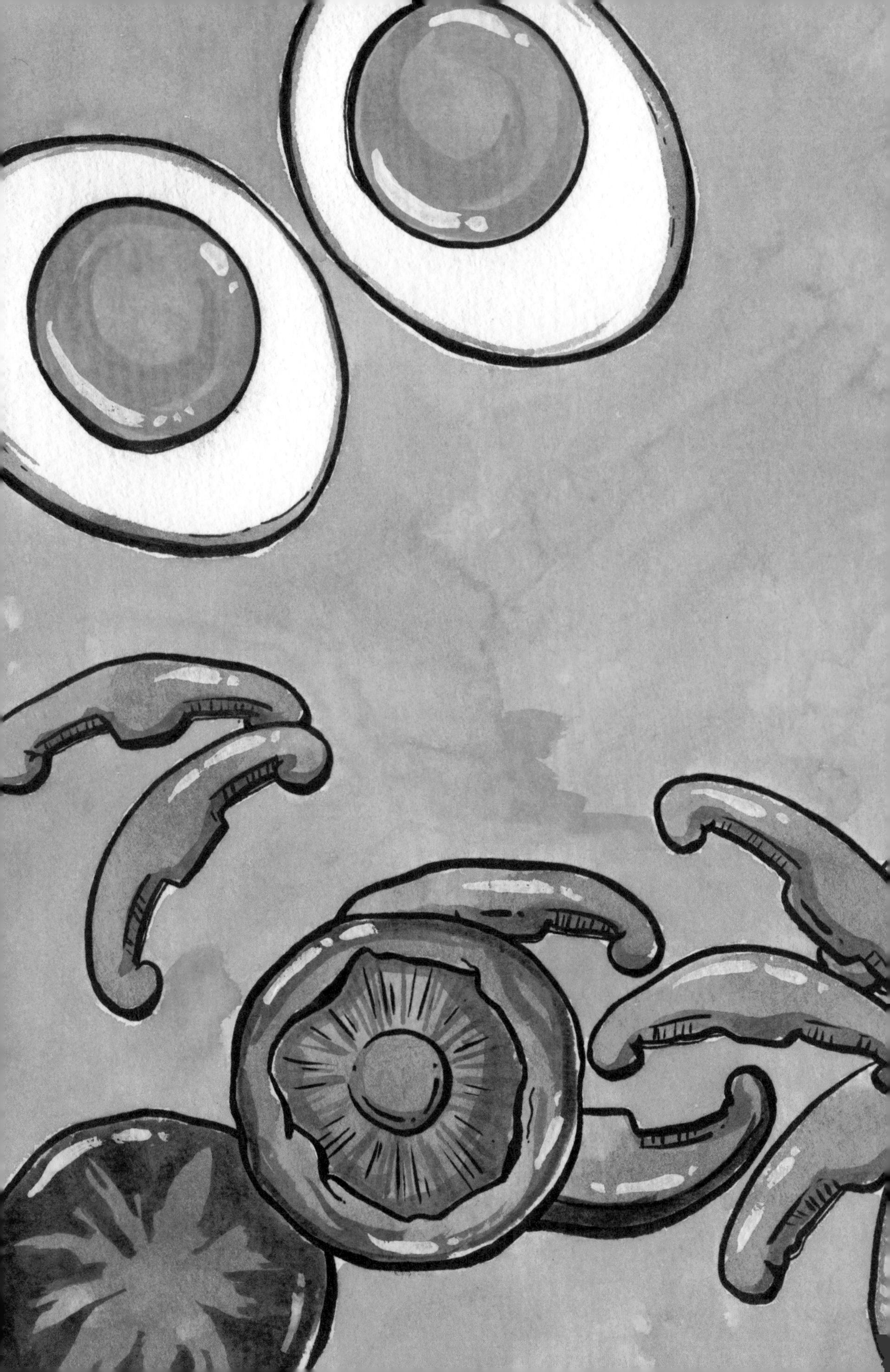

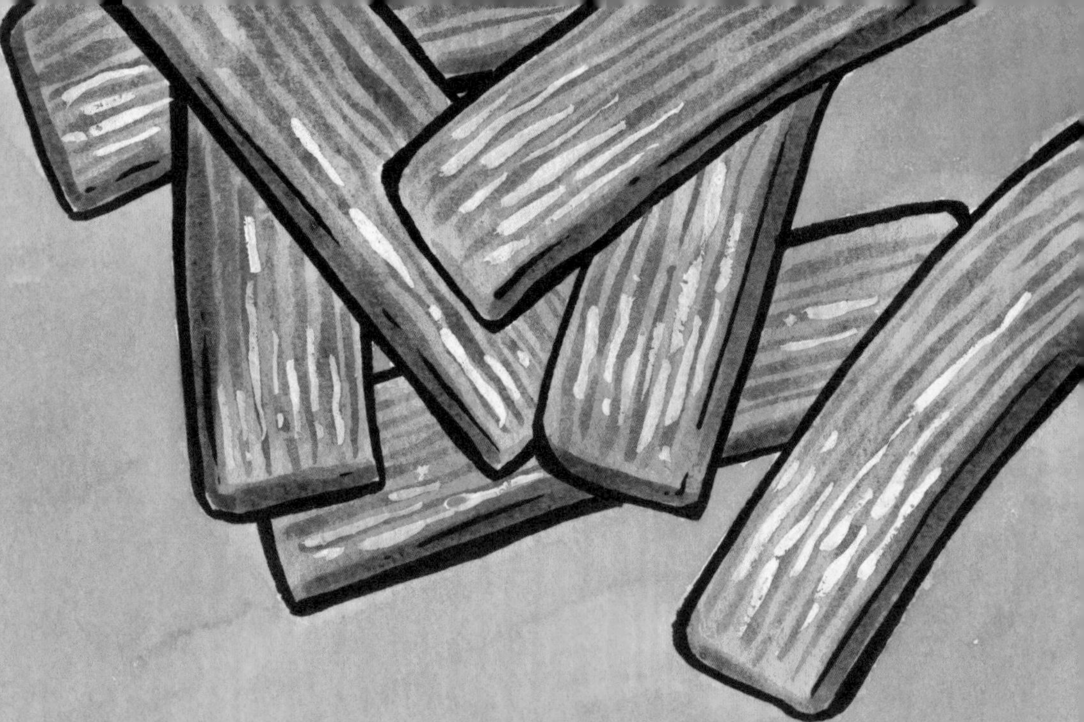

# ACCOMPANIMENTS

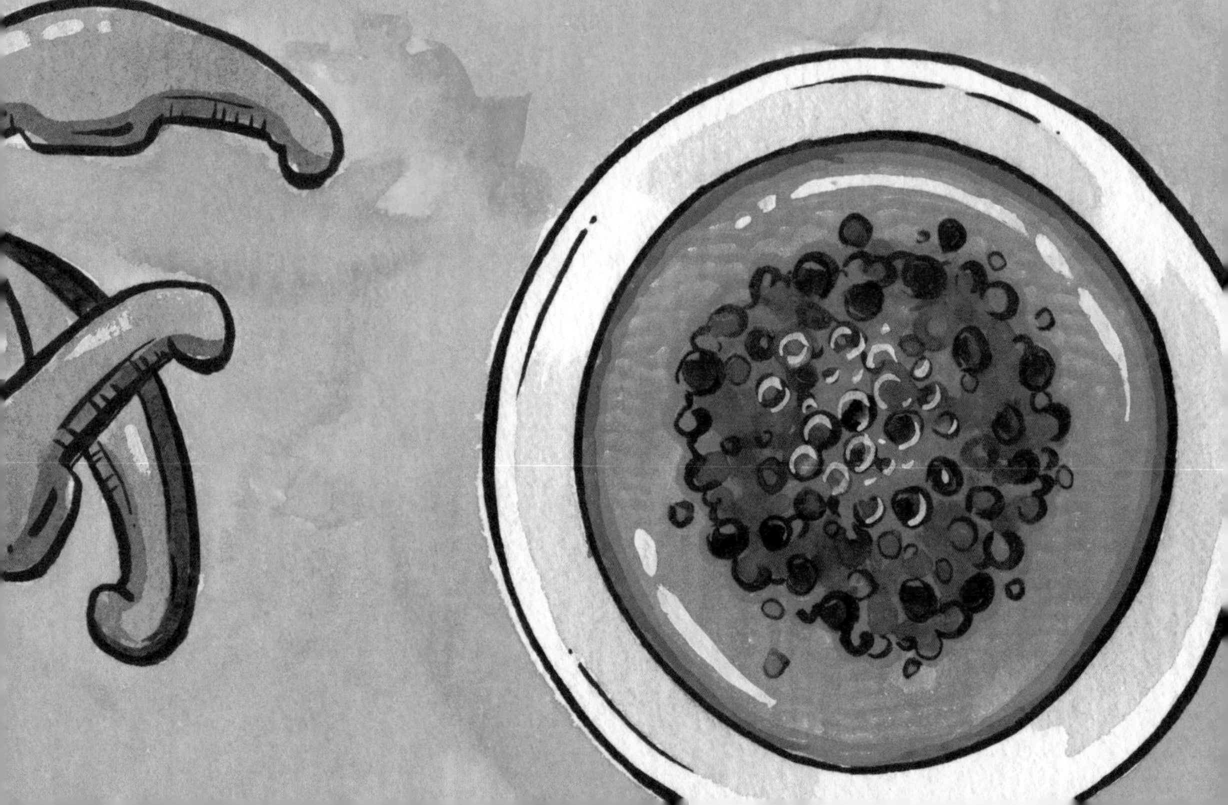

# a word about AJITSUKE TAMAGO

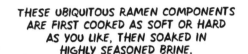

THESE UBIQUITOUS RAMEN COMPONENTS ARE FIRST COOKED AS SOFT OR HARD AS YOU LIKE, THEN SOAKED IN HIGHLY SEASONED BRINE.

WITH YOLKS RANGING IN TEXTURE FROM SOFT AND MOLTEN TO YOUR STANDARD HARD-BOILED EGG, THEY HOLD FORM MORE THAN THEIR UNSEASONED (BUT DELIGHTFULLY UNCTUOUS) COUSIN, THE ONSEN EGG (P. 108).

AJITSUKE 味付け = SEASONED
TAMAGO 玉子 = EGG

WE LOVE AJITSUKE TAMAGO WHEN MADE WITH A 6-MINUTE EGG, BUT PLAY AROUND AND FIND YOUR PREFERRED TIME!

(THE CHASHU LIQUID MAY FIRM UP WHEN COLD, SO EXTRACT YOUR EGGS GENTLY.)

YOU CAN MAKE THE SEASONING BRINE FOR THESE EGGS AS DIRECTED, OR SUBSTITUTE A MIXTURE OF ONE CUP RESERVED COOKING LIQUID FROM YOUR CHASHU (P. 89) AND ONE CUP WATER FOR A LOUDER, MORE PORKY MARINADE.

AJITSUKE TAMAGO WILL TASTE GREAT AFTER A FEW HOURS,

BUT WE RECOMMEND LETTING THEM SOAK OVERNIGHT.

TO REFINE YOUR EGG BOILING TECHNIQUE, PRICK THE WIDER END OF EACH EGG WITH A THUMBTACK OR NEEDLE.

THIS GIVES THE EGG A PLACE TO RELEASE AIR AS IT COOKS, HELPING TO PREVENT CRACKING,

YOU CAN LET THEM GO LONGER, EVEN DAYS LONGER;

JUST NOTE THAT THIS WILL PICKLE YOUR EGGS AND THEY WILL BECOME FIRMER THE LONGER THEY ARE IN THE BRINE — A DELICIOUS BAR SNACK!

AND GIVING THE FINAL PRODUCT A SMOOTHER, TRUER EGG SHAPE.

# AJITSUKE TAMAGO
## (SEASONED SOFT-BOILED EGGS)

MAKES 6 EGGS

**INGREDIENTS:**

3 GARLIC CLOVES, SMASHED AND PEELED

2-INCH PIECE FRESH GINGER, UNPEELED AND SLICED 1/4 INCH THICK

1 ARBOL CHILE

1/2 CUP MIRIN

2 TABLESPOONS RICE WINE VINEGAR

1/2 CUP SOY SAUCE

1 TABLESPOON BROWN SUGAR, PACKED

1 CUP WATER

6 LARGE EGGS

COMBINE ALL THE INGREDIENTS EXCEPT FOR THE EGGS IN A SAUCEPAN AND BRING TO A SIMMER, STIRRING TO DISSOLVE THE SUGAR, THEN REMOVE FROM THE HEAT.

TRANSFER TO A 4-CUP CONTAINER AND LET COOL FULLY.

MEANWHILE, BRING A LARGE POT OF WATER TO A BOIL OVER HIGH HEAT.

GENTLY LOWER THE EGGS INTO THE WATER AND COOK, ADJUSTING THE HEAT TO MAINTAIN A SIMMER.

**SIMMER YOUR EGGS FOR:**

6 MINUTES FOR CREAMY, DELICATE YOLKS

8 MINUTES FOR FIRMER, YET STILL SMOOTH YOLKS

10 MINUTES FOR STANDARD HARD-BOILED EGGS

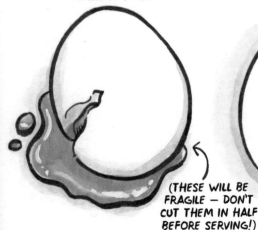

(THESE WILL BE FRAGILE — DON'T CUT THEM IN HALF BEFORE SERVING!)

(8- AND 10-MINUTE EGGS CAN BE CUT IN HALF BEFORE SERVING)

REMOVE FROM THE HEAT, POUR OUT AS MUCH HOT WATER AS POSSIBLE,

AND PLACE THE POT UNDER COLD RUNNING WATER.

STIR THE EGGS GENTLY WITH YOUR HAND AS THE WATER IN THE POT COOLS, POURING WARM WATER OUT OF THE POT TO ALLOW COLDER WATER TO FILL IT.

WHEN THE WATER IS COOL, TURN OFF THE FAUCET AND LET THE EGGS SIT FOR 5 MINUTES,

THEN PEEL.

PLACE THEM IN THE COOLED MARINADE AND LET SOAK OVERNIGHT, REFRIGERATED, REDISTRIBUTING THE EGGS NOW AND THEN FOR EVEN MARINATING.

REMOVE FROM THE MARINADE AND STORE THE EGGS, REFRIGERATED AND COVERED, FOR UP TO ONE WEEK.

1 WEEK

USE AJITSUKE TAMAGO AS DIRECTED IN THE MASTER RAMEN BOWL RECIPE (P. 24), OR EAT THESE DELICIOUS EGGS ON THEIR OWN FOR A QUICK SNACK!

THE MARINADE CAN BE REFRIGERATED AND REUSED UP TO 3 TIMES OVER 1 MONTH.

# a word about ONSEN EGGS

THESE LOVELY EGGS GET THEIR CUSTARDY TEXTURE FROM AN EASY, GENTLE SOAK IN HOT WATER, RESULTING IN A MAGICALLY POACHED-IN-THE-SHELL END PRODUCT.

ONSEN 温泉 = HOT SPRING

TRADITIONALLY, YOU'D TAKE A BUCKET OF EGGS DOWN TO THE ONSEN (JAPANESE HOT SPRING), DIP IT IN TO FILL IT WITH THE GEOTHERMALLY HEATED WATER, AND SET IT ASIDE WHILE YOU BATHED.

ONCE BACK HOME, YOUR EGGS WERE READY TO EAT, CRACKED INTO A BOWL AND ADORNED HOWEVER YOU LIKE.

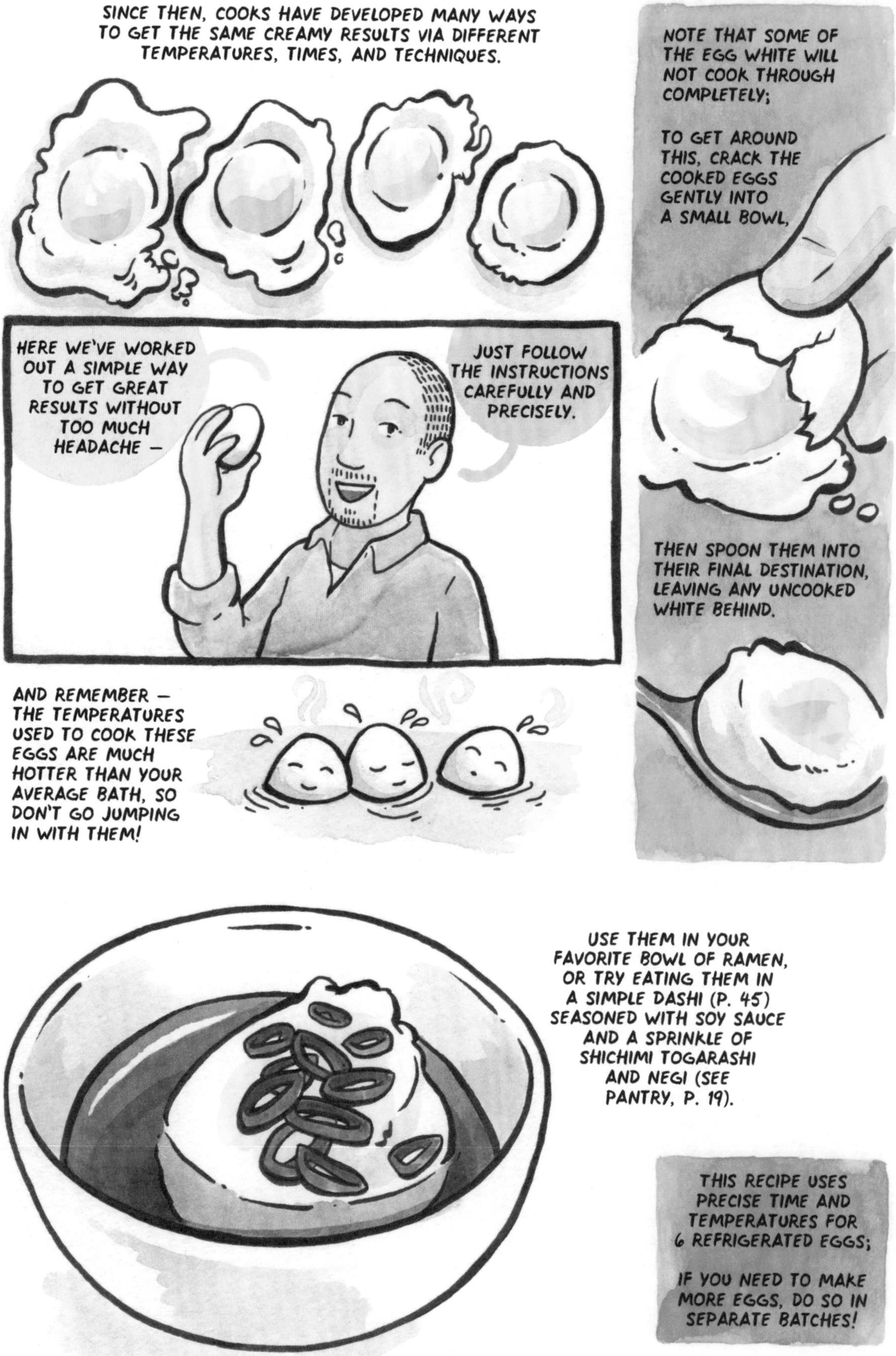
SINCE THEN, COOKS HAVE DEVELOPED MANY WAYS TO GET THE SAME CREAMY RESULTS VIA DIFFERENT TEMPERATURES, TIMES, AND TECHNIQUES.
HERE WE'VE WORKED OUT A SIMPLE WAY TO GET GREAT RESULTS WITHOUT TOO MUCH HEADACHE –
JUST FOLLOW THE INSTRUCTIONS CAREFULLY AND PRECISELY.
AND REMEMBER – THE TEMPERATURES USED TO COOK THESE EGGS ARE MUCH HOTTER THAN YOUR AVERAGE BATH, SO DON'T GO JUMPING IN WITH THEM!
NOTE THAT SOME OF THE EGG WHITE WILL NOT COOK THROUGH COMPLETELY;
TO GET AROUND THIS, CRACK THE COOKED EGGS GENTLY INTO A SMALL BOWL,
THEN SPOON THEM INTO THEIR FINAL DESTINATION, LEAVING ANY UNCOOKED WHITE BEHIND.
USE THEM IN YOUR FAVORITE BOWL OF RAMEN, OR TRY EATING THEM IN A SIMPLE DASHI (P. 45) SEASONED WITH SOY SAUCE AND A SPRINKLE OF SHICHIMI TOGARASHI AND NEGI (SEE PANTRY, P. 19).
THIS RECIPE USES PRECISE TIME AND TEMPERATURES FOR 6 REFRIGERATED EGGS;
IF YOU NEED TO MAKE MORE EGGS, DO SO IN SEPARATE BATCHES!

# ONSEN EGG
## (SLOW-COOKED SOFT-BOILED EGGS)

MAKES 6 EGGS

**INGREDIENTS:**

6 LARGE EGGS, STRAIGHT FROM THE REFRIGERATOR

FILL A MEDIUM LIDDED SAUCEPAN WITH 8 CUPS WATER AND BRING TO 185°F OVER MEDIUM-HIGH HEAT, MEASURING THE TEMPERATURE WITH A DIGITAL THERMOMETER.

AS SOON AS THE TEMPERATURE REACHES 185°F, GENTLY LOWER THE EGGS INTO THE WATER, COVER THE PAN, AND TURN OFF THE HEAT.

LET SIT FOR 17 MINUTES,

THEN POUR AS MUCH HOT WATER OUT OF THE PAN AS POSSIBLE AND PLACE IT UNDER COLD RUNNING WATER FOR ABOUT A MINUTE, UNTIL THE EGGS HAVE COOLED A BIT.

CRACK AN EGG INTO A SMALL BOWL AND REMOVE ANY EGG WHITE THAT LOOKS LIKE IT MAY NOT HAVE COOKED ALL THE WAY,

THEN SPOON THE EGG ON TOP OF RAMEN, OR EAT IT ON ITS OWN WITH WHATEVER GARNISHES YOU LIKE.

UNUSED EGGS CAN BE STORED IN THEIR SHELLS, REFRIGERATED, FOR UP TO ONE WEEK.

1 WEEK

WHEN READY TO USE, LET THE EGGS SIT IN HOT TAP WATER FOR A COUPLE OF MINUTES TO TAKE THE CHILL OFF BEFORE CRACKING INTO A BOWL AND SERVING AS DIRECTED.

# a word about MENMA

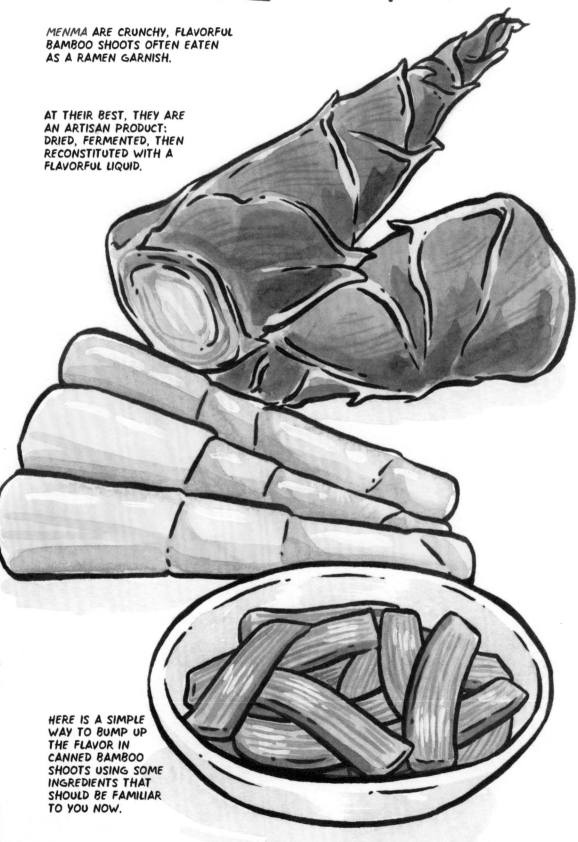

MENMA ARE CRUNCHY, FLAVORFUL BAMBOO SHOOTS OFTEN EATEN AS A RAMEN GARNISH.

AT THEIR BEST, THEY ARE AN ARTISAN PRODUCT: DRIED, FERMENTED, THEN RECONSTITUTED WITH A FLAVORFUL LIQUID.

HERE IS A SIMPLE WAY TO BUMP UP THE FLAVOR IN CANNED BAMBOO SHOOTS USING SOME INGREDIENTS THAT SHOULD BE FAMILIAR TO YOU NOW.

# M E N M A

MAKES ENOUGH FOR 6 TO 8 BOWLS OF RAMEN

## INGREDIENTS:

ONE 8-OUNCE CAN BAMBOO SHOOTS IN WATER

1 CUP WATER

ABOUT 2 TABLESPOONS KATSUOBUSHI

¼ CUP MIRIN

¼ CUP SOY SAUCE

1 GARLIC CLOVE, SMASHED WITH THE SIDE OF YOUR KNIFE

1 ARBOL CHILE

¼ CUP SAKE (OPTIONAL)

DRAIN THE BAMBOO AND RINSE WELL.

SET ASIDE.

BRING THE WATER TO A BOIL IN A SMALL POT OVER HIGH HEAT.

PLACE THE KATSUOBUSHI IN A SMALL BOWL AND COVER WITH BOILING WATER.

LET STEEP FOR 10 MINUTES, THEN STRAIN THE LIQUID BACK INTO THE POT. DISCARD THE KATSUOBUSHI.

ADD THE REMAINING INGREDIENTS AND THE BAMBOO TO THE LIQUID IN THE POT AND BRING TO A SIMMER OVER MEDIUM-HIGH HEAT.

LOWER THE HEAT TO A SIMMER AND COOK FOR 10 MINUTES.

REMOVE FROM THE HEAT AND LET COOL TO ROOM TEMPERATURE.

USE SLICES OF MENMA ON TOP OF THE RAMEN, STORING EXTRA REFRIGERATED IN THE COOKING LIQUID FOR UP TO 1 WEEK.

# PICKLED SHIITAKE MUSHROOMS

MAKES ENOUGH FOR 8 TO 10 BOWLS OF RAMEN

**INGREDIENTS:**

ABOUT 2 CUPS RESERVED SHIITAKE MUSHROOMS FROM DASHI (P. 45) OR YASAI BROTH (P. 60), OR 2 OUNCES DRIED SHIITAKE MUSHROOMS (REHYDRATED WITH A 15-MINUTE SOAK IN HOT WATER), SLICED

½ CUP RICE WINE VINEGAR

¼ CUP SOY SAUCE

¼ CUP WATER

1-INCH PIECE FRESH GINGER, PEELED AND GRATED ON A MICROPLANE (OPTIONAL)

PLACE THE MUSHROOMS IN A HEATPROOF STORAGE CONTAINER.

PLACE THE REMAINING INGREDIENTS IN A SMALL POT OVER HIGH HEAT

AND BRING TO A BOIL.

POUR THE MIXTURE OVER THE MUSHROOMS AND LET COOL TO ROOM TEMPERATURE.

USE IMMEDIATELY, OR COVER TIGHTLY AND REFRIGERATE FOR UP TO ONE WEEK.

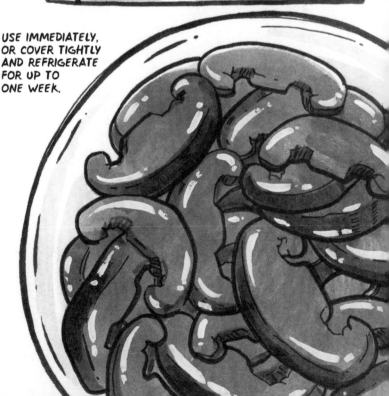

# a word about WOK-FRIED VEGETABLES

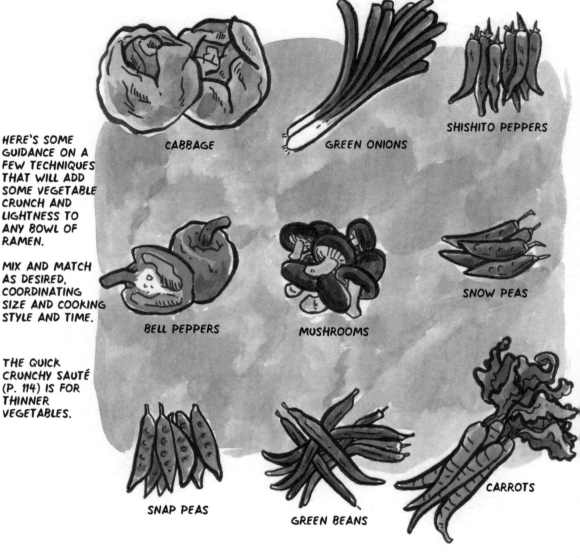

HERE'S SOME GUIDANCE ON A FEW TECHNIQUES THAT WILL ADD SOME VEGETABLE CRUNCH AND LIGHTNESS TO ANY BOWL OF RAMEN.

MIX AND MATCH AS DESIRED, COORDINATING SIZE AND COOKING STYLE AND TIME.

THE QUICK CRUNCHY SAUTÉ (P. 114) IS FOR THINNER VEGETABLES.

CABBAGE

GREEN ONIONS

SHISHITO PEPPERS

BELL PEPPERS

MUSHROOMS

SNOW PEAS

SNAP PEAS

GREEN BEANS

CARROTS

REMEMBER THAT TOTAL COOKING TIMES MAY VARY DEPENDING ON THE HEFT OF EACH INDIVIDUAL VEGETABLE,

SO UTILIZE YOUR SENSES AND PAY HEED TO THE REQUIREMENTS OF YOUR VEGETABLE AND YOUR PALATE —

WE LIKE TO KEEP THINGS ON THE CRISP AND VIBRANT SIDE!

BOK CHOY

BROCCOLI

CAULIFLOWER

THE SAUTÉ & STEAM (P. 115) IS FOR THICKER CUTS THAT NEED THE POWER OF STEAM TO COOK THROUGH.

RADISHES

DAIKON

ASPARAGUS

AND THE GREENS SAUTÉ (P. 116) IS FOR LEAFY VEG THAT WILL RELEASE A GOOD AMOUNT OF LIQUID.

SPINACH

WATERCRESS

WATER SPINACH

CHARD

KALE

WORK IN BATCHES IF NECESSARY TO AVOID OVERCROWDING YOUR WOK,

DON'T BE AFRAID OF GETTING SOME DELICIOUS CHAR ON YOUR VEG,

AND TRY FINISHING WITH A SEASONED OIL (P. 121) TO ADD FLAVOR AND FRAGRANCE.

# QUICK CRUNCHY SAUTÉ

MAKES ENOUGH FOR 4 BOWLS OF RAMEN

## INGREDIENTS:

2 TABLESPOONS CANOLA OIL, OR CHICKEN OR PORK FAT (P. 42)

1 TO 2 CUPS YOUR CHOICE OF:

CABBAGE, CUT INTO ROUGHLY 1-INCH SQUARES

GREEN ONIONS, TRIMMED AND CUT INTO 1- TO 2-INCH PIECES

SHISHITO PEPPERS

BELL PEPPERS, SEEDED AND CUT INTO STRIPS

½-INCH WIDE MUSHROOMS, CUT INTO NO LARGER THAN 1-INCH PIECES

SNOW PEAS, TRIMMED

SNAP PEAS, TRIMMED

GREEN BEANS, TRIMMED

CARROTS, CUT DIAGONALLY ¼-INCH THICK

SALT

HEAT A WOK OR CAST IRON PAN OVER HIGH HEAT.

ADD OIL OR FAT AND WHEN SMOKING,

ADD VEGETABLES OF YOUR CHOICE AND SEASON WITH SALT.

COOK, STIRRING FREQUENTLY, UNTIL THE VEGETABLES HAVE BEGUN TO SOFTEN BUT STILL RETAIN CRUNCH, 1 TO 3 MINUTES.

SERVE ATOP RAMEN IMMEDIATELY.

# SAUTÉ AND STEAM

MAKES ENOUGH FOR 4 BOWLS OF RAMEN

**INGREDIENTS:**

2 TABLESPOONS
CANOLA OIL, OR
CHICKEN OR PORK
FAT (P. 42)

1 TO 2 CUPS
YOUR CHOICE OF:

BOK CHOY, TRIMMED
AND QUARTERED

BROCCOLI FLORETS

CAULIFLOWER FLORETS

RADISHES, QUARTERED

DAIKON, PEELED
AND CUT INTO HALF
MOONS ABOUT
½ INCH THICK

ASPARAGUS, CUT INTO
1- TO 2-INCH PIECES

SALT

HEAT A WOK OR
CAST IRON PAN
OVER HIGH HEAT.

ADD OIL OR FAT
AND WHEN
SMOKING,

ADD VEGETABLES OF
YOUR CHOICE AND
COOK FOR 1 MINUTE,
STIRRING ONCE.

ADD ¼ CUP WATER AND
COOK FOR AN ADDITIONAL
2 TO 3 MINUTES,

STIRRING OCCASIONALLY,
UNTIL THE VEGETABLES
BECOME VIBRANT AND
TENDER AND THE WATER
HAS EVAPORATED.

SERVE ATOP
RAMEN
IMMEDIATELY.

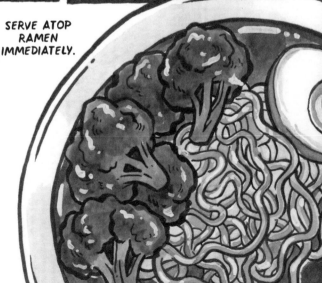

# GREENS SAUTÉ

MAKES ENOUGH FOR 4 BOWLS OF RAMEN

INGREDIENTS:

6 TO 10 CUPS
YOUR CHOICE OF:

SPINACH, TORN INTO
PIECES

WATERCRESS, TORN
INTO PIECES

WATER SPINACH,
TORN INTO PIECES

CHARD, STEMS
REMOVED AND
LEAVES TORN INTO
PIECES

KALE, STEMS
REMOVED AND
LEAVES TORN INTO
PIECES

SALT

HEAT A WOK OR
CAST IRON PAN
OVER HIGH HEAT.

ADD VEGETABLES
OF YOUR CHOICE,

THEN ADD ¼ CUP
WATER SO THE LEAVES
CAPTURE STEAM.

COOK, STIRRING
FREQUENTLY, UNTIL
THE LEAVES ARE
WILTED BUT VIBRANT,
1 TO 4 MINUTES.

SEASON WITH SALT AND SQUEEZE
THE LEAVES SLIGHTLY TO LEAVE
EXCESS LIQUID IN THE WOK.

SERVE ATOP
RAMEN
IMMEDIATELY.

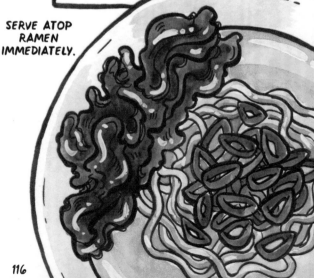

# CRISPY CHICKEN SKINS

MAKES 4 SKINS

## INGREDIENTS:

4 WHOLE SKINS
FROM CHICKEN
THIGHS (RAW,
OR FROM PULLED
CHICKEN, P. 94,
KIMCHI BRAISED
CHICKEN RAMEN,
P. 156, OR ADOBO
CHICKEN RAMEN,
P. 163)

½ TEASPOON SALT

SHICHIMI TOGARASHI
TO TASTE (SEE
PANTRY, P. 17)

PREHEAT THE OVEN TO 350°F.

PLACE THE CHICKEN SKINS
FLAT ON A PARCHMENT
PAPER-LINED BAKING SHEET
AND SEASON WITH SALT.

COVER WITH
ANOTHER SHEET
OF PARCHMENT
PAPER, THEN
TOP WITH
ANOTHER BAKING
SHEET TO KEEP
THE SKINS FROM
CURLING AS
THEY COOK.

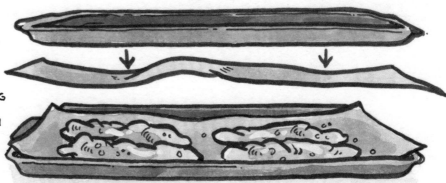

COOK UNTIL GOLDEN
BROWN AND CRISP:

45 TO 60 MINUTES IF RAW,
30 TO 45 MINUTES IF
PREVIOUSLY COOKED.

DUST WITH SHICHIMI
TOGARASHI AND
USE IMMEDIATELY
AS A RAMEN
TOPPING OR
SNACK,

OR LET THEM COOL
FULLY, THEN STORE IN
AN AIRTIGHT CONTAINER
AT ROOM TEMPERATURE
FOR UP TO TWO DAYS.

# G A R I
## (PICKLED GINGER)
### MAKES ENOUGH FOR 6 BOWLS OF RAMEN

## INGREDIENTS:

3 PIECES FRESH GINGER, ABOUT 3 INCHES LONG EACH, AS SOLID AND STRAIGHT AS POSSIBLE

½ CUP WATER

½ CUP RICE WINE VINEGAR

1 TABLESPOON SUGAR

1 TEASPOON SALT

1 ARBOL CHILE

PEEL THE GINGER USING THE SIDE OF A SPOON,

THEN CUT LENGTHWISE INTO STRIPS AS THIN AS POSSIBLE, PREFERABLY ON A MANDOLINE.

SAVE ANY SCRAPS FOR STOCKS!

THOUGH YOU MAY FIND SWEET *BENI SHŌGA* (RED PICKLED GINGER MADE WITH LIQUID FROM THE PICKLED PLUM KNOWN AS *UMEBOSHI*) ON RAMEN FROM TIME TO TIME,

PLACE THE GINGER IN A SMALL HEATPROOF CONTAINER.

PLACE THE REMAINING INGREDIENTS IN A SMALL SAUCEPAN AND BRING TO A SIMMER OVER MEDIUM-HIGH HEAT.

STIR UNTIL THE SALT AND SUGAR ARE DISSOLVED,

THEN POUR THE SOLUTION OVER THE GINGER. LET SIT AT ROOM TEMPERATURE FOR 30 MINUTES.

WE LIKE OUR MILDER VERSION — COMMONLY SERVED WITH SUSHI — FOR ITS BRIGHT, ACIDIC POP AND SLIGHT HEAT,

ESPECIALLY IN RICHER BOWLS OF MISO (P. 48) OR TONKOTSU RAMEN (P. 52).

THE GARI IS NOW READY TO USE AS A RAMEN TOPPING — A FEW STRIPS PER SERVING WILL DO, DEPENDING ON YOUR TASTE.

STORE THE REMAINING PICKLED GINGER IN ITS LIQUID, REFRIGERATED, FOR UP TO ONE MONTH.

# CHARRED SHALLOT & SCALLION

MAKES ENOUGH FOR 4 BOWLS OF RAMEN

## INGREDIENTS:

¼ CUP CANOLA OIL

3 LARGE SHALLOTS, PEELED AND JULIENNED (ABOUT 1½ CUPS)

1 BUNCH SCALLIONS, GREENS CUT INTO THIN DIAGONAL SLICES AND WHITES CUT INTO ¼ INCH THICK SLICES, SEPARATED

1 TEASPOON MINCED FRESH HOT RED CHILE (OPTIONAL)

1 TABLESPOON MIRIN

2 TABLESPOONS SOY SAUCE

2 TEASPOONS SESAME OIL

1 TEASPOON RICE WINE VINEGAR

THIS RAMEN GARNISH COMES TOGETHER QUICKLY AND ADDS GREAT SAVORY FLAVOR TO ANY BOWL.

BE SURE TO REMAIN CALM AND PATIENT IN THE INTERVALS BETWEEN STIRRING TO ENSURE GOOD CHAR ON YOUR SHALLOTS!

SIZZZZZLE

HEAT A WOK OR CAST IRON PAN OVER HIGH HEAT UNTIL SMOKING.

ADD THE CANOLA OIL AND SWIRL AROUND IN THE PAN,

THEN ADD THE SHALLOTS IN AN EVEN LAYER.

LET SIT FOR 30 SECONDS,

THEN STIR THOROUGHLY.

LET SIT ANOTHER 30 SECONDS,

ADD THE SCALLION WHITES, AND STIR.

LET SIT FOR
ANOTHER
30 SECONDS,

THEN STIR.

LET SIT A FINAL
30 SECONDS,

THEN ADD THE
GREENS AND CHILE,
STIR, AND REMOVE
FROM THE HEAT.

IMMEDIATELY TRANSFER
TO A SMALL BOWL AND
STIR IN THE REMAINING
INGREDIENTS.

TO SERVE, PLACE A BIG HEAP
(ABOUT ¼ CUP) ON TOP OF YOUR
RAMEN, DRIZZLING ANY LIQUID
AROUND THE BOWL.

KEEPS, REFRIGERATED,
FOR UP TO 3 DAYS.

3 DAYS

# a word about SEASONED OILS

JUST LIKE THE PORK AND CHICKEN FAT USED IN OUR RAMEN BROTHS, THESE SEASONED OILS WILL BRING A LOAD OF FLAVOR (NOT TO MENTION BEAUTIFUL PATTERNS) TO YOUR BOWL WHEN DRIZZLED ON TOP.

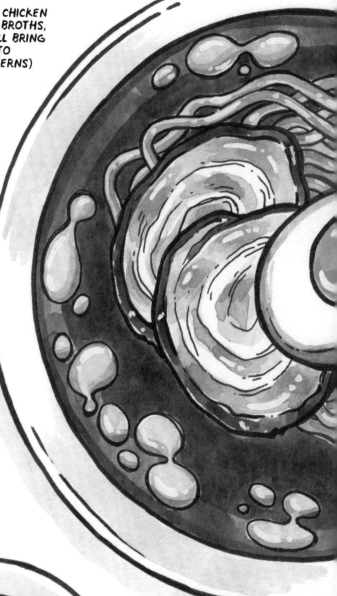

THE AROMATIC GARLIC AND SHALLOT OIL IS NICELY BALANCED, AND ITS SAVORY FRAGRANCE WILL GO WITH JUST ABOUT ANYTHING.

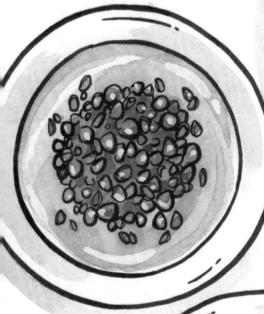

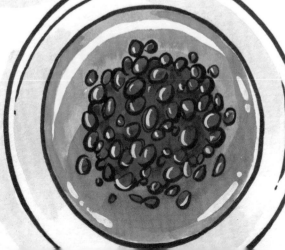

RAYU IS A CHILI OIL THAT OFFERS NOT JUST CHILI HEAT, BUT COMPLEMENTARY FLAVORS OF GINGER, GARLIC, AND GREEN ONIONS TO ANY RAMEN.

MAYU IS THE MOST CHALLENGING OF THE THREE TO "GET," BUT WHEN YOU DO, IT IS MAGICAL.

IT'S MADE WHEN GARLIC IS ESSENTIALLY BURNED SLOWLY IN FRAGRANT SESAME OIL.

THE RESULT IS A DARK, BITTER CONCOCTION: NOT VERY PALATABLE BY ITSELF, BUT DELICIOUSLY PERFECT FOR OFFSETTING THE RICHNESS OF PAITAN BROTHS LIKE TONKOTSU AND TORIKOTSU — A LITTLE GOES A LONG WAY!

A COUPLE OF NOTES: THE MAIN FUNCTION OF THESE OILS IS TO DELIVER AROMA (AND IN SOME CASES SPICE),

SO WE INTENTIONALLY LEAVE OUT SALTY ELEMENTS SINCE YOUR BOWLS WILL ALREADY BE SEASONED WITH TARE.

AND DON'T FORGET TO GIVE A STIR AND SCOOP FROM THE BOTTOM OF THE JAR WHEN USING SEASONED OILS — THERE'S GOOD STUFF DOWN THERE!

# AROMATIC GARLIC & SHALLOT OIL

MAKES ABOUT 1 CUP

**INGREDIENTS:**

1 CUP CANOLA OIL

1 HEAD GARLIC CLOVES, PEELED AND MINCED

2 LARGE SHALLOTS, PEELED AND MINCED

PLACE ALL THE INGREDIENTS IN A SMALL, HEAVY SAUCEPAN OVER LOW HEAT.

COOK NICE AND SLOW TO EXTRACT THE AROMA AND FLAVOR OF THE GARLIC AND SHALLOTS INTO THE OIL, STIRRING OCCASIONALLY.

WHEN THE GARLIC AND SHALLOTS BEGIN TO BROWN, ANYWHERE BETWEEN 20 AND 30 MINUTES,

BEGIN TO STIR CONSTANTLY FOR 2 TO 5 ADDITIONAL MINUTES UNTIL THE GARLIC IS A NICE, LIGHT, EVEN BROWN,

THEN REMOVE FROM THE HEAT AND LET COOL TO ROOM TEMPERATURE.

STORE REFRIGERATED IN AN AIRTIGHT CONTAINER FOR UP TO 1 MONTH, DOLLOPING A TABLESPOON OR SO ON TOP OF RAMEN AS DESIRED.

1 MONTH

 # RAYU

## (JAPANESE CHILI OIL)

MAKES ABOUT 1½ CUPS

**INGREDIENTS:**

½ CUP CANOLA OIL

3-INCH PIECE OF GINGER, PEELED AND MINCED

6 CLOVES GARLIC, PEELED AND MINCED

WHITE PARTS OF 3 GREEN ONIONS, TRIMMED AND MINCED

1 TABLESPOON SHICHIMI TOGARASHI (SEE PANTRY, P. 17)

1 TEASPOON CRUSHED RED PEPPER FLAKES

½ CUP SESAME OIL

PLACE THE CANOLA OIL, GINGER, GARLIC, AND GREEN ONIONS IN A SMALL SAUCEPAN OVER MEDIUM HEAT.

BRING TO A SIMMER,

STIRRING OCCASIONALLY, COOKING OUT THE RAWNESS OF THE VEGETABLES UNTIL FRAGRANT WITHOUT BROWNING THEM, ABOUT 5 MINUTES.

REMOVE FROM THE HEAT AND STIR IN THE REMAINING INGREDIENTS.

LET COOL,

THEN STORE REFRIGERATED IN AN AIRTIGHT CONTAINER FOR UP TO 1 MONTH, DRIZZLING ON TOP OF RAMEN AS DESIRED.

1 MONTH

# M A Y U
## (BLACK GARLIC OIL)
### MAKES ABOUT ½ CUP

**INGREDIENTS:**

½ CUP SESAME OIL

¼ CUP MINCED GARLIC CLOVES (1 TO 2 HEADS)

PLACE THE OIL AND GARLIC IN A SMALL SAUCEPAN OVER MEDIUM-LOW HEAT.

COOK, STIRRING FREQUENTLY, UNTIL THE GARLIC STARTS TO BROWN, 10 TO 15 MINUTES.

MAYU WILL BE ACRID AND DISAGREEABLE WHEN TASTED ON ITS OWN,

BLEH.

BUT BRINGS BEAUTIFUL CONTRAST AND BEGUILING AROMA TO RICH PAITAN BROTHS!

THE GARLIC WILL GET STICKY AND THE OIL WILL BECOME LESS VISCOUS.

WHEN THE GARLIC IS DEEPLY BROWN, PAY EVEN CLOSER ATTENTION, AND BRAVELY CONTINUE COOKING,

UNTIL THE GARLIC JUST BEGINS TO TURN BLACK (YOU MAY EVEN SEE WISPS OF SMOKE),

20 TO 30 MINUTES TOTAL DEPENDING ON THE SUGAR AND WATER CONTENT OF YOUR GARLIC.

REMOVE FROM THE HEAT AND IMMEDIATELY TRANSFER TO A BLENDER.

CAREFULLY BLEND UNTIL THOROUGHLY PUREED,

THEN STORE REFRIGERATED IN AN AIRTIGHT CONTAINER FOR UP TO 3 MONTHS, DRIZZLING ON RICHER BOWLS OF RAMEN AS DESIRED.

3 MONTHS

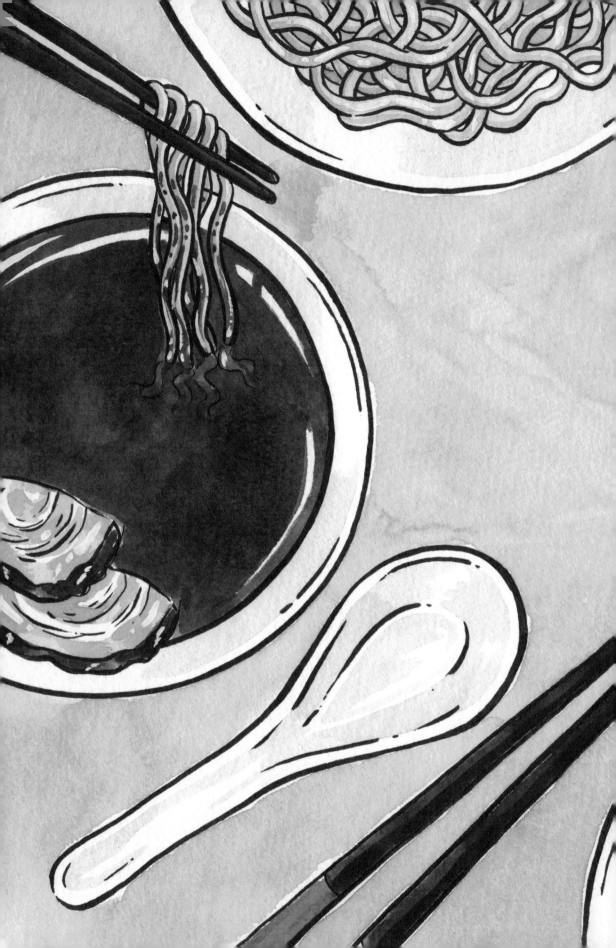

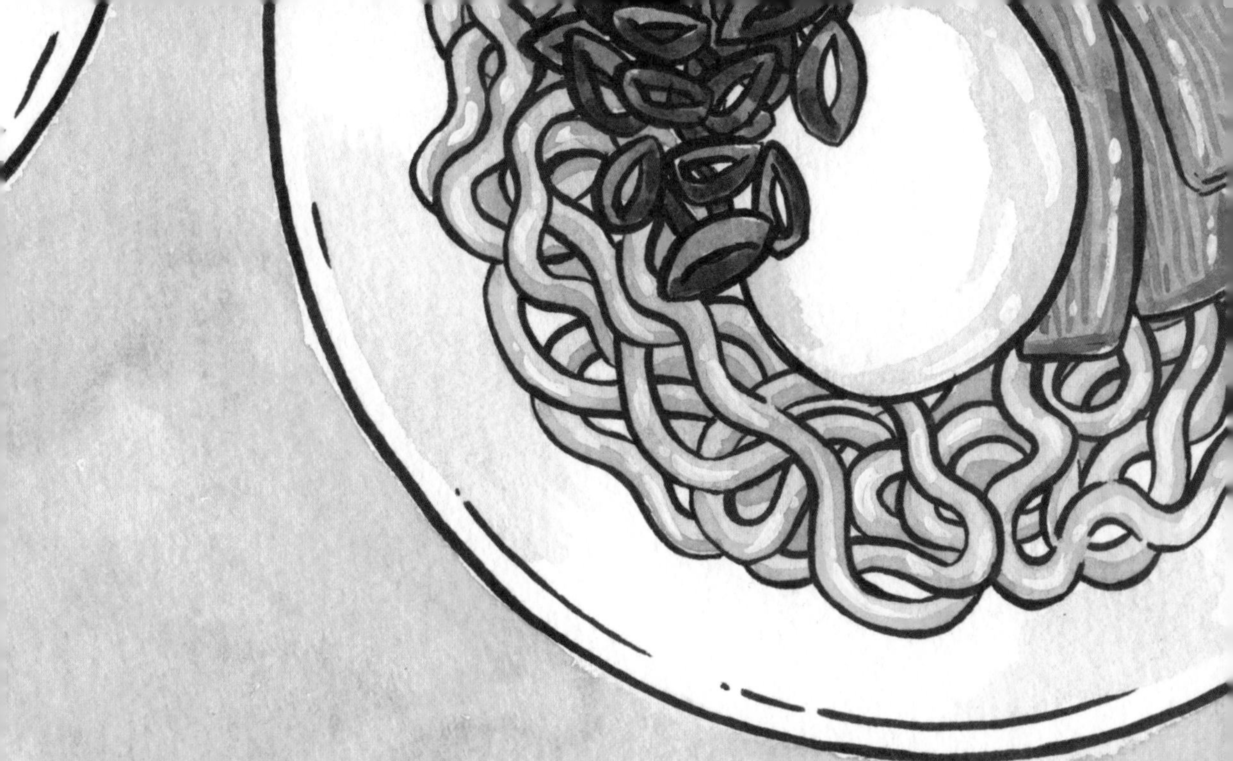

# OFFSHOOTS & RIFFS

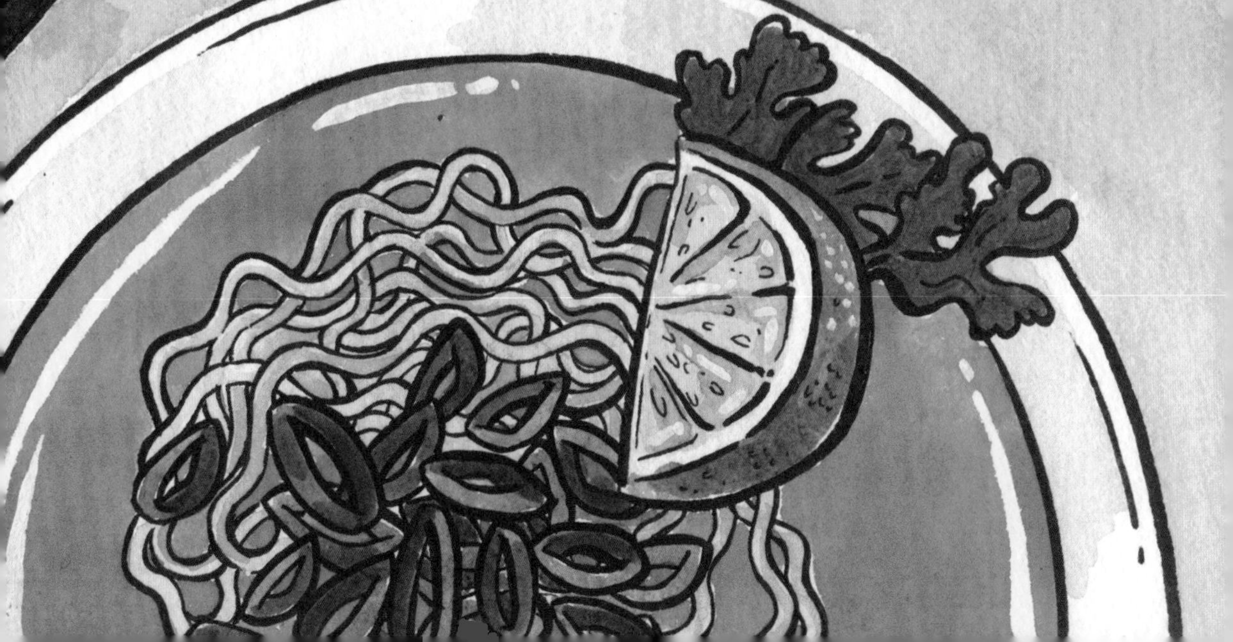

# a word about TSUKEMEN

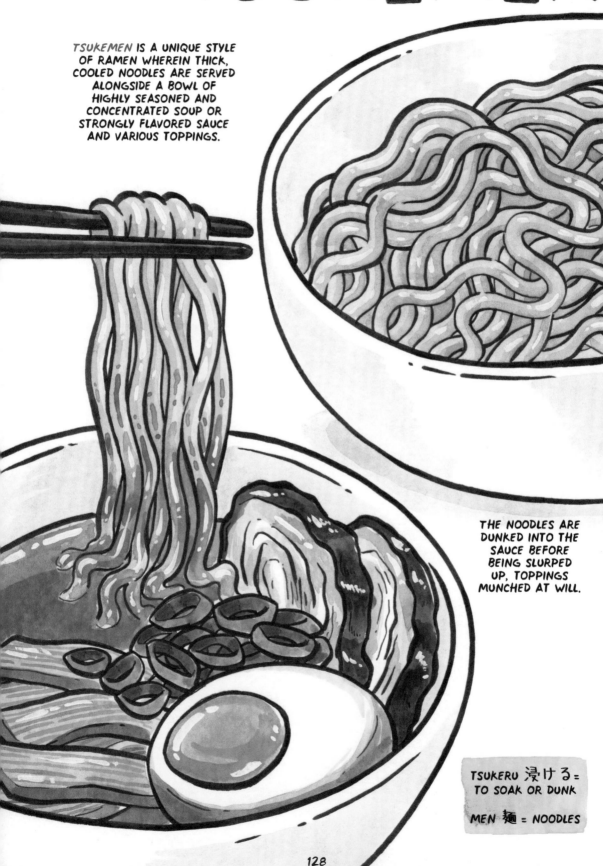

TSUKEMEN IS A UNIQUE STYLE OF RAMEN WHEREIN THICK, COOLED NOODLES ARE SERVED ALONGSIDE A BOWL OF HIGHLY SEASONED AND CONCENTRATED SOUP OR STRONGLY FLAVORED SAUCE AND VARIOUS TOPPINGS.

THE NOODLES ARE DUNKED INTO THE SAUCE BEFORE BEING SLURPED UP, TOPPINGS MUNCHED AT WILL.

TSUKERU 浸ける = TO SOAK OR DUNK

MEN 麺 = NOODLES

TSUKEMEN WAS DEVELOPED BY THE RAMEN LEGEND KAZUO YAMAGISHI IN THE MID-1950S WHEN HE WAS STILL AN APPRENTICE AT A RAMEN SHOP.

A REGULAR CUSTOMER ASKED TO JOIN THE STAFF MEAL — FOR WHICH YAMAGISHI-SAN HAD PREPARED NOODLES SOAKED IN SMALL BOWLS OF PRECIOUS BROTH, STRETCHED WITH HEAVY SEASONING.

THE CUSTOMER LOVED IT, SPURRING YAMAGISHI-SAN TO PERFECT HIS RECIPE.

HE SOON OPENED HIS OWN SHOP, TAISHOKEN, AND HIS LEGION OF DISCIPLES BEGAN TO GROW.

AS DECADES PASSED AND YAMAGISHI-SAN GREW OLDER, HE REMAINED IN CHARGE, TASTING THE SOUPS AND NOODLES DAILY BEFORE MAKING HIS WAY TO A PERCH OUTSIDE HIS FLAGSHIP SHOP (TAISHOKEN IS NOW A WELL-KNOWN AND WELL-RUN CHAIN),

WHERE HE WOULD SIT, A RAMEN ICON GREETING CUSTOMERS IN THE EVER-LONG LINE OUTSIDE HIS RAMEN PALACE.

129

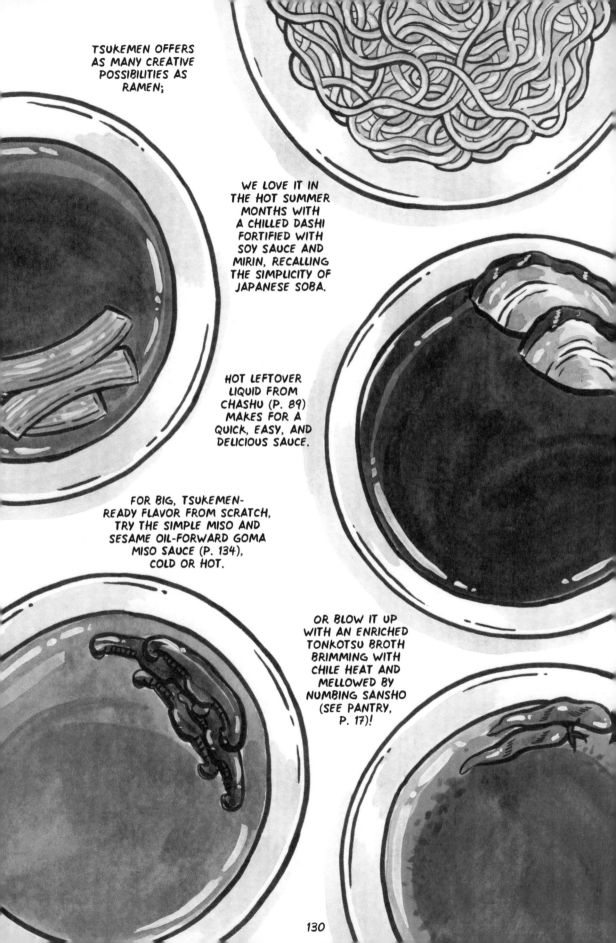

TSUKEMEN OFFERS AS MANY CREATIVE POSSIBILITIES AS RAMEN;

WE LOVE IT IN THE HOT SUMMER MONTHS WITH A CHILLED DASHI FORTIFIED WITH SOY SAUCE AND MIRIN, RECALLING THE SIMPLICITY OF JAPANESE SOBA.

HOT LEFTOVER LIQUID FROM CHASHU (P. 89) MAKES FOR A QUICK, EASY, AND DELICIOUS SAUCE.

FOR BIG, TSUKEMEN-READY FLAVOR FROM SCRATCH, TRY THE SIMPLE MISO AND SESAME OIL-FORWARD GOMA MISO SAUCE (P. 134), COLD OR HOT.

OR BLOW IT UP WITH AN ENRICHED TONKOTSU BROTH BRIMMING WITH CHILE HEAT AND MELLOWED BY NUMBING SANSHO (SEE PANTRY, P. 17)!

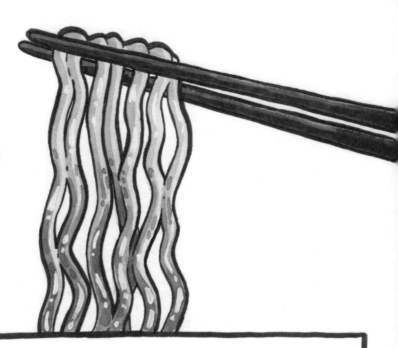

WHICHEVER SAUCE YOU USE, PAIR IT WITH THICKER NOODLES TO HIGHLIGHT THEIR SATISFYING CHEW; THEY'LL ALSO GIVE THE SAUCE MORE TO ADHERE TO.

AND NOTE THAT NOODLE PORTIONS FOR TSUKEMEN ARE USUALLY LARGER THAN FOR A STANDARD BOWL OF RAMEN, SINCE YOU WON'T BE CONSUMING A BIG BOWL OF SOUP AS WELL.

BUT ADJUST AS YOU SEE FIT, AND WHEN YOU'VE FINISHED ALL YOUR NOODLES, DON'T BE AFRAID TO REPLENISH WITH MORE,

OR EVEN ADD A LITTLE HOT STOCK OR WATER TO THE SAUCE AND DRINK IT DOWN!

# TSUKEMEN
## (DIPPED NOODLES)
MAKES 1 SERVING

**INGREDIENTS:**

6 TO 8 OUNCES FRESH RAMEN NOODLES (THE THICKER THE BETTER)

6 OUNCES FORTIFIED DASHI OR CHASHU LIQUID FOR TSUKEMEN, OR 4 OUNCES GOMA MISO SAUCE OR SPICY TSUKEMEN BROTH (RECIPES FOLLOW)

1 SLICE CHASHU (P. 89)

1 AJITSUKE TAMAGO (P. 104), SLICED IN HALF

5 OR 6 PIECES MENMA (P. 110)

SMALL HANDFUL NEGI (SEE PANTRY, P. 17)

A HEARTY PINCH OF TOASTED SESAME SEEDS

RAYU (P. 124) OR AROMATIC GARLIC AND SHALLOT OIL (P. 123) AS DESIRED

SHICHIMI TOGARASHI, NORI, YAKITORI (P. 96) OR CRISPY CHICKEN SKINS (P. 117) AS DESIRED

FIRST, PREPARE THE NOODLES.

BRING A LARGE POT OF WATER TO A BOIL OVER HIGH HEAT.

COOK THE NOODLES UNTIL AL DENTE,

THEN DRAIN,

AND PLUNGE INTO A BOWL UNDER RUNNING COLD WATER.

AGITATE THE NOODLES GENTLY UNTIL COMPLETELY COOLED,

THEN DRAIN WELL.

TRANSFER TO A BOWL AND SET ASIDE.

IF USING FORTIFIED DASHI OR COLD GOMA MISO SAUCE, PLACE IT IN A SMALL BOWL.

IF USING CHASHU LIQUID FOR TSUKEMEN, HOT GOMA MISO SAUCE, OR SPICY TSUKEMEN BROTH, HEAT IT IN A SAUCEPAN, THEN TRANSFER TO A SMALL BOWL.

SEAR THE CHASHU IN A DRY PAN OVER MEDIUM-HIGH HEAT, AND PLACE AGAINST THE SIDE OF THE SAUCE BOWL,

FOLLOWED BY THE AJITSUKE TAMAGO, MENMA, NEGI, AND SESAME SEEDS.

DRIZZLE THE OILS AND ARRANGE ANY OPTIONAL GARNISHES AROUND SAUCE BOWL (DON'T FORGET THE SANSHO OR SICHUAN PEPPERCORN IF USING FOR SPICY TSUKEMEN BROTH!)

AND SERVE IMMEDIATELY ALONG WITH THE NOODLES.

DIP THE NOODLES INTO THE SAUCE AND SLURP HEARTILY!

LIFT!

DUNK!

SLURP!

# FORTIFIED DASHI

MAKES ONE 6-OUNCE SERVING

**INGREDIENTS:**

½ CUP DASHI (P. 45)

2 TABLESPOONS SOY SAUCE

2 TABLESPOONS MIRIN

COMBINE ALL THE INGREDIENTS AND REFRIGERATE FOR AT LEAST 30 MINUTES BEFORE USING AS DIRECTED FORTSUKEMEN.

# GOMA MISO SAUCE

MAKES ABOUT 4 SERVINGS

**INGREDIENTS:**

3 TABLESPOONS SESAME OIL

2 TABLESPOONS MISO OF YOUR CHOICE

2 TABLESPOONS SOY SAUCE

2 TEASPOONS RICE WINE VINEGAR

½ CUP SAKE

½ CUP WATER

½ CUP DASHI (P. 45) OR WATER PLUS 1 ADDITIONAL TEASPOON SOY SAUCE

1-INCH PIECE FRESH GINGER, PEELED AND GRATED ON A MICROPLANE OR MINCED

2 CLOVES GARLIC, GRATED ON A MICROPLANE, OR MINCED

WHISK THE SESAME OIL, MISO, SOY SAUCE, VINEGAR, SAKE, WATER, AND DASHI TOGETHER IN A SMALL STOCKPOT.

BRING TO A SIMMER OVER MEDIUM-HIGH HEAT, WHISKING OCCASIONALLY, AND COOK FOR 2 MINUTES TO BURN OFF THE ALCOHOL.

REMOVE FROM THE HEAT, THEN WHISK IN THE GINGER AND GARLIC.

SERVE IMMEDIATELY,

OR COOL, STIRRING BEFORE MEASURING EACH PORTION TO REDISTRIBUTE INGREDIENTS,

AND REFRIGERATE ANY UNUSED SAUCE FOR UP TO 2 WEEKS, OR FREEZE FOR UP TO 3 MONTHS.

2 WEEKS

3 MONTHS

# CHASHU LIQUID for TSUKEMEN

## MAKES ONE 6-OUNCE SERVING

**INGREDIENTS:**

½ CUP LIQUID LEFT OVER FROM COOKING CHASHU (P. 89)

¼ CUP WATER

THIN THE CHASHU LIQUID WITH WATER,

USING MORE OR LESS DEPENDING ON THE STRENGTH OF YOUR CHASHU LIQUID AND YOUR PERSONAL TASTE, AND HEAT BEFORE SERVING.

# SPICY TSUKEMEN BROTH

## MAKES ABOUT 4 SERVINGS

**INGREDIENTS:**

2 CUPS TONKOTSU (P. 52), TORIKOTSU (P. 54), OR GYOKAI BROTH (P. 63)

3 TABLESPOONS PORK (P. 42) OR CHICKEN FAT (P. 43)

½ CUP SOY SAUCE

1 TABLESPOON RICE WINE VINEGAR

1 TABLESPOON SUGAR

1-2 TEASPOONS CRUSHED RED PEPPER FLAKES

¼ TO ½ TEASPOON PER SERVING SANSHO OR SICHUAN PEPPERCORNS, GROUND AND SIFTED (OPTIONAL, SEE PANTRY, P. 17)

COMBINE ALL THE INGREDIENTS EXCEPT THE SANSHO IN A SAUCEPAN AND BRING TO A SIMMER.

LOWER HEAT TO MAINTAIN A SIMMER AND COOK FOR 5 MINUTES.

REMOVE FROM THE HEAT, THEN USE AS DIRECTED FOR TSUKEMEN, STIRRING WELL BETWEEN EACH SERVING TO ENSURE DISTRIBUTION OF THE INGREDIENTS,

SPRINKLING SANSHO ATOP EACH SERVING OF BROTH IF USING.

REFRIGERATE ANY UNUSED SAUCE FOR UP TO 2 WEEKS, OR FREEZE FOR UP TO 3 MONTHS.

2 WEEKS

3 MONTHS

# a word about ABURA SOBA

THIS RELATIVELY NEW STYLE OF RAMEN EMBRACES THE BEAUTY OF FAT, RELYING ON IT TO DELIVER FLAVOR AND KEEP THE SOUPLESS NOODLES FLOWING FREELY.

OFTEN SERVED WITH A RAW EGG ON TOP, IT'S MEANT TO BE MIXED UP — THE HEAT FROM THE NOODLES COMBINING THE EGG AND FAT INTO A CARBONARA-LIKE SAUCE —

AND CONTINUALLY DOCTORED WITH VINEGAR AND RAYU AS YOU SLURP YOUR WAY TO THE BOTTOM OF THE BOWL.

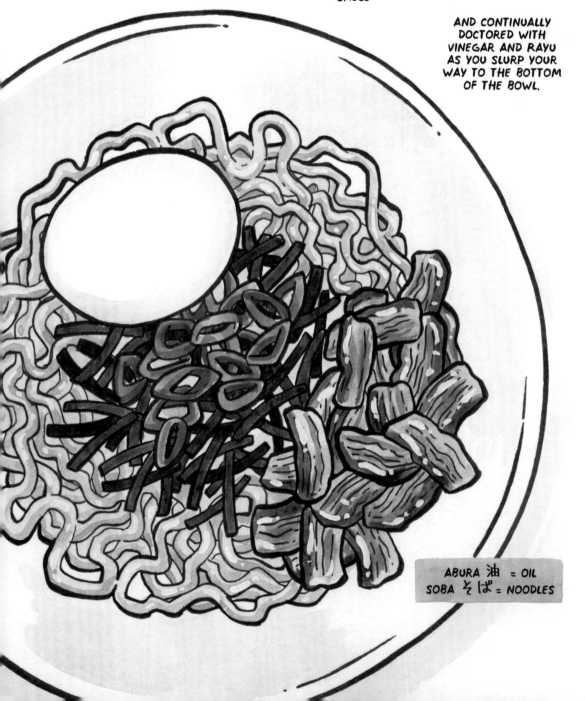

ABURA 油 = OIL
SOBA そば = NOODLES

THOSE WITH AN AVERSION TO RAW EGGS CAN USE AN ONSEN EGG (P. 108) OR A SOFT AJITSUKE TAMAGO (P. 104).

ABURA SOBA IS LONG ON FLAVOR AND SATISFYING CHEW, AND EASY TO MAKE SINCE THERE'S NO NEED FOR LONG-BUBBLING STOCKS.

THIS IS OUR FAVORITE WAY TO SERVE IT USING SEVERAL RECIPES FROM THIS BOOK — FOR A SIMILAR STYLE, CHECK THE MAZEMEN RECIPE (P. 141), WHICH GETS EVEN SAUCIER WITH THE ADDITION OF BROTH.

OR GO AHEAD AND PLAY WITH DIFFERENT FATS AND VARIOUS TOPPINGS AS YOU LIKE, LOAD IT UP, AND FIND YOUR FAVORITE BLEND!

# ABURA SOBA
## (OIL NOODLES)
### MAKES 1 SERVING

**INGREDIENTS:**

2 TABLESPOONS PORK FAT (P.43) OR CHICKEN FAT (P. 42)

1 SLICE CHASHU (P. 89), CUT INTO BATONS ABOUT 1 BY ¼ INCH

½ TEASPOON SESAME OIL

1 TEASPOON RICE WINE VINEGAR, PLUS MORE FOR SERVING

2 TEASPOONS SOY SAUCE

5 OUNCES HANDMADE RAMEN NOODLES (P. 79) OR OTHER FRESH RAMEN NOODLES

1 RAW EGG OR ONSEN EGG (P. 108) OR SOFT AJITSUKE TAMAGO (P. 104)

A FEW PIECES MENMA (P. 110)

A FEW PIECES GARI (P. 118)

SMALL HANDFUL NEGI (SEE PANTRY, P. 17)

1 TEASPOON SESAME SEEDS

2 BY 4-INCH PIECE NORI, JULIENNED

RAYU (P. 124)

BRING A LARGE POT OF WATER TO A BOIL OVER HIGH HEAT.

MEANWHILE, MELT THE FAT IN A PAN OR WOK OVER MEDIUM-HIGH HEAT,

THEN ADD THE CHASHU AND COOK, STIRRING FREQUENTLY, UNTIL HEATED THROUGH, ABOUT 1 MINUTE.

REMOVE AND RESERVE THE CHASHU.

SPOON ABOUT 2 TABLESPOONS OF THE FAT INTO A SERVING BOWL

AND ADD THE SESAME OIL, VINEGAR, AND SOY SAUCE.

COOK THE NOODLES AS DIRECTED IN HANDMADE RAMEN NOODLES (P. 79), DRAIN WELL, AND PLACE ON TOP OF THE SAUCE.

CRACK OR PEEL YOUR EGG AND PLACE IT ON TOP OF THE NOODLES, ALONG WITH THE CHASHU, MENMA, GARI, NEGI, SESAME SEEDS, AND NORI.

SERVE IMMEDIATELY WITH RAYU AND ADDITIONAL VINEGAR ON THE SIDE.

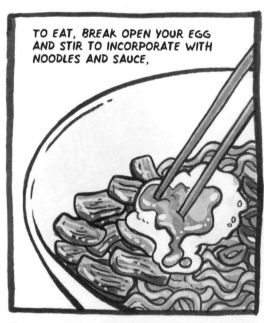

TO EAT, BREAK OPEN YOUR EGG AND STIR TO INCORPORATE WITH NOODLES AND SAUCE,

SEASONING WITH MORE VINEGAR AND RAYU AS YOU GO.

# a word about MAZEMEN

WHILE ABURA SOBA'S (P. 138) STRENGTH LIES IN ITS USE OF SAVORY OILS AND FATS,

ITS COUSIN MAZEMEN USES A SMALL AMOUNT OF HIGHLY FLAVORED BROTH AND TASTY TOPPINGS, MEANT TO BE MIXED UP THOROUGHLY AT THE TABLE BEFORE SLURPING.

THINK OF A REALLY WELL-COOKED PASTA DISH, WHERE THE STARCHES FROM THE NOODLES COMBINE WITH SAUCE (IN THIS CASE THE REDUCED STOCK) TO COAT THE NOODLES WITH FULL FLAVOR IN EACH BITE.

YOU CAN REALLY GO WILD HERE (CHECK IVAN ORKIN'S GREAT BOOK IVAN RAMEN FOR SOME DELICIOUSLY IMAGINATIVE RECIPES, INCLUDING A BLT MAZEMEN!), SO GET CREATIVE!

MAZE 混ぜ = MIX
MEN 麺 = NOODLES

OUR BASIC RECIPE IS AN UNCOMPLICATED INTRODUCTION TO THE STYLE, BUT SEE OUR RIFFS THAT FOLLOW THE RECIPE FOR MORE OPTIONS, AND FEEL FREE TO SWAP OUT TOPPINGS AS YOU LIKE!

# MAZEMEN

## (MIXED NOODLES)

MAKES 4 SERVINGS

## INGREDIENTS:

3 CUPS PORK (P. 43) OR CHICKEN STOCK (P. 42) OR TONKOTSU (P. 52) OR TORIKOTSU BROTH (P. 54)

4 TABLESPOONS PORK (P. 43) OR CHICKEN FAT (P. 42), OMIT IF USING TONKOTSU OR TORIKOTSU BROTH

8 TABLESPOONS SHOYU (P. 47) OR MISO TARE (P. 48) OR 4 TABLESPOONS SHIO TARE (P. 46)

4 TABLESPOONS RAYU (P. 124) OR AROMATIC GARLIC OIL (P. 123), CHUNKS INCLUDED

2 TEASPOONS RICE WINE VINEGAR

5 OUNCES HANDMADE RAMEN NOODLES (P. 79) OR OTHER FRESH RAMEN NOODLES

ONSEN EGG (P. 108) OR AJITSUKE TAMAGO (P. 104)

BRING A LARGE POT OF WATER TO A BOIL OVER HIGH HEAT.

PLACE THE STOCK IN A SMALL SAUCEPAN AND COOK OVER HIGH HEAT

UNTIL REDUCED BY ABOUT HALF, TO 1½ CUPS.

ADD THE FAT AND LOWER THE HEAT TO LOW.

MEANWHILE, EVENLY DIVIDE THE TARE, RAYU, AND VINEGAR AMONG 4 BOWLS.

COOK THE NOODLES AS DIRECTED IN HANDMADE RAMEN NOODLES (P. 79),

AND WHEN ALMOST DONE, DIVIDE THE HOT BROTH AND FAT AMONG THE BOWLS.

DRAIN THE NOODLES WELL AND PLACE ON TOP OF THE SAUCE.

TOP WITH THE EGG AND OTHER DESIRED TOPPINGS, AND SERVE IMMEDIATELY WITH RAYU AND ADDITIONAL VINEGAR ON THE SIDE.

TO EAT, BREAK THE EGG AND STIR TO INCORPORATE WITH THE NOODLES AND SAUCE, SEASONING WITH MORE VINEGAR AND RAYU AS YOU GO.

SUGGESTED ACCOMPANIMENTS:

CHASHU (P. 89)

SHREDDED PORK (P. 92)

PICKLED SHIITAKE MUSHROOMS (P. 111)

NEGI (P. 19)

SESAME SEEDS

GARI (P. 118)

EXTRA RAYU

EXTRA RICE WINE VINEGAR

# CREAMY MUSHROOM MAZEMEN

MAKES 1 SERVING

## INGREDIENTS:

2 TABLESPOONS BUTTER

4 OUNCES (ABOUT 2 CUPS) SHIITAKE MUSHROOMS, SLICED

1 LARGE SHALLOT, JULIENNED

1 CLOVE GARLIC, THINLY SLICED

2 GREEN ONIONS, TRIMMED AND SEPARATED, WHITES MINCED AND GREENS THINLY SLICED DIAGONALLY

½ CUP CHICKEN STOCK (P. 42) OR TORIKOTSU BROTH (P. 54)

¼ CUP HEAVY CREAM

½ TEASPOON SESAME OIL

1 TEASPOON RAYU (P. 124) PLUS MORE FOR SERVING

SALT AND FRESHLY GROUND BLACK PEPPER

5 OUNCES HANDMADE RAMEN NOODLES (P. 79) OR OTHER FRESH RAMEN NOODLES

1 RAW EGG YOLK (OPTIONAL)

SHICHIMI TOGARASHI

BRING A LARGE POT OF WATER TO A BOIL OVER HIGH HEAT.

MEANWHILE, MELT THE BUTTER IN A CAST IRON PAN OR WOK OVER MEDIUM-HIGH HEAT,

THEN ADD THE MUSHROOMS AND COOK UNTIL THEY ARE JUST BEGINNING TO SOFTEN, ABOUT 2 MINUTES.

THIS DISH MAY NOT SCREAM TRADITIONAL JAPANESE FLAVORS, BUT IT'S A DELICIOUS, INDULGENT TAKE ON THE MAZEMEN STYLE, AND EASY TO MAKE IN NO TIME.

NOTE THAT IT IS WRITTEN FOR ONE SERVING — YOU CAN MULTIPLY THE RECIPE FOR UP TO 4 SERVINGS WITH GOOD RESULTS, BUT BE SURE TO ALLOW A BIT MORE COOKING TIME AS NEEDED TO REDUCE LARGER QUANTITIES OF LIQUIDS.

ADD THE SHALLOT, GARLIC, AND GREEN ONION WHITES AND COOK, STIRRING, UNTIL SOFT AND STARTING TO BROWN, ANOTHER 2 TO 3 MINUTES.

ADD THE STOCK AND INCREASE THE HEAT TO HIGH, COOKING UNTIL THE LIQUID HAS REDUCED BY ABOUT HALF, 2 TO 3 MINUTES.

ADD THE CREAM AND COOK 1 ADDITIONAL MINUTE TO COMBINE THE FLAVORS AND REDUCE A BIT MORE.

STIR IN THE SESAME OIL, THE 1 TEASPOON RAYU, AND GREEN ONION GREENS.

REMOVE FROM THE HEAT AND ADJUST SEASONING.

SUGGESTED ACCOMPANIMENTS:

PULLED CHICKEN (P. 94)

TSUKUNE (P. 98)

YAKITORI (P. 96)

ONSEN EGG (P. 108)
OR AJITSUKE TAMAGO (P. 104)

NEGI (P. 19)

CRISPY CHICKEN SKINS (P. 117)

COOK THE NOODLES AS DIRECTED IN HANDMADE RAMEN NOODLES (P. 79), DRAIN WELL, AND PLACE IN A BOWL.

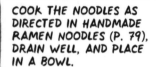

POUR THE MUSHROOM MIXTURE OVER THE NOODLES, ARRANGING MUSHROOMS ATTRACTIVELY.

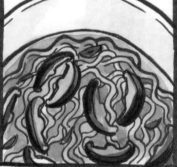

TOP WITH THE YOLK AND DESIRED ACCOMPANIMENTS, PLENTY OF BLACK PEPPER, AND SHICHIMI TOGARASHI.

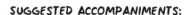

SERVE IMMEDIATELY, BREAKING THE YOLK AND MIXING WELL TO INCORPORATE THE NOODLES AND SAUCE, WITH RAYU ON THE SIDE.

# HOT & COLD SUMMER TOMATO MAZEMEN

MAKES 1 SERVING

## INGREDIENTS:

1 SMALL SHALLOT, JULIENNED

A FEW CROSSWISE SLICES OF FRESNO, JALAPEÑO, OR SERRANO PEPPER, MORE OR LESS TO TASTE

½ TEASPOON BROWN SUGAR, PACKED

JUICE OF 1 LIME (ABOUT 2 TABLESPOONS)

1 TABLESPOON CANE OR RICE WINE VINEGAR

2 TEASPOONS FISH SAUCE, MORE OR LESS TO TASTE

1 TEASPOON SOY SAUCE

1 TEASPOON CANOLA OIL

½ TEASPOON SESAME OIL

2 GREEN ONIONS, TRIMMED AND SEPARATED, WHITES THINLY SLICED CROSSWISE AND GREENS THINLY SLICED DIAGONALLY

1 LARGE HANDFUL RIPE CHERRY TOMATOES, HALVED

5 OUNCES HANDMADE RAMEN NOODLES (P. 79) OR OTHER FRESH RAMEN NOODLES

SEVERAL LEAVES THAI OR GENOVESE BASIL, TORN INTO PIECES

COMBINE THE SHALLOT, PEPPER, SUGAR, LIME JUICE, VINEGAR, FISH SAUCE, SOY SAUCE, OILS, GREEN ONION WHITES, AND TOMATOES IN A BOWL AND STIR WELL TO INCORPORATE AND DISSOLVE THE SUGAR.

COVER AND REFRIGERATE FOR 30 MINUTES.

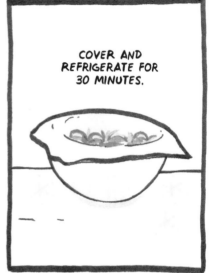

BRING A LARGE POT OF WATER TO A BOIL OVER HIGH HEAT.

COOK THE NOODLES AS DIRECTED, DRAIN WELL, AND ADD DIRECTLY TO THE CHILLED SAUCE.

THIS IS ANOTHER UNIQUE TAKE ON THE MAZEMEN STYLE, PERFECT FOR THE SUMMER MONTHS WHEN YOU WANT TO CELEBRATE AN ABUNDANCE OF TOMATOES. IT UNITES THE BRIGHTNESS OF SOUTHEAST ASIAN FLAVORS WITH A BEGUILING HOT NOODLES/COLD SAUCE TECHNIQUE.

THE ADDITION OF FISH SAUCE BRINGS A RICH UMAMI DEPTH — DON'T SKIMP!

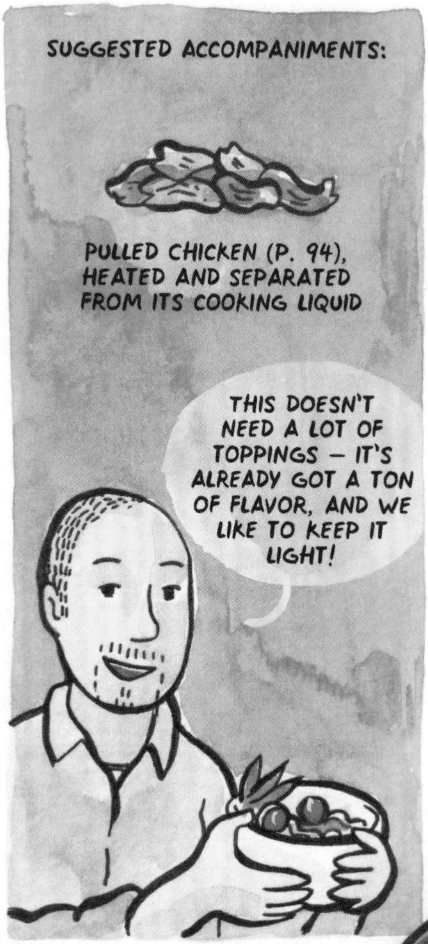
SUGGESTED ACCOMPANIMENTS:
PULLED CHICKEN (P. 94), HEATED AND SEPARATED FROM ITS COOKING LIQUID
THIS DOESN'T NEED A LOT OF TOPPINGS – IT'S ALREADY GOT A TON OF FLAVOR, AND WE LIKE TO KEEP IT LIGHT!

ADD THE GREEN ONION GREENS AND HALF OF THE BASIL AND QUICKLY MIX WELL.

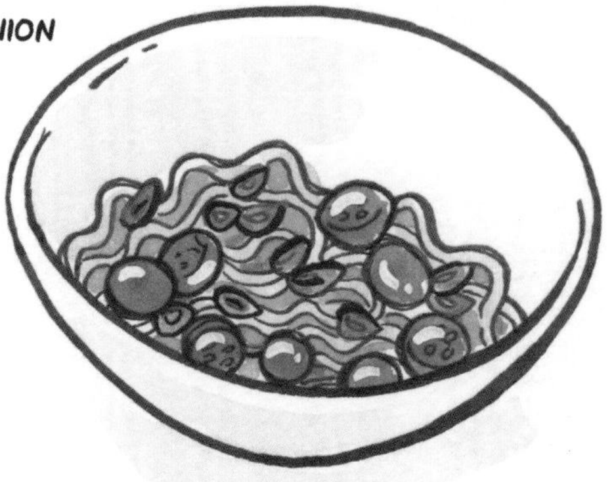

TRANSFER TO A BOWL. ARRANGE THE TOMATOES ATTRACTIVELY AND POUR ALL THE LIQUID OVER THE NOODLES.

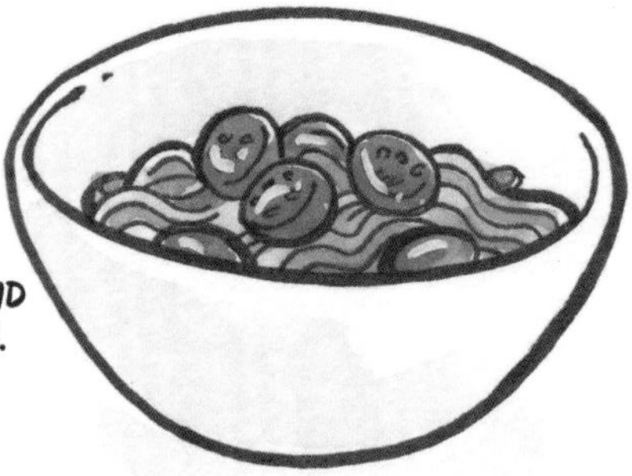

GARNISH WITH THE REMAINING BASIL AND SERVE IMMEDIATELY.

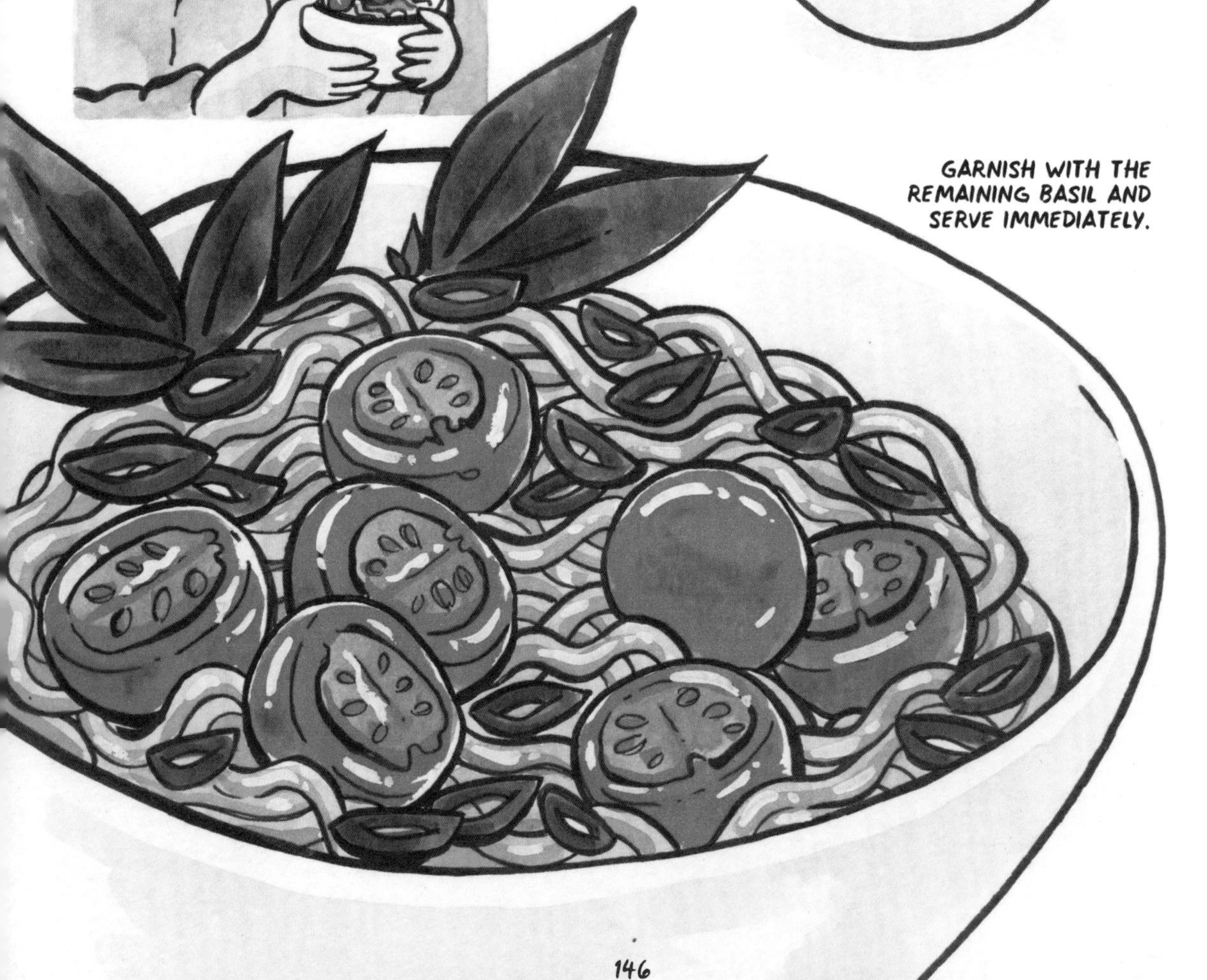

# a word about TANTANMEN

THIS IS OUR TAKE ON A POPULAR BOWL THAT DESCENDS FROM CHINESE *DANDAN* NOODLES,

A SICHUAN DISH OF WHEAT NOODLES TOPPED WITH GROUND PORK, SURGING WITH CHILI HEAT COUNTERACTED WITH NUMBING SICHUAN PEPPERCORN.

THE JAPANESE EVOLUTION KNOWN AS *TANTANMEN* IS SOMETIMES BROTHY, SOMETIMES MORE DRY LIKE MAZEMEN, AND OFTEN RED WITH THE CHILI OIL LYING IN WAIT.

OURS READS A BIT MORE LIKE A THICK TONKOTSU BROTH, DUE TO THE RICH SESAME PASTE USED, BUT TRUST US — THE HEAT IS THERE!

TO CAPTURE THE DEPTH OF THE TRADITIONAL CHINESE FLAVOR OF DANDAN OFTEN FOUND IN YOUR TANTANMEN,

USE THE FERMENTED VEGETABLE KNOWN AS *YA CAI* AND THE SWEET BEAN PASTE CALLED *TIANMIANJIANG*, BOTH FOUND IN MOST ASIAN MARKETS.

IF YOU CAN'T GET YOUR HANDS ON THEM — DON'T WORRY, THIS DISH WILL STILL BE DELICIOUS!

# TANTANMEN
## (SPICY GROUND PORK RAMEN)
### MAKES 1 SERVING

**INGREDIENTS:**

¾ CUP PORK OR TOFU FOR TANTANMEN (P. 150)

1¼ CUP UNSEASONED STOCK OR BROTH OF YOUR CHOICE

5 OUNCES PER PORTION OF HANDMADE RAMEN NOODLES (P. 79) OR OTHER RAMEN NOODLES

1 TO 2 TEASPOONS RAYU (P. 124)

BRING A LARGE POT OF UNSALTED WATER TO A BOIL OVER HIGH HEAT.

MEANWHILE, HEAT THE PORK IN A WOK OR CAST IRON PAN OVER MEDIUM-HIGH HEAT,

WE LIKE YASAI BROTH (P. 60) FOR THIS RICH SOUP!

THEN ADD THE STOCK AND BRING TO A SIMMER.

THIS DISH WORKS EQUALLY WELL WITH EXTRA FIRM TOFU — JUST FINELY CHOP 12 TO 16 OUNCES AND SUBSTITUTE IT FOR THE PORK IN THE PORK FOR TANTANMEN RECIPE.

YOU CAN USE ANY STOCK WITHOUT TARE IN THIS RECIPE — ULTIMATELY, THE FINISHED PORK AND ITS LIQUID BECOME THE TARE TO SEASON THE SOUP.

COOK THE NOODLES AS DIRECTED,

DRAIN WELL, AND PUT IN A SERVING BOWL.

SUGGESTED ACCOMPANIMENTS:

AJITSUKE TAMAGO (P. 104)

ONSEN EGG (P. 108)

WOK-FRIED VEGETABLES
(P. 112)

MENMA (P. 110)

GARI (P. 118)

NEGI (P. 19)

CRUSHED RED PEPPER FLAKES

SANSHO (P. 17)

RAW PEA SHOOTS OR
SUNFLOWER SPROUTS

POUR THE HOT BROTH
OVER THE NOODLES,

ARRANGING THE
PORK ATTRACTIVELY
OVER THE NOODLES.

DRIZZLE THE RAYU
AROUND THE BOWL,

THEN TOP WITH
THE DESIRED
ACCOMPANIMENTS.

SERVE
IMMEDIATELY.

# PORK FOR TANTANMEN

MAKES ENOUGH FOR 4 BOWLS OF RAMEN

## INGREDIENTS:

¼ CUP TAHINI

¼ CUP SESAME OIL

2 TABLESPOONS RAYU (P. 124)

¼ CUP SOY SAUCE

2 TABLESPOONS RICE WINE VINEGAR

1 TEASPOON SANSHO OR SICHUAN PEPPERCORNS, GROUND AND SIFTED (OPTIONAL, SEE PANTRY, P. 17)

1 TEASPOON CRUSHED RED PEPPER FLAKES (OPTIONAL)

2 TABLESPOONS PORK FAT OR CANOLA OIL

3-INCH PIECE FRESH GINGER, PEELED AND MINCED

4 GARLIC CLOVES, MINCED

1 BUNCH SCALLIONS, TRIMMED AND SEPARATED, WHITES MINCED AND GREENS THINLY SLICED DIAGONALLY

1 TABLESPOON YA CAI (CHINESE FERMENTED VEGETABLE, OPTIONAL; P. 147)

1 TABLESPOON TIANMIANJIANG (CHINESE SWEET BEAN PASTE, OPTIONAL; P. 147)

1 POUND GROUND PORK

½ CUP STOCK OF YOUR CHOOSING (SEE BROTHS, P. 42–43) OR WATER

WHISK TOGETHER THE TAHINI, SESAME OIL, RAYU, SOY SAUCE, VINEGAR, SANSHO, AND PEPPER FLAKES IN A SMALL BOWL AND SET ASIDE.

HEAT A WOK OR CAST IRON PAN OVER HIGH HEAT AND ADD THE FAT.

WHEN THE FAT IS MELTED, ADD THE GINGER, GARLIC, SCALLION WHITES, YA CAI, AND TIANMIANJIANG AND FRY, STIRRING CONSTANTLY, UNTIL AROMATIC AND STARTING TO BROWN, 30 TO 60 SECONDS.

ADD THE PORK AND COOK, STIRRING TO BREAK IT UP, UNTIL IT IS COOKED THROUGH AND CRUMBLY, ABOUT 3 MORE MINUTES.

ADD THE TAHINI MIXTURE AND STIR UNTIL THOROUGHLY COMBINED.

ADD THE STOCK AND CONTINUE TO COOK AND STIR FOR 1 MORE MINUTE,

THEN STIR IN THE GREEN ONION GREENS.

ADJUST THE SEASONING AND SPICINESS AND REMOVE FROM THE HEAT.

USE AS DIRECTED FOR TANTANMEN, AND REFRIGERATE THE LEFTOVER PORK MIXTURE FOR UP TO 3 DAYS, OR FREEZE FOR 3 MONTHS.

3 DAYS

3 MONTHS

# YAKISOBA
## (WOK-FRIED RAMEN)

MAKES 4 SERVINGS

## INGREDIENTS:

ABOUT 15 OUNCES HANDMADE RAMEN NOODLES (P. 79) OR OTHER FRESH RAMEN NOODLES

7 TABLESPOONS CANOLA OIL

3 TABLESPOONS SOY SAUCE

3 TABLESPOONS MIRIN

2 TEASPOONS RICE WINE VINEGAR

1 TABLESPOON SESAME OIL

½ POUND BONELESS CHICKEN THIGHS OR BREASTS; BEEF RIBEYE, FLANK, OR SKIRT STEAK; OR PORK LOIN OR TENDERLOIN, CUT INTO THIN STRIPS ABOUT 2-INCHES LONG AND ¼-INCH THICK, OR ½ POUND PEELED AND DEVEINED SHRIMP

1 SMALL HEAD BROCCOLI, CUT INTO ROUGHLY 1-INCH FLORETS, ABOUT 2 CUPS

½ CUP WATER

2 GARLIC CLOVES, CUT INTO THIN SLICES

1 BUNCH GREEN ONIONS, TRIMMED, ENTIRE ONION CUT INTO 1-INCH PIECES

1 TO 2 RED PEPPERS, JULIENNED

2 CUPS JULIENNED CABBAGE

1 TEASPOON SHICHIMI TOGARASHI

SEVERAL STRIPS OF GARI (P. 118), OPTIONAL

TO USE SHRIMP, OMIT THE FIRST WOK STEP, AND SIMPLY ADD THE SHRIMP WITH THE ONIONS AND PEPPERS!

COOK AND COOL THE NOODLES AS DIRECTED FOR TSUKEMEN (P. 132). DRAIN WELL, TOSS WITH 1 TABLESPOON OF THE CANOLA OIL, AND SET ASIDE.

COMBINE THE SOY SAUCE, MIRIN, VINEGAR, AND SESAME OIL IN A SMALL BOWL AND SET ASIDE.

HEAT A WOK OVER HIGH HEAT, THEN ADD 2 TABLESPOONS OF THE CANOLA OIL.

WHEN SMOKING, ADD THE MEAT AND COOK FOR 2 MINUTES, STIRRING EVERY 30 SECONDS.

TRANSFER TO A MEDIUM BOWL.

YOU'RE PROBABLY FAMILIAR WITH THIS FRIED NOODLE DISH (OR ITS CHINESE COUSIN *LO MEIN*) FROM YOUR FAVORITE GUT-BUSTING TAKE-OUT JOINTS — IT'S INDULGENTLY CHEWY, AND CHOCK-FULL OF DELIGHTFUL TEXTURES AND FLAVORS.

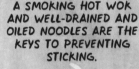

A SMOKING HOT WOK AND WELL-DRAINED AND OILED NOODLES ARE THE KEYS TO PREVENTING STICKING.

THIS RECIPE WILL WORK WITH MOST MEATS AND VEGGIES, SO MIX AND MATCH TO PERSONALIZE THE DISH AS YOU LIKE — AND DON'T BE AFRAID TO LOAD IT UP WITH PLENTY OF MIX-INS!

WIPE OUT THE WOK WITH A DRY PAPER TOWEL,

RETURN IT TO THE HEAT, AND ADD 1 TABLESPOON OIL.

REMEMBER THAT HOT INGREDIENTS WILL CONTINUE TO COOK WHILE THEY WAIT ON THE SIDELINES FOR THEIR BUDDIES TO FINISH COOKING,

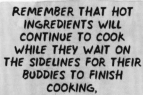

WHEN SMOKING, ADD THE BROCCOLI AND COOK FOR 1 MINUTE, STIRRING ONCE, LETTING IT CHAR A BIT.

ADD THE WATER AND COOK FOR AN ADDITIONAL 2 TO 3 MINUTES, STIRRING OCCASIONALLY, UNTIL THE BROCCOLI IS BRIGHT GREEN AND TENDER AND THE WATER HAS EVAPORATED.

SO MOVE THROUGH THE RECIPE WITHOUT INTERRUPTION, AND PULL THINGS FROM THE HEAT JUST SHY OF BEING DONE SO THEY ALL ARRIVE AT THE FINISH LINE AT THE SAME TIME.

ADD 1 TABLESPOON OF OIL AND THE GARLIC, ONIONS, PEPPERS, AND CABBAGE

AND COOK, STIRRING OCCASIONALLY, UNTIL THE ONIONS ARE TENDER, 1 TO 2 MINUTES.

TRANSFER TO THE BOWL WITH THE MEAT.

WIPE OUT THE WOK,

RETURN IT TO THE HEAT, AND ADD 2 TABLESPOONS OIL.

WHEN IT SMOKES, ADD THE NOODLES AND STIR WELL TO COAT WITH OIL.

ADD RESERVED MEAT AND VEGETABLES, SOY MIXTURE, AND SHICHIMI TOGARASHI AND STIR WELL.

TRANSFER TO INDIVIDUAL BOWLS AND TOP WITH GARI, OR PLATE ON A LARGE SERVING DISH WITH GARI ON THE SIDE.

SERVE IMMEDIATELY.

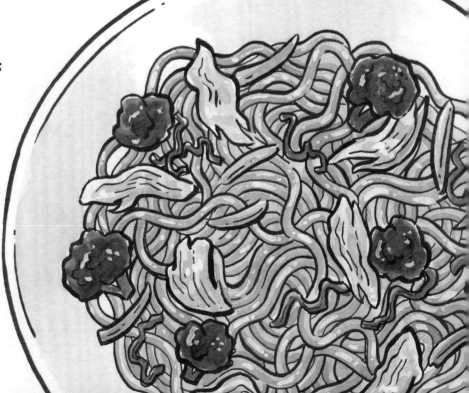

# CURRY RAMEN

MAKES ABOUT 4 SERVINGS

## INGREDIENTS:

2 TABLESPOONS COCONUT OR CANOLA OIL

2 LARGE SHALLOTS, MINCED

3 CLOVES GARLIC, MINCED

2-INCH PIECE FRESH GINGER, PEELED AND MINCED

1 JALAPEÑO OR FRESNO CHILE, STEMMED, SEEDED, AND MINCED

½ TART APPLE, GRATED

2 TABLESPOONS CURRY POWDER

4 CUPS PORK OR CHICKEN STOCK (P. 42), OR A COMBINATION, OR YASAI BROTH (P. 60)

14-OUNCE CAN COCONUT MILK

1 TABLESPOON FISH SAUCE OR MORE (OPTIONAL)

5 OUNCES PER PORTION OF HANDMADE RAMEN NOODLES, OR OTHER RAMEN NOODLES

SALT

HEAT THE OIL IN A MEDIUM SAUCEPAN OVER MEDIUM HEAT.

ADD THE SHALLOTS, GARLIC, GINGER, CHILE, AND APPLE AND COOK, STIRRING OCCASIONALLY, UNTIL SOFT AND JUST STARTING TO BROWN, 2 TO 3 MINUTES.

IF YOU LIKE CURRY, THIS NONTRADITIONAL SOUP IS FOR YOU!

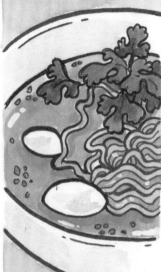

IT'S MUCH THINNER THAN THE DECADENTLY THICK, ROUX-BASED SAUCE TRADITIONALLY LADLED OVER *KATSU* (JAPANESE FRIED CUTLETS) AND IS REMINISCENT OF A BURMESE-STYLE *KHAO SOI* NOODLE SOUP.

STIR IN THE CURRY POWDER,

THEN ADD THE STOCK AND COCONUT MILK AND STIR WELL.

SKIP HEAVY CHASHU AND GO WITH PULLED CHICKEN (P. 94) OR JAPANESE MEATBALLS (P. 98) AS AN ACCOMPANIMENT, AND CUT THE RICHNESS OF THE COCONUT MILK WITH FRESH LIME, SHALLOTS, AND GARI (P. 118) FOR SERVING.

INCREASE THE HEAT AND BRING TO A BOIL,

THEN LOWER THE HEAT TO MAINTAIN A SIMMER FOR 15 MINUTES.

REMOVE FROM THE HEAT AND ADD THE FISH SAUCE AND SEASON WITH SALT.

USE AS DIRECTED FOR THE MASTER RAMEN BOWL (P. 24) ALONG WITH ANY TOPPINGS AND NOODLES YOU LIKE —

WE LOVE IT WITH LIME-DRESSED SHALLOTS, CILANTRO, GARI, AJITSUKE TAMAGO, AND PULLED CHICKEN.

SUGGESTED ACCOMPANIMENTS:

PULLED CHICKEN (P. 94)

JAPANESE MEATBALLS (P. 98)

AJITSUKE TAMAGO (P. 104)

GARI (P. 118)

THINLY SLICED SHALLOTS DRESSED WITH A SQUEEZE OF LIME

LIME WEDGES

FRESH CILANTRO, CHOPPED

# KIMCHI-BRAISED CHICKEN RAMEN

## INGREDIENTS:

4 STRIPS SMOKY BACON, CUT INTO ¼-INCH LARDONS

2½ CUPS WATER

6 CHICKEN THIGHS, PREFERABLY BONE-IN AND SKIN-ON

1½ TEASPOONS SALT, PLUS MORE FOR FINAL SEASONING

1 ONION, CUT INTO A ROUGH 1-INCH DICE

4 GARLIC CLOVES, CUT INTO THIN SLICES

1 POUND RIPE TOMATOES, DICED, OR ONE 14-OUNCE CAN DICED TOMATOES

2 CUPS KIMCHI, ROUGHLY CHOPPED INTO 1-INCH PIECES

2 TABLESPOONS SOY SAUCE

1 TABLESPOON RICE WINE VINEGAR

1 TO 2 CUPS CHICKEN OR PORK STOCK (P. 42) AS NEEDED

5 OUNCES PER PORTION OF HANDMADE RAMEN NOODLES OR OTHER RAMEN NOODLES

PLACE THE BACON IN A DUTCH OVEN AND ADD ½ CUP OF THE WATER.

COOK OVER MEDIUM-HIGH HEAT, STIRRING NOW AND THEN, UNTIL THE WATER EVAPORATES AND THE BACON BEGINS FRYING IN ITS OWN RENDERED FAT, 3 TO 4 MINUTES.

FLAVOR IS EVERYWHERE IN THE KITCHEN! WE LOVE TO USE BYPRODUCTS FROM BRAISING AS BASES OF FLAVOR IN OTHER DISHES, AND NOWHERE BETTER THAN IN RAMEN BROTH.

IN THIS RECIPE, THE FUNKILY DELICIOUS KOREAN CONDIMENT KIMCHI BRINGS GREAT DEPTH TO TENDER BRAISED CHICKEN, AND THE LEFTOVER LIQUID PROVIDES THE BASE FOR A DELICIOUS RAMEN BROTH.

LOWER THE HEAT TO MEDIUM-LOW AND COOK UNTIL THE BACON IS CRISPY, ANOTHER 5 TO 6 MINUTES.

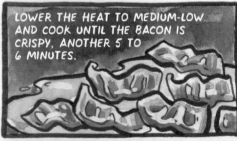

REMOVE THE BACON, LEAVING BEHIND ENOUGH RENDERED FAT TO COAT THE BOTTOM OF THE POT, AND INCREASE THE HEAT TO MEDIUM-HIGH.

SEASON THE CHICKEN THIGHS WITH SALT AND LAY THEM IN THE POT, SKIN SIDE DOWN.

COOK UNTIL GOLDEN BROWN AND NOT STICKING, 3 TO 4 MINUTES, THEN FLIP.

COOK AN ADDITIONAL 3 MINUTES, THEN REMOVE FROM THE POT.

ADD THE ONION AND GARLIC, SEASON WITH SALT, AND COOK, STIRRING OCCASIONALLY, UNTIL THE ONIONS HAVE SOFTENED, 3 TO 4 MINUTES.

ADD THE TOMATOES AND ALL THEIR JUICES, KIMCHI, SOY SAUCE, VINEGAR, RESERVED BACON, AND REMAINING 2 CUPS WATER AND STIR,

SCRAPING UP ANY TASTY BROWNED BITS FROM THE BOTTOM OF THE PAN.

NESTLE THE BACON AND CHICKEN BACK INTO THE POT,

LOWER THE HEAT TO MAINTAIN A SLOW SIMMER, AND COVER TIGHTLY.

COOK UNTIL THE CHICKEN IS TENDER AND PULLS APART EASILY, 20 TO 25 MINUTES (15 MINUTES IF USING BONELESS THIGHS).

REMOVE FROM THE HEAT AND LET COOL, UNCOVERED, UNTIL THE CHICKEN IS COOL ENOUGH TO HANDLE.

REMOVE THE SKINS AND USE FOR CRISPY CHICKEN SKINS (P. 117), OR DISCARD.

PULL THE CHICKEN INTO BITE-SIZED CHUNKS, MAKING SURE TO REMOVE THE CARTILAGE CONNECTING THE MEAT TO THE BONE,

AND PLACE THE CHICKEN BACK IN THE POT.

STRAIN ALL THE COOKING LIQUID

AND TOP OFF WITH ENOUGH STOCK TO MAKE A TOTAL OF 48 OUNCES, AND SEASON WITH SALT.

DIVIDE THE CHICKEN AND KIMCHI INTO 4 EQUAL PORTIONS.

WHEN READY TO USE, PROCEED AS DIRECTED FOR THE MASTER RAMEN BOWL (P. 24), USING 12 OUNCES OF THE BROTH AND ¼ OF THE CHICKEN AND KIMCHI MIXTURE FOR EACH BOWL ALONG WITH ANY TOPPINGS YOU LIKE.

PORTION ANY EXTRA INTO INDIVIDUAL CONTAINERS AND REFRIGERATE FOR UP TO 3 DAYS, OR FREEZE FOR UP TO 3 MONTHS.

SUGGESTED ACCOMPANIMENTS:

CHASHU (P. 89)

JAPANESE MEATBALLS (P. 98)

ONSEN EGG (P. 108)

AJITSUKE TAMAGO (P. 104)

CRISPY CHICKEN SKINS (P. 117)

WOK-FRIED VEGETABLES (P. 112)

GARI (P. 118)

NORI (P. 18)

NEGI (P. 19)

SESAME SEEDS

# SHRIMP AND ROASTED TOMATO RAMEN

MAKES 4 SERVINGS

## INGREDIENTS:

1 PINT RIPE CHERRY TOMATOES, HALVED

1 TEASPOON SALT

1 POUND SHRIMP OR PRAWNS, PREFERABLY UNPEELED WITH HEADS ON

8 TABLESPOONS BUTTER

2 LARGE SHALLOTS, MINCED

4 CLOVES GARLIC, MINCED

1 2-INCH PIECE FRESH GINGER, PEELED AND MINCED

1 BUNCH GREEN ONIONS, TRIMMED AND SEPARATED, WHITES MINCED AND GREENS THINLY SLICED DIAGONALLY

½ CUP SAKE

1 QUART YASAI BROTH (P. 60)

1 PINT DASHI (P. 45)

3 OUNCES (6 TABLESPOONS) SHIO TARE (P. 46), MORE OR LESS TO TASTE

1 TABLESPOON SHICHIMI TOGARASHI (SEE PANTRY, P. 17)

5 OUNCES PER PORTION OF HANDMADE RAMEN NOODLES OR OTHER RAMEN NOODLES

PREHEAT THE OVEN TO 300°F.

LAY THE TOMATOES FACE UP ON A PARCHMENT PAPER–LINED BAKING SHEET AND SPRINKLE WITH SALT.

ROAST UNTIL SHRIVELED BUT STILL JUICY, 45 TO 60 MINUTES,

THE SEAFOOD RAMEN FOUND IN RAMEN-YAS OFTEN CONTAINS PORK OR CHICKEN BROTH, AND THE DEEP OCEANIC FLAVORS OF OUR GYOKAI BROTH (P. 13) MIGHT BE TOO ASSERTIVE FOR SOME,

SO WE'VE INCLUDED THIS LIGHTER, TRULY PESCATARIAN BROTH FOR THOSE WHO DON'T EAT LAND ANIMALS.

ROASTING THE TOMATOES CONCENTRATES THEIR FLAVORS AND COMPLEMENTS THE GARLICKY SAUTÉED SHRIMP FOR A DELICIOUS (IF UNORTHODOX) BOWL.

THEN REMOVE FROM THE OVEN AND LET COOL SLIGHTLY.

IF ANY LIQUID HAS SEEPED OUT OF THE TOMATOES, SAVE IT AND RESERVE.

THIS IS BEST MADE WITH WHOLE, UNPEELED, HEAD-ON SHRIMP, BUT IF YOU CAN ONLY FIND PEELED SHRIMP, SKIP THE STEP OF SAUTÉING THE SHELLS AND PROCEED WITH THE GARLIC AND OTHER AROMATICS.

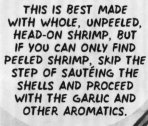

PEEL AND DEVEIN THE SHRIMP, RESERVING THE HEADS AND SHELLS.

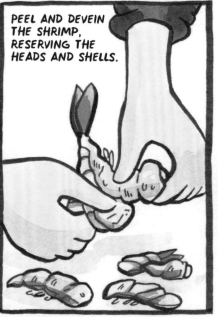

HEAT A MEDIUM SAUCE POT OVER MEDIUM-HIGH HEAT AND ADD 4 TABLESPOONS OF THE BUTTER.

WHEN MELTED, ADD THE RESERVED SHRIMP HEADS AND SHELLS, SEASON WITH SALT,

AND COOK, FREQUENTLY STIRRING AND MASHING THE HEADS, UNTIL PINK, ABOUT 2 MINUTES.

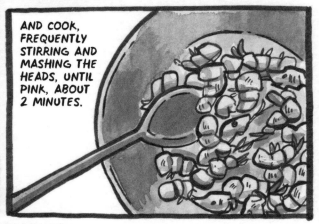

ADD THE SHALLOTS, GARLIC, GINGER, AND GREEN ONION WHITES AND CONTINUE TO COOK UNTIL THE VEGETABLES ARE FRAGRANT AND BECOMING SOFT, WITH SLIGHT BROWNING ON THE BOTTOM OF THE POT, 2 TO 3 MORE MINUTES.

IT SMELLS AMAZING!

INCREASE THE HEAT TO HIGH, ADD THE SAKE,

AND STIR, SCRAPING ANY BROWN BITS FROM THE BOTTOM OF THE PAN AND LETTING THE SAKE REDUCE UNTIL THE PAN IS NEARLY DRY, 60 TO 90 SECONDS.

ADD THE BROTH, DASHI, AND ANY RESERVED TOMATO LIQUID, STIR, AND BRING TO A SIMMER.

LOWER THE HEAT TO MAINTAIN A SLOW SIMMER FOR 20 MINUTES.

REMOVE FROM THE HEAT AND STIR IN THE TARE,

SOY OR MISO TARE WOULD OVERPOWER THIS BROTH'S SUBTLE FLAVORS — SHIO LETS THEM SHINE THROUGH!

THEN STRAIN THROUGH A FINE MESH STRAINER, PRESSING ON THE SHELLS TO RELEASE ANY EXTRA JUICES.

MEASURE THE REDUCED LIQUID AND ADD ENOUGH WATER FOR A TOTAL OF 48 OUNCES AND ADJUST THE SEASONING WITH MORE TARE IF NECESSARY.

AT THIS POINT, THE BROTH MAY BE REFRIGERATED FOR UP TO 3 DAYS OR FROZEN FOR UP TO 3 MONTHS.

3 DAYS

3 MONTHS

PREPARE THE SHRIMP FOR A HOT GARNISH: HEAT A PAN OVER MEDIUM-HIGH HEAT AND ADD THE REMAINING 4 TABLESPOONS BUTTER.

WHEN MELTED, SEASON THE SHRIMP WITH SALT AND ADD TO THE PAN.

LET SEAR ON ONE SIDE FOR 60 TO 90 SECONDS UNTIL PINK AND LIGHTLY BROWNED,

THEN FLIP AND COOK FOR AN ADDITIONAL 60 TO 90 SECONDS UNTIL COOKED THROUGH.

ADD THE GREEN ONION GREENS AND SHICHIMI TOGARASHI AND STIR,

THEN PROCEED AS DIRECTED IN THE MASTER RAMEN BOWL (P. 24), GARNISHING WITH SHRIMP AND TOMATOES

AND DRIZZLING THE MELTED BUTTER AROUND THE BOWL.

SUGGESTED ACCOMPANIMENTS:

ONSEN EGG (P. 108)

AJITSUKE TAMAGO (P. 104)

WOK-FRIED VEGETABLES (P. 112)

GARI (P. 118)

AROMATIC GARLIC AND SHALLOT OIL (P. 123)

RAYU (P. 124)

CHARRED SHALLOT AND SCALLION (P. 119)

NEGI (P. 19)

SESAME SEEDS

# ADOBO CHICKEN RAMEN

MAKES 4 SERVINGS

## INGREDIENTS:

1 POUND SMOKY BACON, CUT INTO 1-INCH PIECES

½ CUP WATER

6 CHICKEN THIGHS, PREFERABLY BONE-IN AND SKIN-ON

SALT

4 SHALLOTS, JULIENNED

8 CLOVES GARLIC, SMASHED WITH THE SIDE OF YOUR KNIFE

¾ CUP VINEGAR (CANE, RICE WINE, OR CIDER)

¼ CUP FISH SAUCE

¼ CUP SOY SAUCE

4 BAY LEAVES

5 OUNCES PER PORTION OF HANDMADE RAMEN NOODLES (P. 79) OR OTHER RAMEN NOODLES

NEGI (SEE PANTRY, P. 19)

GARI (P. 118)

ONSEN EGG (P. 108) OR SOFT AJITSUKE TAMAGO (P. 104)

PLACE BACON IN A DUTCH OVEN AND ADD ½ CUP WATER.

COOK OVER MEDIUM-HIGH HEAT, STIRRING NOW AND THEN, UNTIL THE WATER EVAPORATES AND THE BACON BEGINS FRYING IN ITS OWN RENDERED FAT, 3 TO 4 MINUTES.

LOWER THE HEAT TO MEDIUM-LOW AND COOK UNTIL THE BACON IS CRISPY, ANOTHER 5 TO 6 MINUTES.

ADOBO CHICKEN IS A FILIPINO DISH LONG ON FLAVOR AND GREAT FOR RAMEN.

A RICH SAUCE AND DELECTABLE TOPPING PERFECT FOR SOUPLESS MAZEMEN-STYLE RAMEN (P. 141) IS PRODUCED WHEN CHICKEN IS COOKED WITH SMOKY BACON, SHALLOTS, VINEGAR, AND FISH SAUCE UNTIL REDUCED TO A BRAWNY UMAMI GOLDMINE.

THIS SEEMS LIKE A LOT OF VINEGAR AND FISH SAUCE, BUT TRUST US — THE RESULT IS ONE OF A KIND!

REMOVE THE BACON, LEAVING BEHIND ALL RENDERED FAT, AND INCREASE THE HEAT TO MEDIUM-HIGH.

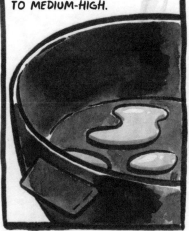

SEASON THE CHICKEN THIGHS WITH SALT AND LAY THEM IN THE POT, SKIN SIDE DOWN.

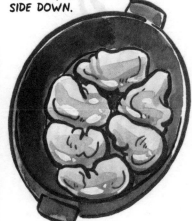

COOK UNTIL GOLDEN BROWN AND NOT STICKING, 3 TO 4 MINUTES, THEN FLIP.

COOK AN ADDITIONAL 3 MINUTES, THEN REMOVE FROM THE POT AND RESERVE.

ADD THE SHALLOTS AND GARLIC TO THE POT AND COOK, STIRRING OCCASIONALLY, UNTIL THE SHALLOTS HAVE SOFTENED, ABOUT 2 MINUTES.

ADD THE VINEGAR, FISH SAUCE, SOY SAUCE, AND BAY LEAVES AND STIR, SCRAPING UP ANY TASTY BROWNED BITS FROM THE BOTTOM OF THE PAN.

NESTLE THE BACON AND CHICKEN BACK INTO THE POT, AND BRING TO A SIMMER.

ADJUST THE HEAT TO MAINTAIN A LOW SIMMER, COVER THE POT, AND COOK,

BASTING AND FLIPPING A COUPLE OF TIMES,

UNTIL THE CHICKEN IS TENDER AND CAN BE PULLED FROM THE BONE, 20 TO 25 MINUTES (15 IF USING BONELESS THIGHS).

REMOVE FROM THE HEAT AND LET COOL, UNCOVERED, UNTIL THE CHICKEN IS COOL ENOUGH TO HANDLE.

REMOVE THE SKINS AND USE FOR CRISPY CHICKEN SKINS (P. 117) OR DISCARD, AND DISCARD THE BAY LEAVES.

PULL THE CHICKEN INTO NICE-SIZED CHUNKS, MAKING SURE TO REMOVE THE CARTILAGE CONNECTING THE MEAT TO THE BONE.

MIX THE CHICKEN WITH THE REMAINING SAUCE IN THE POT.

BRING A LARGE POT OF WATER TO A BOIL.

SUGGESTED ACCOMPANIMENTS:

WOK-FRIED VEGETABLES (P. 112)

CRISPY CHICKEN SKINS (P. 117)

MEANWHILE, BRING THE CHICKEN BACK TO A SIMMER.

COOK THE NOODLES AS DIRECTED IN THE RECIPE OR ON THE PACKAGE, DRAIN WELL, AND PUT IN A SERVING BOWL.

TOP WITH ¼ OF THE HOT CHICKEN AND SAUCE, FAT AND ALL, THEN THE REMAINING TOPPINGS.

SERVE IMMEDIATELY, BREAKING THE EGG AND STIRRING ALL THE INGREDIENTS TOGETHER UNTIL THE NOODLES ARE WELL COATED.

REFRIGERATE ANY UNUSED PORTIONS OF CHICKEN AND SAUCE TOGETHER IN THE REFRIGERATOR FOR UP TO 3 DAYS, OR FREEZE FOR UP TO 3 MONTHS. TO SERVE, REHEAT IN A SMALL POT.

3 DAYS

3 MONTHS

# a word about PRESSURE COOKERS

THERE ARE MANY KINDS OF PRESSURE COOKERS OUT THERE, SOME FOR STOVETOP USE AND SOME ELECTRIC. BUT THEY ALL WORK ON THE SAME PRINCIPLE:

THE HIGH PRESSURE CREATED IN THE SEALED CHAMBER RAISES WATER'S BOILING POINT, INCREASING TEMPERATURES INSIDE THE POT, AND RESULTING IN MUCH QUICKER COOKING TIMES.

ALL PRESSURE COOKERS HAVE SECURE-FITTING LIDS TO KEEP THE PRESSURIZED WATER VAPOR IN THE POT; FOR SAFETY'S SAKE, THIS STEAM MUST BE RELEASED GRADUALLY OVER TIME OR THROUGH A CONTROLLED RELEASE VALVE.

ALWAYS FOLLOW THE GUIDELINES IN YOUR PRESSURE COOKER'S MANUAL.

HERE ARE 2 RECIPES ADAPTED FOR PRESSURE COOKERS; WE ENCOURAGE YOU TO EXPERIMENT TO ADAPT OTHER RECIPES TO FIT YOUR COOKER.

THE FIRST USES A TECHNIQUE SHOWN TO US BY MIKE SATINOVER, AKA RAMEN_LORD (P. 170).

NORMALLY, THE LONG, RAPID BOIL OF A TONKOTSU BROTH EXTRACTS AND AGITATES TO EMULSIFY THE PORK GELATIN AND FAT IN THE STOCK.

HERE, A PRESSURE COOK FOLLOWED BY A QUICK SPIN IN A BLENDER MAKES UP FOR THE RELATIVELY QUICK COOK TIME AND LACK OF AGITATION, AND MAKES AN EVEN RICHER, CREAMIER BROTH THAN OUR STANDARD TONKOTSU BROTH (P. 52).

IT NOT ONLY SAVES TIME BUT ALSO MAKES A VERY STRONG BROTH.

IT COMES OUT OF THE PRESSURE COOKER LOOKING PRETTY CLEAR AND THIN, BUT GET READY — WHEN BLENDED, THIS CREAM OF PORK SOUP GETS SUPER WHITE!

THE SECOND RECIPE DOESN'T REALLY SAVE TIME, BUT IT MAKES EGGS MUCH EASIER TO PEEL.

NOTE THAT YOLK TEXTURES CAN VARY SLIGHTLY DUE TO THE QUICKER COOK TIMES IN A PRESSURE COOKER;

THIS RECIPE WILL YIELD SOFT, CREAMY YOLKS. ADJUST COOK TIMES TO YOUR LIKING AND REPLACE THE PEELED EGGS IN AJITSUKE TAMAGO (P. 104) WITH THESE!

# PRESSURE COOKER TONKOTSU BROTH

MAKES ABOUT 2½ QUARTS

## INGREDIENTS:

1 PORK TROTTER

3 POUNDS PORK NECK BONES, RIBS, OR CHICKEN CARCASSES

1 BUNCH GREEN ONIONS, TRIMMED AND CUT IN HALF CROSS-WISE

¼ POUND GINGER, UNPEELED AND SLICED ¼ INCH THICK

PLACE ALL THE INGREDIENTS IN A PRESSURE COOKER AND ADD 2 QUARTS WATER, MAKING SURE NOT TO EXCEED YOUR COOKER'S RECOMMENDED LIQUID LIMIT.

SEAL AND COOK ON HIGH PRESSURE FOR 2 HOURS.

LET COOL TO RELEASE THE PRESSURE NATURALLY, THEN UNSEAL.

STRAIN THE BROTH, THEN PUT IN A BLENDER (WORK IN BATCHES IF NECESSARY), AND BLEND AT AN INCREASING SPEED UNTIL ALL THE FAT AND STOCK HAS EMULSIFIED INTO A CREAMY WHITE BROTH.

PORTION INTO 12-OUNCE SERVINGS AND STORE REFRIGERATED FOR UP TO 5 DAYS, OR FROZEN FOR 6 MONTHS.

5 DAYS

6 MONTHS

WHEN READY TO USE, SEASON USING THE FOLLOWING AMOUNTS OF YOUR DESIRED TARE PER 12-OUNCE SERVING — THE ADDITION OF FAT IS NOT NECESSARY BECAUSE IT IS EMULSIFIED IN THE BROTH.

| TARE | AMOUNT PER 12 OZ OF STOCK |
|---|---|
| SHIO (P. 46) | 1 OZ (2 TABLESPOONS) |
| SHOYU (P. 47) | 2 OZ (¼ CUP) |
| MISO (P. 48) | 2 OZ (¼ CUP) |

# PRESSURE COOKER AJITSUKE TAMAGO

MAKES 6 EGGS

**INGREDIENTS:**

6 EGGS

SET UP YOUR PRESSURE COOKER WITH A STEAM RACK AND PLACE THE EGGS ON THE RACK.

ADD 1 CUP OF WATER,

SEAL, AND COOK ON LOW PRESSURE FOR 5 MINUTES.

QUICK-RELEASE THE PRESSURE, REMOVE THE EGGS FROM THE COOKER,

AND PLACE IN A BOWL UNDER COLD RUNNING WATER.

WHEN COOL, PEEL THE EGGS, THEN SOAK IN MARINADE AS DIRECTED IN THE AJITSUKE TAMAGO RECIPE (P. 104).

# MIKE SATINOVER
## ON SIMPLIFYING RAMEN IN THE HOME KITCHEN

IF YOU EVER FEEL LIKE YOU DON'T HAVE THE SPACE, TIME, OR GENERAL WHEREWITHAL TO COOK RAMEN IN YOUR HOME KITCHEN, YOU NEED LOOK NO FURTHER THAN MIKE SATINOVER (AKA REDDIT'S RAMEN_LORD) FOR INSPIRATION.

HE'S NOT ONLY A PASSIONATE SOURCE OF RAMEN KNOWLEDGE AND RECIPES (GOOGLE HIS HANDLE PLUS WHATEVER RECIPE YOU'RE LOOKING FOR) BUT ALSO ONE OF THE BEST RAMEN COOKS WE KNOW (LUCKY SLURPERS CAN SNAG A SEAT AT HIS AKAHOSHI RAMEN POP-UPS) — AND IT ALL STARTS IN HIS HOME KITCHEN.

PEOPLE REACH OUT TO ME ALL THE TIME SAYING, "RAMEN SEEMS TO TAKE SO MUCH TIME! THERE'S SO MANY STEPS BEFORE YOU CAN PUT IT ALL TOGETHER TO MAKE A GOOD BOWL! CAN'T THIS BE SIMPLIFIED?"

MY RESPONSE IS ALWAYS THE SAME: "YOU'VE ANSWERED YOUR OWN QUESTION — TAKE IT ONE STEP AT A TIME AND SPREAD THE WORK OUT AS NEEDED!"

DON'T TRY TO DO IT ALL IN ONE DAY, BECAUSE YOU'LL BURN OUT. MAKE THE COMPONENTS IN ADVANCE OVER TIME, AND BUILD AN ARSENAL OF INGREDIENTS IN THE FREEZER.

FOCUS ON SIMPLER THINGS FIRST TO BUILD YOUR CONFIDENCE: MAKE A COUPLE OF STOCKS, SOME TARE, A BRAISED PIECE OF CHASHU.

IF YOU DON'T IMMEDIATELY RUSH INTO MAKING HOMEMADE NOODLES, DON'T SWEAT IT!

BUY PREMADE NOODLES AND ALLOW FOR SOME FAILED ATTEMPTS. BUILD A SOLID FOUNDATION OF BASICS FIRST — THEN MASTER NOODLES!

I WAS OVERWHELMED WHEN I STARTED, TOO. WHAT HELPED ME GET BETTER WAS ISOLATING EACH COMPONENT, LETTING RAMEN BE A PASSION PROJECT.

I LEARNED TO PUT FOCUS AND ENERGY INTO EACH INDIVIDUAL COMPONENT, AND THIS ALLOWED ME TO GAIN A DEEPER UNDERSTANDING OF EACH PIECE OF THE RAMEN PUZZLE.

ONCE YOUR COMPONENTS ARE PREPARED, A GREAT BOWL IS JUST ABOUT ASSEMBLY!

OTHER TIPS:

MAKE TARE IN LARGE BATCHES AHEAD OF TIME, NOT EVERY SINGLE TIME YOU MAKE RAMEN. LET IT HANG OUT! TARE EVEN GETS BETTER AS IT AGES.

STAY SIMPLE AT FIRST. YOU DON'T NEED TO GO OUT AND BUY A BUNCH OF SPECIALIZED GEAR! RAMEN IS ABOUT FOCUS ON COMPONENTS, NOT FANCY EQUIPMENT.

PINT- AND QUART-SIZE DELI CONTAINERS (AND OTHER PLASTIC STORAGE CONTAINERS) ARE A RAMEN MVP! THEY ARE A GREAT SIZE FOR PORTIONING, SUPER INEXPENSIVE, AND REUSABLE.

ONLY A FEW SIMPLE THINGS NEED TO BE DONE LAST MINUTE, LIKE SLICING NEGI, OR WOK-FRYING FRESH VEGETABLES.

I ALWAYS THINK: YOU DO THESE SIMPLE STEPS, BUILD THESE BEAUTIFUL COMPONENTS, AND YOU CAN HAVE HOMEMADE RAMEN ON YOUR TABLE ANYTIME YOU WANT. HOW AWESOME IS THAT?

# GOCHISOSAMA

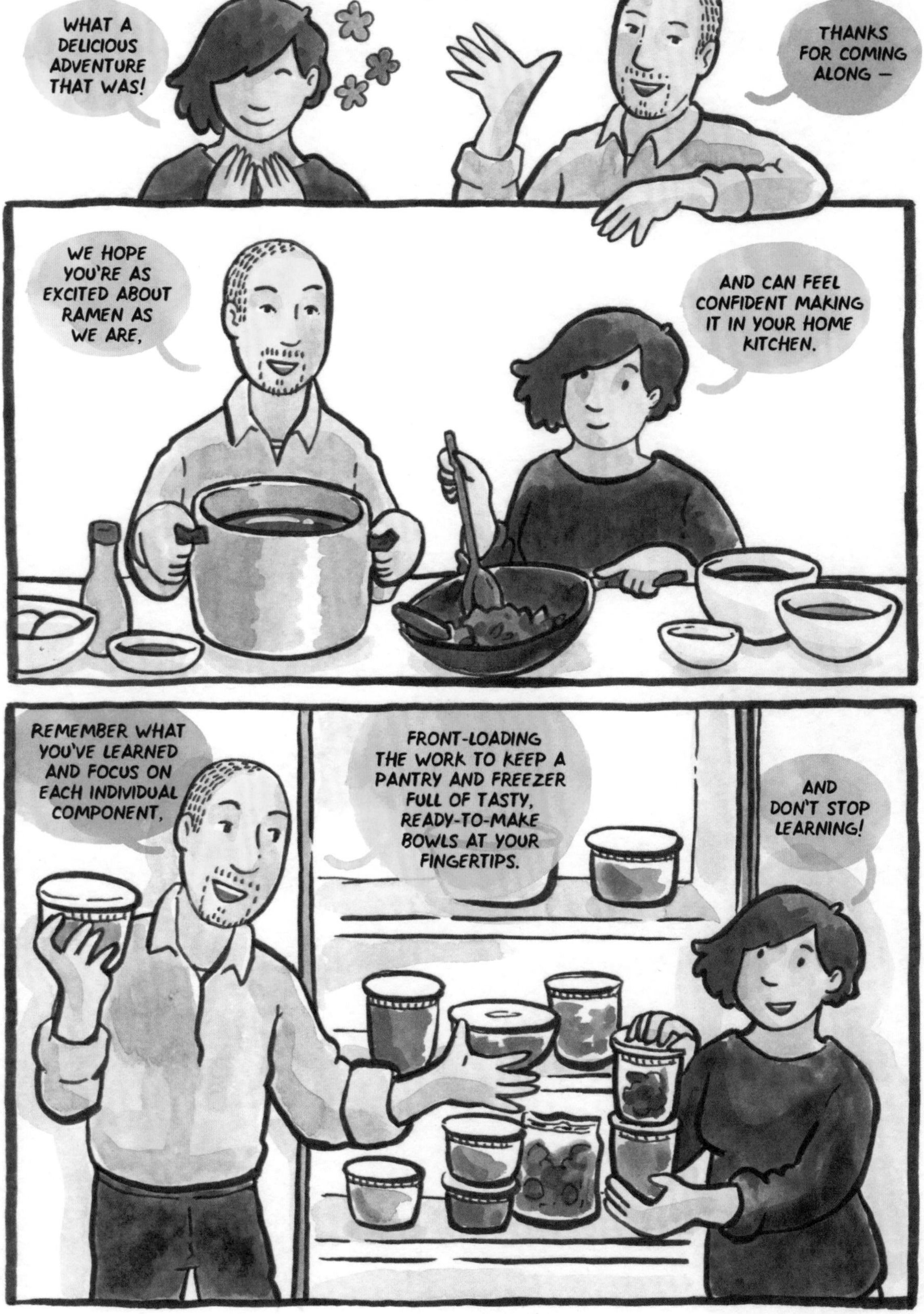
WHAT A DELICIOUS ADVENTURE THAT WAS!
THANKS FOR COMING ALONG –
WE HOPE YOU'RE AS EXCITED ABOUT RAMEN AS WE ARE,
AND CAN FEEL CONFIDENT MAKING IT IN YOUR HOME KITCHEN.
REMEMBER WHAT YOU'VE LEARNED AND FOCUS ON EACH INDIVIDUAL COMPONENT,
FRONT-LOADING THE WORK TO KEEP A PANTRY AND FREEZER FULL OF TASTY, READY-TO-MAKE BOWLS AT YOUR FINGERTIPS.
AND DON'T STOP LEARNING!

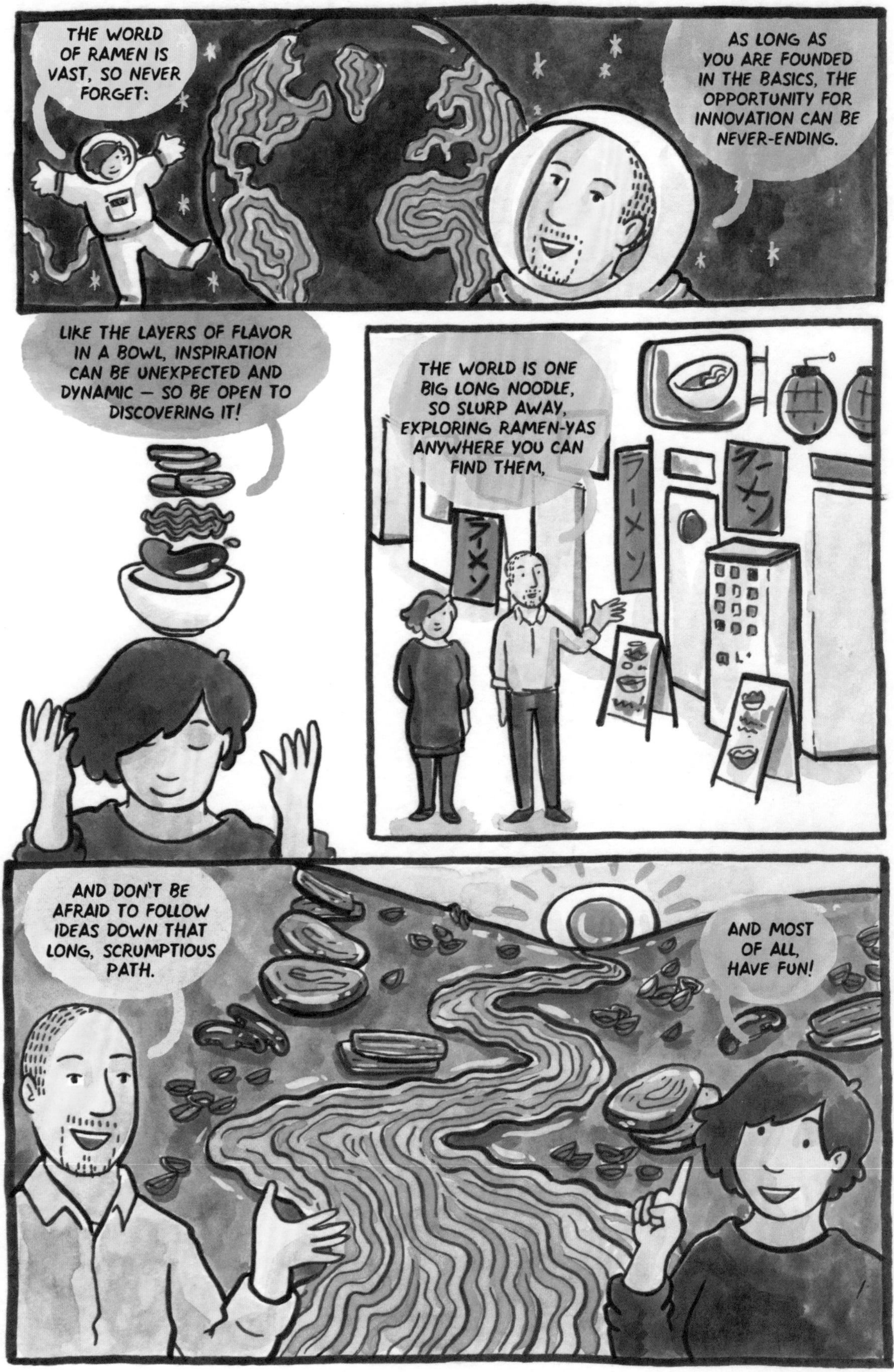
THE WORLD OF RAMEN IS VAST, SO NEVER FORGET:
AS LONG AS YOU ARE FOUNDED IN THE BASICS, THE OPPORTUNITY FOR INNOVATION CAN BE NEVER-ENDING.
LIKE THE LAYERS OF FLAVOR IN A BOWL, INSPIRATION CAN BE UNEXPECTED AND DYNAMIC — SO BE OPEN TO DISCOVERING IT!
THE WORLD IS ONE BIG LONG NOODLE, SO SLURP AWAY, EXPLORING RAMEN-YAS ANYWHERE YOU CAN FIND THEM,
ラーメン
ラーメン
ラーメン
AND DON'T BE AFRAID TO FOLLOW IDEAS DOWN THAT LONG, SCRUMPTIOUS PATH.
AND MOST OF ALL, HAVE FUN!

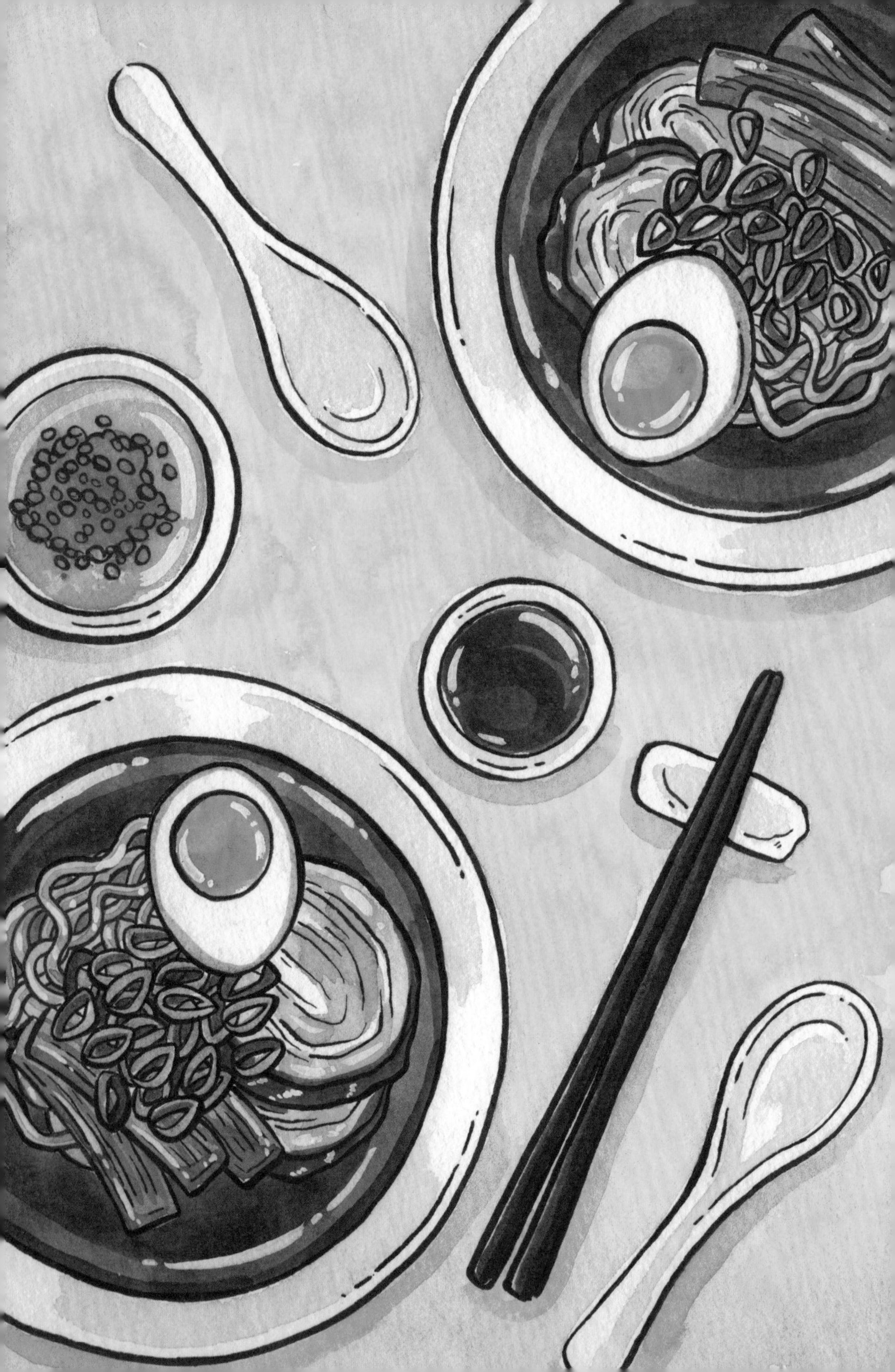

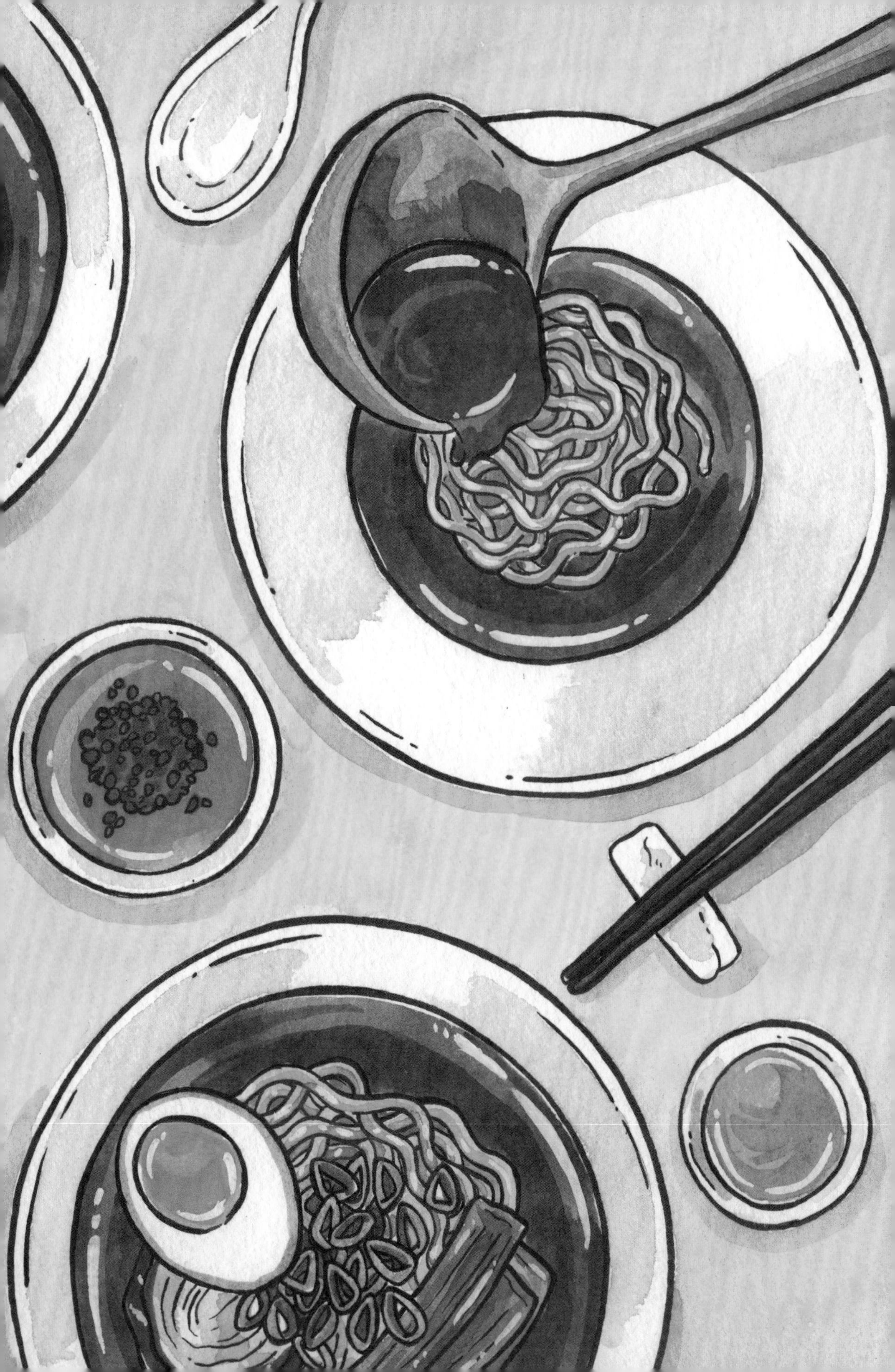

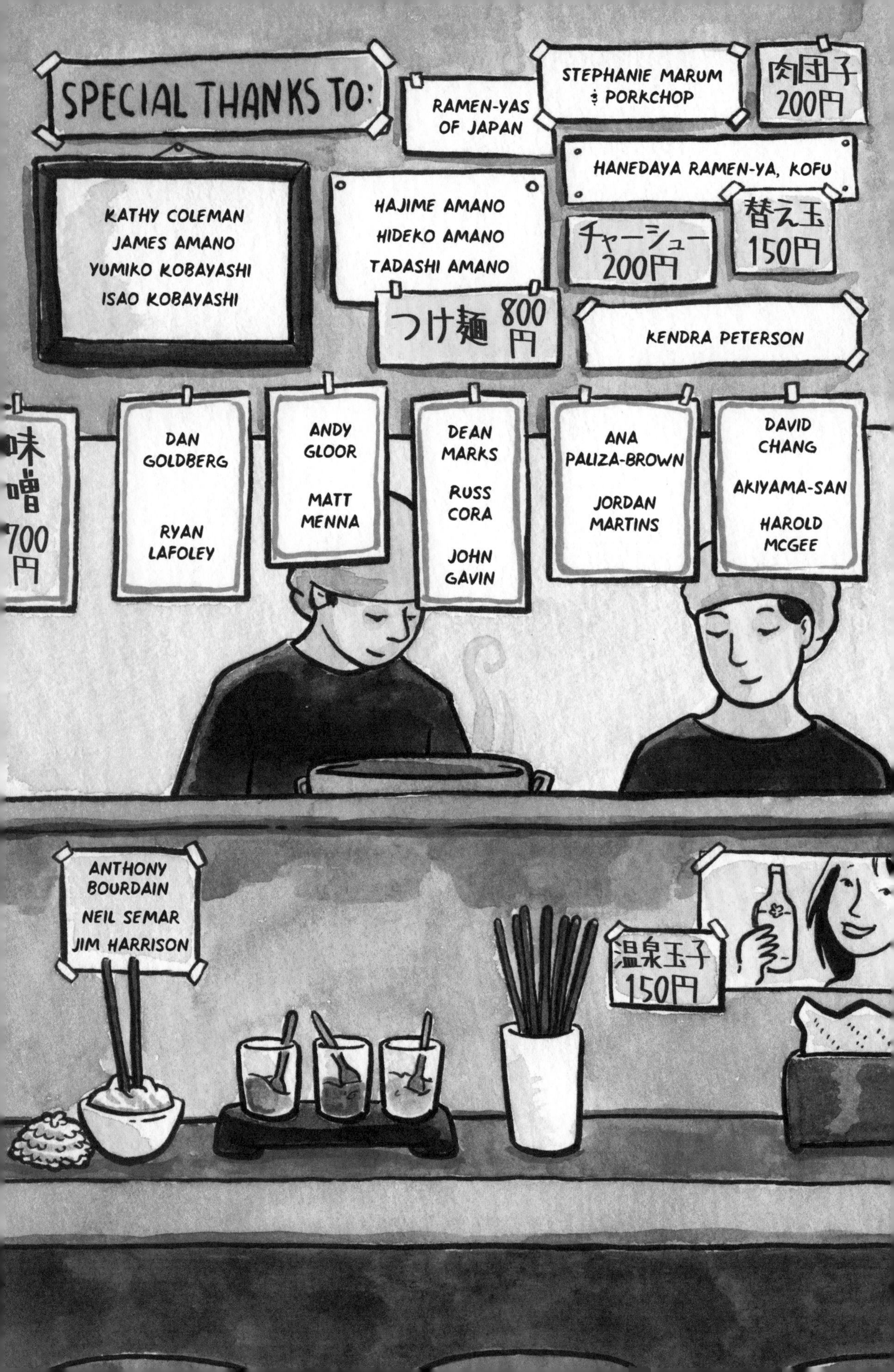

SPECIAL THANKS TO:
RAMEN-YAS OF JAPAN
STEPHANIE MARUM & PORKCHOP
肉団子 200円
HANEDAYA RAMEN-YA, KOFU
KATHY COLEMAN
JAMES AMANO
YUMIKO KOBAYASHI
ISAO KOBAYASHI
HAJIME AMANO
HIDEKO AMANO
TADASHI AMANO
チャーシュー 200円
替え玉 150円
つけ麺 800円
KENDRA PETERSON
味噌 700円
DAN GOLDBERG
RYAN LAFOLEY
ANDY GLOOR
MATT MENNA
DEAN MARKS
RUSS CORA
JOHN GAVIN
ANA PALIZA-BROWN
JORDAN MARTINS
DAVID CHANG
AKIYAMA-SAN
HAROLD MCGEE
ANTHONY BOURDAIN
NEIL SEMAR
JIM HARRISON
温泉玉子 150円

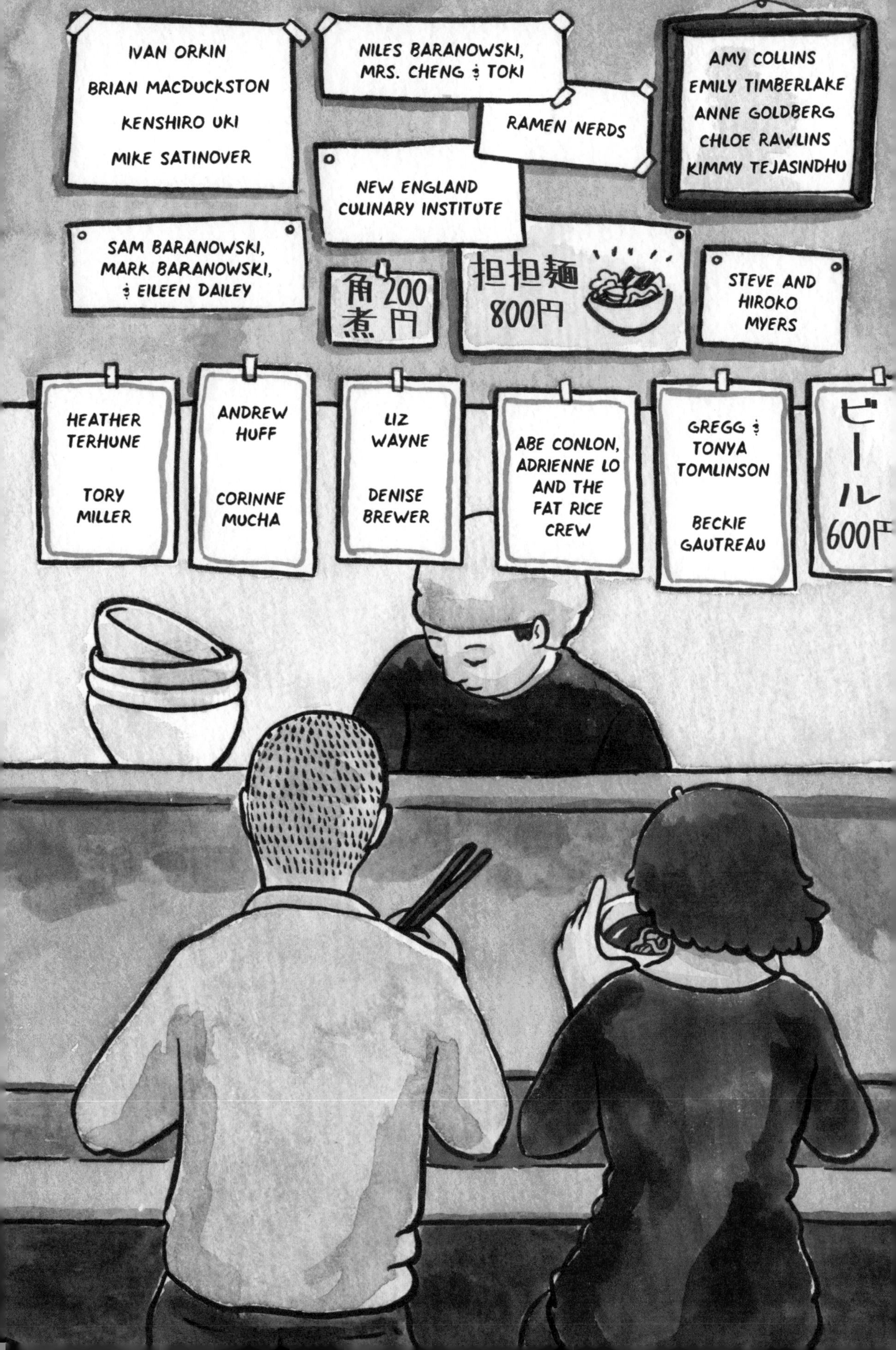
IVAN ORKIN
BRIAN MACDUCKSTON
KENSHIRO UKI
MIKE SATINOVER
NILES BARANOWSKI, MRS. CHENG & TOKI
RAMEN NERDS
AMY COLLINS
EMILY TIMBERLAKE
ANNE GOLDBERG
CHLOE RAWLINS
KIMMY TEJASINDHU
NEW ENGLAND CULINARY INSTITUTE
SAM BARANOWSKI, MARK BARANOWSKI, & EILEEN DAILEY
角煮 200円
担担麺 800円
STEVE AND HIROKO MYERS
HEATHER TERHUNE
TORY MILLER
ANDREW HUFF
CORINNE MUCHA
LIZ WAYNE
DENISE BREWER
ABE CONLON, ADRIENNE LO AND THE FAT RICE CREW
GREGG & TONYA TOMLINSON
BECKIE GAUTREAU
ビール 600円

# HUGH AMANO

HUGH AMANO GREW UP SPENDING MOST SUMMERS IN JAPAN VISITING HIS FATHER'S SIDE OF THE FAMILY. BEING A HALF-JAPANESE AMERICAN ADRIFT IN A CULTURE WORLDS APART FROM HIS SMALL COLORADO HOMETOWN LED TO AN EARLY LOVE OF RAMEN AS HE DEFIED ALL PARENTAL WARNINGS OF SODIUM CONTENT AND SLURPED IT UP DAILY IN HIS FATHER'S KYOTO APARTMENT. BACK IN HIS MOUNTAIN HOMETOWN, WHILE OTHER KIDS BINGED ON BURGERS AND ICE CREAM, HUGH WAITED ANXIOUSLY FOR PACKAGES SENT FROM KYOTO CONTAINING POCKY STICKS, MILKY CANDY, AND MOST IMPORTANTLY, ICHIBAN RAMEN — IN HIS MIND, SO DIFFERENT FROM THE AMERICAN STORE-BOUGHT PACKS AVAILABLE TO THE SKI BUMS AND COLLEGE STUDENTS IN TOWN. AS HE GOT OLDER, HIS INTEREST (AND TASTE) IN RAMEN MATURED, AND TRIPS TO JAPAN INCLUDED A LARGE ITINERARY OF RAMEN SHOP VISITS; BACK STATESIDE, HIS STUDY OF RAMEN CONTINUED, AS HE APPLIED HIS TRAINING AND EXPERIENCE AS A CHEF TO HIS HISTORY WITH RAMEN, DEVELOPING RECIPES OF HIS OWN TO BE MADE AT HOME.

HUGH NOW LIVES IN CHICAGO, WHERE HE WORKS AS A CHEF AND A WRITER, MOST RECENTLY COAUTHORING *THE ADVENTURES OF FAT RICE* (TEN SPEED PRESS), ILLUSTRATED BY NONE OTHER THAN SARAH BECAN!

# SARAH BECAN

SARAH BECAN IS AN ILLUSTRATOR, COMICS ARTIST, AND DESIGNER BASED IN CHICAGO. SHE'S BEEN DRAWING COMICS ABOUT FOOD SINCE 2010, CREATING THE FOOD-CENTRIC AUTOBIOGRAPHICAL WEBCOMIC "I THINK YOU'RE SAUCEOME" AND PUBLISHING WORK IN SAVEUR MAGAZINE, EATER.COM, RODALE'S ORGANIC LIFE, STARCHEFS, TASTING TABLE, TRUTHOUT, AND THE CHICAGO READER. SHE WAS AWARDED A XERIC AWARD AND A STUMPTOWN TROPHY FOR OUTSTANDING DEBUT FOR HER FIRST GRAPHIC NOVEL, THE COMPLETE OUIJA INTERVIEWS, AND HER SECOND GRAPHIC NOVEL, SHUTEYE, WAS RELEASED IN EARLY 2012. SARAH FIRST DEVELOPED AN INTEREST IN JAPANESE FOOD THROUGH COMICS LIKE TETSU KARIYA'S OISHINBO AND OTHER GURUME (GOURMET) MANGA, LEADING TO A TRIP TO VISIT FAMILY AND FRIENDS IN JAPAN, WHERE SHE FELL IN LOVE WITH ALL THINGS RAMEN (ESPECIALLY MISO RAMEN WITH PLENTY OF CHASHU, ROASTED GARLIC, AND AN EXTRA AJITSUKE TAMAGO!), AND ABSOLUTELY ANYTHING AT THE SHIN-YOKOHAMA RAUMEN MUSEUM.

LATELY, SHE'S BEEN ILLUSTRATING COOKBOOKS, SUCH AS THE ADVENTURES OF FAT RICE (TEN SPEED PRESS), COAUTHORED BY HUGH AMANO, AND SMOOTHIE BOWLS (STERLING PUBLISHING), AND IF SHE HAD HER WAY, SHE'D DO NOTHING BUT DRAW PICTURES OF FOOD ALL DAY.

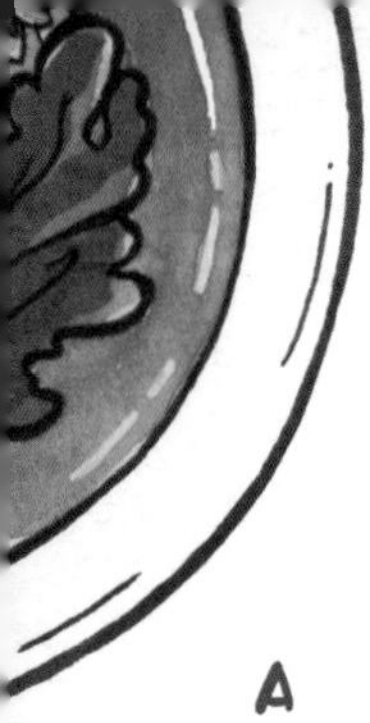

# INDEX



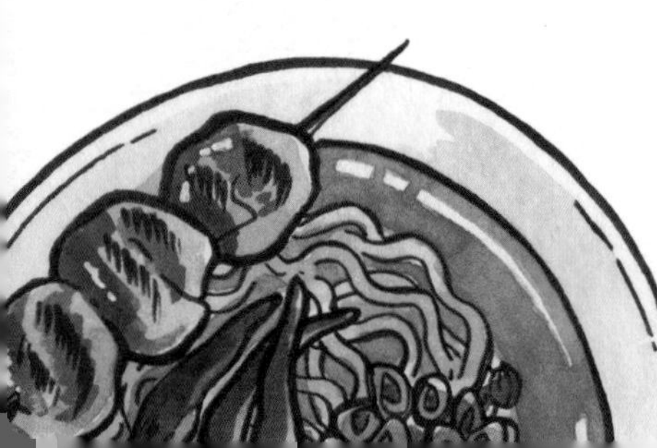

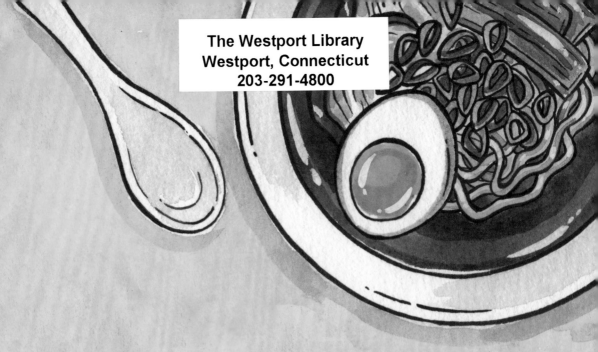

COPYRIGHT © 2019 BY HUGH AMANO AND SARAH BECAN
ILLUSTRATIONS COPYRIGHT © 2019 BY SARAH BECAN

PUBLISHED IN THE UNITED STATES BY TEN SPEED PRESS,
AN IMPRINT OF THE CROWN PUBLISHING GROUP, A DIVISION
OF PENGUIN RANDOM HOUSE LLC, NEW YORK.
WWW.CROWNPUBLISHING.COM
WWW.TENSPEED.COM

TEN SPEED PRESS AND THE TEN SPEED PRESS COLOPHON
ARE REGISTERED TRADEMARKS OF PENGUIN RANDOM HOUSE LLC.

LIBRARY OF CONGRESS CATALOGING-IN-PUBLICATION DATA
NAMES: AMANO, HUGH, AUTHOR. | BECAN, SARAH, 1976- AUTHOR.
TITLE: LET'S MAKE RAMEN! : A COMIC BOOK COOKBOOK / HUGH AMANO AND SARAH BECAN.
DESCRIPTION: FIRST EDITION. | NEW YORK : TEN SPEED PRESS, AN IMPRINT OF THE
    CROWN PUBLISHING GROUP, A DIVISION OF PENGUIN RANDOM HOUSE LLC, 2019 |
    INCLUDES BIBLIOGRAPHICAL REFERENCES AND INDEX. |
IDENTIFIERS: LCCN 2019000621 (PRINT) | LCCN 2019000792 (EBOOK)
SUBJECTS: LCSH: RAMEN. | COOKING, JAPANESE. | LCGFT: COOKBOOKS.
CLASSIFICATION: LCC TX809.N65 (EBOOK) | LCC TX809.N65 A43 2019 (PRINT) |
    DDC 641.82/2—DC23
LC RECORD AVAILABLE AT HTTPS://LCCN.LOC.GOV/2019000621

TRADE PAPERBACK ISBN: 978-0-399-58199-1
EBOOK ISBN: 978-0-399-58200-4

PRINTED IN CHINA

DESIGN BY CHLOE RAWLINS

10 9 8 7 6

FIRST EDITION